CW00349570

Victorian Fiction and the
Insights of Sympathy

Anthem Nineteenth Century Studies

Series editor: Robert Douglas-Fairhurst

Tim Youngs (ed.) *Travel Writing in the Nineteenth Century* (2006)

David Clifford, Elisabeth Wadge, Alex Warwick and Martin Willis (eds)
Repositioning Victorian Sciences (2006)

Ian St John *Disraeli and the Art of Victorian Politics* (2005)

John D Rosenberg *Elegy for an Age* (2005)

Anne-Julia Zwierlein (ed.) *Unmapped Countries* (2005)

Michael Diamond *Victorian Sensation* (2004)

Kirstie Blair *John Keble in Context* (2004)

David Clifford and Laurence Roussillon (eds) *Outsiders Looking In* (2004)

Simon James *Unsettled Accounts* (2003)

Bharat Tandon *Jane Austen and the Morality of Conversation* (2003)

Victorian Fiction and the Insights of Sympathy

An Alternative to the Hermeneutics of Suspicion

Brigid Lowe

ANTHEM PRESS
LONDON · NEW YORK · DELHI

Anthem Press
An imprint of Wimbledon Publishing Company
www.anthempress.com

This edition first published in UK and USA 2007
by ANTHEM PRESS
75-76 Blackfriars Road, London SE1 8HA, UK
or PO Box 9779, London SW19 7ZG, UK
and
244 Madison Ave. #116, New York, NY 10016, USA

Brigid Lowe © 2007

The moral right of the author has been asserted.

All rights reserved. Without limiting the rights under copyright reserved above, no
part of this publication may be reproduced, stored or introduced into a retrieval
system, or transmitted, in any form or by any means (electronic, mechanical,
photocopying, recording or otherwise), without the prior written permission
of both the copyright owner and the above publisher of this book.

British Library Cataloguing in Publication Data
A catalogue record for this book is available from the British Library.

Library of Congress Cataloging in Publication Data
A catalog record for this book has been requested.

1 3 5 7 9 10 8 6 4 2

ISBN 1 84331 233 6 (Hbk)
ISBN-13 978 1 84331 233 8 (Hbk)

Cover illustration: 'Portrait of Juliette Courbet as a Sleeping Child,' 1841.
Courtesy of Photo RMN. © Jean-Gilles Berizzi.

Printed in India

For My Mother

... that splendid brotherhood of fiction-writers in England, whose graphic and eloquent pages have issued to the world more political and social truths than have been uttered by all the professional politicians, publicists and moralists put together.

—Karl Marx

I cannot forego [the] opportunity of saying farewell to my readers in this greeting-place, though I have only to acknowledge the unbounded warmth and earnestness of their sympathy in every stage of the journey we have just concluded.

—Charles Dickens

CONTENTS

		Page
Acknowledgements		xi
Introduction: Critical Missiles and Sympathetic Ink		1
1.	Charles Dickens, Uncommercial Space-Time Traveller: *Dombey and Son* and the Ethics of History	23
2.	Other People's Shoes: Realism, Imagination and Sympathy	61
3.	The Personal, the Political and the Human, Part I: Sympathy – a Family Affair?	123
4.	The Personal, the Political and the Human, Part II: Which Family Values?	157
5.	The Personal, the Political and the Human, Part III: 'The Torn Nest is Pierced by the Thorns'– Sympathy after the Family	203
Envoi: Sympathetic Magic		241
Bibliography		243
Index		251

Acknowledgments

I recall with the greatest warmth and gratitude the suggestions and help of friends and colleagues at Oxford and Sheffield, foremost amongst them being Stephen Gill, Valentine Cunningham, David Paroissien, Stefano Maria Evangelista, Dinah Birch, Elisabeth Jay, Sally Shuttleworth, and, in particular, Matthew Bevis, who has been an ideal reader and friend: discriminating and balanced in his advice, and whole-hearted and partisan in his encouragement. I also have to thank the Masters and Fellows of Trinity College, Cambridge, for their generous support and their sympathy for the gadfly, and for breaking with centuries of tradition in electing me, a non-Trinity alumnus, to my Fellowship. The championship and advice of Adrian Poole and Eric Griffiths, especially, have been indispensable: I certainly feel I would not be where I am, were it not for the intellectual trail-blazing of the latter. I am also grateful to all at Anthem for their faith in a controversial manuscript.

The ideas and feelings behind this book were born, however, around a kitchen table in Wales where all the most fundamental ideals of sympathy are incarnate. A million thanks to Fergus Lowe, a truly maternal father, and Catrin Lowe, the embodiment of loving sisterhood, for keeping chat so constantly exciting. Discussions and debates with Sean Crawford (my very own G H Lewes, but with a better beard) have shaped every argument in this book, and his cheerful sustenance is the paper it is written on. And I have to thank my daughter Ide, for proving to me beyond all further question the unparalleled joys of being a non-autonomous human animal. She is a tiny, tender radicle of all the boundless beauty, intelligence, curiosity and friendliness that make our species so poignantly loveable.

This book is dedicated to my mother Pat, 'the last intellectual', and a pioneer of sympathetic realms in life and letters. The extent and importance of her help has been beyond expression.

Introduction: Critical Missiles and Sympathetic Ink

Only we, who are now living, can give a 'meaning' to the past ... It is pointless to complain that the bourgeoisie have not been communitarians, or that the Levellers did not introduce an anarcho-syndicalist society. What we may do, rather, is identify with certain values which past actors upheld ... In the end we also will be dead, and our own lives will lie inert within the finished process, our intentions assimilated within a past event which we never intended. What we may hope is that the men and women of the future will reach back to us, will affirm and renew our meanings, and make our history intelligible within their own present tense ...and ...transmute some part of our process into their progress.

E.P. THOMPSON

In 1988, DA Miller made an influential diagnosis of 'a radical *entanglement* between the nature of the novel and the practice of the police'.[1] His book, *The Novel and the Police*, was designed to challenge what he saw as a politically conservative 'consensus' in departments of English that 'literature exercises a destabilising function in our culture'.[2] In opposition to that 'consensus' a new school of critics, authors of books with valiant titles like *Resisting Novels*, set themselves to argue that the function of literature was to act as vehicle for ideological control.[3] The irresistible conclusion was that this was particularly true of literary forms distinctive of the bourgeois era, and thus of the Victorian novel above all.

At this juncture of the twenty-first century, this stance does not seem as oppositional as it may once have appeared. The tone of much work in English studies now suggests that the existing consensus is, if anything, in agreement with Miller's view of canonical literature in general, and the Victorian novel in particular, as fundamentally disciplinary and conservative. Such a view is institutionally enshrined everywhere, from

---

[1] DA Miller, *The Novel and the Police* (London: University of California Press, 1988), p.2.
[2] Miller, xi.
[3] Lennard J. Davis, *Resisting Novels* (New York and London: Methuen, 1987).

monographs published by professors at the world's leading academies to *The Cambridge Companion to the Victorian Novel* and student reading lists in every university. The present study, however, was written in part out of a strong sense that, widely held though it may be, this view is both unproductive and inaccurate. My argument against this view has its roots in a reflection upon the present and recent past of politicized literary criticism, which prompts some embarrassingly basic questions. These questions are no less important than basic, and are often too well wadded in tactful silence.

i. Criticism in existential crisis?

Poor Mr Casaubon himself was lost among small closets and winding stairs, and...in an exposure of other mythologist's ill-considered parallels, easily lost sight of any purpose which had prompted him to these labours. With his taper stuck before him he forgot the absence of window, and in bitter manuscript remarks on other men's notions about the solar deities, he had become indifferent to the sunlight.

GEORGE ELIOT, *MIDDLEMARCH*

For almost 20 years now, the mainstream of theorized, politicized literary criticism has been living with, and more or less evading, a profound contradiction that strikes at the root of its *raison d'être*. For a while now, this contradiction seems either to have been repressed or to have grown comfortably familiar, but at one time it was a cause not only of nihilistic excitement but also of some concern. For instance, Daniel Cottom's 1987 book on George Eliot, in which he systematically relates every aspect of her fiction to the project of bourgeois hegemony, has a predominately eulogistic foreword by Terry Eagleton. Towards the end of his comments, however, Eagleton remarks that Cottom's 'critical, powerfully distancing study' has been almost 'too successful', prompting as it does the question: 'Why, after this, read Eliot at all?'[4]

---

[4] Terry Eagleton, 'Foreword' to Daniel Cottom, *Social Figures: George Eliot, Social History, and Literary Representation* (Minneapolis: University of Minnesota Press, 1987), xvi. Eagleton has very recently written things that suggest he no longer holds the suspicious and simplistic attitude towards the novel which his older writings imply, although he has never made it clear quite how he is able to come to such a wide range of different conclusions without ever explicitly altering his premises, or conceding a change or a tension within his own views. Certainly he played a big role in releasing from a bottle a destructive genie which has by now outstayed its moment, but continues to build itself up on the massive sales of his *Literary Theory*, *The Ideology of the Aesthetic*, etc.

Eagleton does not seem too deeply troubled by this question, which dallies elegantly between qualification and augmentation of his praise of the book. No wonder perhaps, as Cottom gives the appearance of having pre-empted any such challenge in his preface. There he embraces the Eagletonian axiom that 'criticism, like literature, is always political', but asserts that 'the dominant intellectual tradition in the humanities still rejects this idea ... For these contemporary authorities – especially in the field of literature – remain to a great extent bound by the middle-class construction of reality that I analyse in Eliot's writing'.[5] In the very act of reading Eliot's novels as embodiments of the bourgeois ideology of the 1860s and 70s, in other words, Cottom feels he is indirectly engaged in pulling out the linchpin of the ideology of the 1980s embodied by 'contemporary authorities' in departments of literature – the illusion that literature is something more than a system of discipline or of class propaganda. Cottom finds further justification for his focus on Eliot's novels in the suggestion that they also embody more widely just the same 'middle-class construction of reality' that still dominates — so that critiquing Eliot's ideology is basically the same thing as critiquing that of Thatcher's Britain.

It is doubtful, to say the least, whether the intricately over-materially-determined diagram of a 'middle-class construction of reality' that Cottom provides can plausibly be taken as an accurate description of the nature of middle-class thought at both ends of 130 years of rapid social change. But it is certain that in the 18 years since Cottom wrote, his picture of general attitudes to literature within the 'dominant intellectual tradition in the humanities' has become dated. The Eagletonian axiom that criticism and literature are always political is now foundational to a central current of cultural criticism generally, and criticism of the novel in particular, for which the rejection and exposure – on every possible front, and at every level of detail – of the bourgeois 'construction of reality' as embodied in the literature of the past is an assumed critical motivation. That particular way out of the contradiction no longer works.

So after all this, why, from a political point of view (and, for post-Eagletonian criticism, there is no other), read Eliot? She has received so much notice already. If we are to spend any more time on her we must believe that her novels stand in some peculiar relation to ideology – are exceptional, either in distilling ideology to a concentrated essence, or in challenging its evasions.

For much contemporary politico-literary criticism to admit to studying

5 Cottom, *Social Figures: George Eliot, Social History, and Literary Representation* (Minneapolis: University of Minnesota Press, 1987), xx.

literature out of a conviction that it may have some particular merit is to stand convicted of propagating Cottom's reviled 'middle-class construction of reality', and in consequence many follow his assumption that the requisite task is now to demonstrate that the 'literary' texts on which we have lavished so much attention are no more and no less than ideology given a long and humanist name. One might have thought, though, that if what we have in view is no more than a subversive revelation of the insidious deceptions of the ideology of our own time, our highly developed critical reading techniques would be put to better use applied to television programmes like *ER* or newspapers like *The Guardian* or other such currently popular and influential systems of signs. If, on the other hand, we hope to reach some sort of distinctive understanding of the workings of the ideology of the present through an understanding of the ideology of the past, it looks like running before we can walk to give so much scrutiny (always at the expense of journals, conduct books, advertisements and so on) to a literary discourse that was generally aimed at a relatively small and extremely economically diverse audience – a discourse characterized, moreover, by a bewildering sedimentary accretion of the conventions of many historical periods, and an ambiguous, shifting, and often violently hostile relation to the common sense of its era. Lacking any non-porous definition of the political, Eagleton's maxim that criticism is always political is trivially true. But if we construe the political in a stronger sense – as a more or less reasoned, strategic and/or effective intervention in social life – we must concede that some of criticism's tactics for achieving the political effects to which it nowadays aspires are somewhat baffling.

In order to retain the sense of political/ethical responsibility that has characterized the mainstream of recent literary criticism, it seems to me necessary to abandon many of its tactics and replace them with different ones. If politics is to come into the question of the study of what we have called 'literature' (rather than just contributing to the arguments against such study), it will have to justify allowing literature its continued disproportionate claim on our attention.

The scepticism of my own study, then, is levelled not against the monolithically conceived 'liberal humanism' that many suppose to be embodied in the thought of the past, but rather against the creeping solipsism and self-righteousness that seems to me to threaten the future of political critique in the humanities. I will argue that the best Victorian novels, through their atypical profundity, rather than their typical ideological complicity, provide rich, peculiar resources for the task of social criticism.

I do not mean, however, to announce myself one of those notorious though elusive critics who believe in an absolute, unworldly, 'frankly ontological' (as DA Miller so scathingly puts it) distance between literature and non-literature.[6] As a complex cultural phenomenon, a conception of 'great fiction' that has no more distinct edges than our conception of, say, 'stew' or 'shrubs', is serviceable enough. As with these far simpler things, we can understand each other when we talk of 'a great novel', and can provide some explanation of what we mean in more basic terms. I hope to present a small part of the chimerical total explanation of the way great fiction, particularly as instantiated by the mid-nineteenth-century novel, functions in relation to the political ideologies of its time, and ours; to show that these novels convey some quite distinctive and radical effects and messages. It seems to me more interesting, more useful, and much more challenging, to focus rather on their special insights than on their blind spots.

Thus the question of literary value, although it is addressed only obliquely (as perhaps it can only ever be), hovers on the threshold of what I have to say. It seems to me that the degree of force and skill with which a novel commands distinctive, desirable political and ethical effects and ideas tends to correlate directly (if fairly roughly), rather than inversely, with the degree of literary value traditionally ascribed to it.[7] My juxtaposition of canonical texts with others, both minor and non-fictional, serves several purposes. Non-fiction provides contextual or explanatory keys to the great novels, and emphasizes the distinctiveness of the strategies and insight that they contain as novels. The comparison of big novels with little ones brings out the best in the minor fiction, which can be seen to participate in the same crucial struggles with which the major fiction is engaged, if with lesser mastery. But it also reminds us how exceptionally great, even – or especially – in terms of political sophistication and insight great novels really are. The worldliness of the great novels is not opposed to, but rather a large part of, their literary value.

Such a suggestion is often pre-emptively ruled out by the argument (to which Eagleton gives an early formulation in his foreword) that not only the seeming lack of political function, but also the seemingly subversive tendency of the literary tradition must somehow be part of a double bluff. This argument rests on weak foundations. There is no *prima facie* reason to believe that, as Eagleton insists, 'if the humanities seem merely supplementary to a society with quite different priorities of value, that

---

[6] Miller, xii.

[7] This is not to say that great works of literature are necessarily the most politically insightful and effective texts of any kind that you can get; only that great novels (for example) are usually politically insightful, and generally more so than minor ones.

supplementarity [must] fulfil a structural and hence, paradoxically, "central" function' − to believe, that is, that literature's seeming subversiveness *must* function as a homeopathic cordial for cultural confidence, or some inoculation against real subversion. When Eagleton dismisses the nineteenth-century humanities as exhibiting 'a familiar dialectic' in which 'intensified repression in social reality generates evermore fantastic sublimations, the phenomena at once sworn antagonists and comrades in crime', the terms of his argument suggest the unfalsifiable theories of Freudian pseudo-science.[8]

Such counter-intuitive conclusions are produced by the expectation that the cultural critic should be able to pull out of a hat a functionalist political explanation for every cultural phenomenon in terms of its role in an over-determined and self-perpetuating social structure. But one need not be any sort of idealist to hold that there may not be such functional explanations close at hand for all such phenomena. Cultural systems are extremely complex, and to a degree chaotic. They evolve through a combination of something like random mutation and natural selection − which embodies the blindness of mechanical process − and the forethought and passions of man. There are no other shaping forces on earth, and neither nature nor man has the power to construct a flawless and homogeneously self-perpetuating political system. We should not expect optimality. Like a cultural appendix, the humanistic tradition of social criticism may have either no function at all, or an extremely explosive one. Whether any given text, part of this imagined body of 'the humanities', is functionally empty, conservative, subversive, or something far more complex, is a matter which can be determined only by allowing it individual attention, not by some foregone theoretical deduction.

I mean here to supply that individual attention to a number of nineteenth-century literary texts, with the various charges recently brought against the novel in mind. I do not mean to argue for the immaculate political conceptions of Victorian novelists. I do, however, assume that there is little use in dwelling further on their failures, let alone in indulging in argumentative torsions to reveal that even their most liberating moments are really moments of repression.

I have tried to subordinate a negative argument about the misguidedness of some recent critical strategies to a positive argument about the

---

[8]   Eagleton, 'Foreword', ix, x. A similar worry is posed by Cottom's repeated insistence that George Eliot's caustic comments on the abuse of abstract concepts like 'society', 'human nature' and 'duty' can be nothing but the canny ideological means through which she herself propagates such abstractions.

political/ethical insight of the novel, and for this reason what follows is not a comprehensive engagement with contemporary theories or with their principal exponents.[9] Few of my arguments add up to a complete refutation of recent arguments against the novel on their own terms (though some, I think, do). In general, the indirection and obliquity with which such arguments tend to extrapolate from their already contentious founding assumptions makes any such refutation a rather exorbitant task. I have sought to circumscribe and shape my critique through a detailed focus on particular novels – many of the questions at issue are indeed resistant to entirely abstract consideration; it is for this reason that the novelistic perspective on them is so well worth considering. I try to maintain a coherent argument without distorting the literary evidence by forcing it too crudely into the reified categories of contemporary politico-theoretical debate. The tensions within what I think of as the sympathetic critical perspective have meant that the dynamic and focus of my argument with contemporary politicised criticism is partly diffused by something of the patience of empirical historicism, while that patience is in turn stirred by the urgency of argument. I hope these tensions have proved productive rather than self-defeating.

I will consider the political/ethical function of the novel with regard to its formal properties, historical genesis and cultural genetics. The mixedness of the novel genre demands an eclectic methodological approach and broadness of scope in any such endeavour. At times the novel seems to approach the plane of philosophical argument. At others it seems an aesthetic object whose 'meaning' is of quite another order. Often it seems a vehicle of emotion as impossible either to paraphrase, or to objectify aesthetically, as a kiss. To respond flexibly to these shifting manifestations so that novels are felt at their most expressive – rather than to reduce the formal to the thematic, or the thematic to the formal, or the emotional to either – is part of the sympathetic attitude this book is all about.

ii. Sympathy

[*Socialist thought must maintain*] an understanding of the provisional and exploratory nature of all theory, and the openness with which one must approach all knowledge. This must also entail a respect for the continuity of intellectual culture, which is not to be seen as fractured into two halves,

---

[9] Just about every strand of criticism influenced by 'theory' conceives of itself as political to some degree and at some remove. It is the foundations of these self-conceptualisations that I wish to question.

between the BC and AD of Marx's 'epistemological break', and in which all other minds and knowledges are to be measured against the rule of Marxist Science.[10]

Of course, to acknowledge that there may be political enlightenment extractable from literature is not so radical an idea. Eagleton, in his foreword to Cottom, criticizes the latter for omitting to note the way in which 'the bourgeois ...impulse to incorporate the proletariat unavoidably bequeaths to them certain political and cultural goods, which they can turn against their oppressors'.[11] To show that, despite themselves, novels can be made by clever and enlightened critics to say something subversive (which the novelists would rather have cut their tongue out than suggest on purpose) – that the unavoidable 'gaps' are subversive, or the contradictions are subversive, or anything but the intended sense is subversive – is a common strategy. But there is something patronizing in the concession that though novels may be oppressive, *we* can make something of them despite their best efforts. It has perhaps become more difficult, since 1987 when Eagleton wrote these words, to accept the implication that a Marxist or post-Marxist approach necessarily brings scientific illumination where before there was utter darkness – especially since, according to the schematic materialist explanations which still have common, if often tacit, critical currency, the twenty-first-century critic, or, more pertinently, the twenty-first-century critical mainstream, should not have a jot more potential for subversive insight than the socially mobile nineteenth-century intellectuals with whom, demographically, they have so much in common. Much contemporary criticism works from what Catherine Gallagher and Stephen Greenblatt have recently held up as the 'core hermeneutical presumption' that we can and must 'discover meanings that those who left traces of themselves could not have articulated'. Regarding 'explication and paraphrase' as an activity infinitely beneath the contemporary critic, it considers the only authentic goal 'something more, something that the authors we study would not have had sufficient distance upon themselves and their own era to grasp'.[12] This approach excludes the converse realization that the past might be just as capable of opening up perspectives on *our* views that, without its guidance, *we* might not have sufficient distance

[10] EP Thompson, 'The Poverty of Theory', in *The Poverty of Theory and Other Essays* (London: Merlin Press, 1978), p.360.
[11] Eagleton, 'Foreword,' xvi
[12] Catherine Gallagher and Stephen Greenblatt, *Practising New Historicism* (Chicago and London: University of Chicago Press, 2001), pp.8–9.

enough upon ourselves and *our* own era to grasp (and here I mean *us* critics, in our critical function, not the wider society we look down upon). It is in pursuit of that perspective that I invoke the notion of sympathy.

Sympathy, although it has been widely considered in relation to eighteenth-century fiction, has received very little attention in work on nineteenth-century texts. One recent exception is a study by Audrey Jaffe, yet another politicized indictment of the novel, which focuses on sympathy as a primary rhetorical and ideological trope behind Victorian fiction.[13] Jaffe associates sympathy predominantly with the relation between middle-class 'benefactors' and beggars. She treats it as a notion closely aligned to pity or charity. In this regard, she is of her time. Modern usage of the word 'sympathy' has drifted away from the wide eighteenth-century conception of a general faculty of affective communication, towards an implication of a particular moral or emotional attitude – probably because the coining of 'empathy' in the early twentieth century took over much of the earlier meaning of sympathy. The two words are now often opposed to one another, with 'empathy' comprehending feeling with another person from their point of view, the feeling of their feelings, and 'sympathy' indicating a feeling for them from a distinct, outside, or at least still separate, perspective. But to follow this usage uncritically seems to me to represent a fatal misinterpretation of the Victorian sense of the word. For example, of the hundreds of usages of the word by Dickens (Jaffe's prime suspect for the ideological exploitation of sympathy), only five occur in a context remotely approximating the 'vertical' sympathy, sympathy of the richer for the poorer, on which she focuses (and none of them involve beggars). In fact, Dickens uses the word most often with regard to the attitude of the poor towards one another: he is not the only nineteenth-century observer to note a sense of solidarity amongst the poorest which is less common amongst the middle classes, and it is with this solidarity that he links sympathy.

Jaffe takes as paradigmatic Adam Smith's formulation of sympathy. However, as several commentators have pointed out, Smith's conception of sympathy is something of a retreat within the sentimental tradition.[14] Smith's project and, indeed, to an extent that of Hume in his later years also, was to put the radical genie of sympathy back into the bottle out of which, despite the warnings of his predecessors, Hume had released it in the *Treatise of Human Nature*. Smith seeks to replace Hume's celebration of

---

[13] Audrey Jaffe, *Scenes of Sympathy* (Ithaca, NY and London: Cornell University Press, 2000).

[14] See for instance Joan Tronto, *Moral Boundaries* (London: Routledge, 1993), and John Mullan, *Sentiment and Sociability* (Oxford: Clarendon Press, 1988).

sympathy as a fundamental principle of radically intersubjective communication, as the spontaneous and passionate subjective dispersal that is the raw material of society, with a model of sympathy as distance, spectatorship, impartiality, control and subjective consolidation. But the fiction I look at here seems to resist this revision. The 'distancing' critical practice of Gallagher, Greenblatt and Jaffe herself seems to place them far nearer Smith's model of the proper dynamics of intersubjective communication than Victorian novelists ever get. Dickens's characters grow hot, laugh, and eat out of sympathy. It is hard to accommodate these bodily manifestations of sympathy within Jaffe's conception of it as a spectatorial circulation of representations consolidating individual identity.

While explicit discussion of it declines as the nineteenth century goes on, there remains throughout the Victorian period a pervasive sense of the question of sympathy in the intellectual atmosphere. Any concept is open to abuse, and sympathy is perhaps particularly so; Dickens is as aware of that as Jaffe could ever be. In his fiction, the word occurs in the mouths of characters such as Mrs Jellyby, Harold Skimpole, Eugene Rayburn, and Mrs Skewton, and such false sympathy is indeed represented as an evasion of responsibility and a tool in the construction of an idealized and alienated self-image. However, sympathy retains for Dickens, for many of his contemporaries, and for me, its positive potential.

For Hume, 'no quality of human nature is more remarkable, both in itself and in its consequences, than the propensity we have to sympathize with others ...to receive by communication their inclinations and sentiments'. The starting point of sympathy is recognition of similarity: 'The stronger the relation is betwixt ourselves and any object, the more easily does the imagination make the transition'.[15] The more we share, the easier sympathy comes. Marx and Engels, whose inheritance has been of unrivalled importance in the political critique of culture, were both Victorians. They were exercised by the same direct experience, and many of the same theoretical problems as Victorian novelists. Indeed, there is so much common ground between the author of *London Labour and the London Poor* and Dickens, Gaskell and Brontë; and between Eliot, translator of Feuerbach and sceptical disciple of Comte, and that most intimate critic of Feuerbach and French socialism, Karl Marx, that it is hard to understand why the relationship between Victorian fiction and a tradition of criticism that is the (albeit undutiful) legatee of Marx should be characterized not only by so

---

[15]   David Hume, *A Treatise of Human Nature*, LA Selby-Bigge and PH Nidditch (eds) (Oxford: Clarendon Press, 1978), I.XI.316, I.XI.318.

much hostility but also by such a sense of distance.

It is this acknowledgement of commonality, so strictly repressed in 'powerfully distancing' politicized criticism – of commonality not only between Victorian writers and ourselves, but also between the political condition of literature and that of criticism – with which I begin, and for which I will argue in the first chapter. If we recognize the vitality of our own political struggles, we should recognize that of theirs.

And if we make such a concession, why should we start *always* with the 'powerfully distancing' attitude of suspicion? Even granting the epistemological value of such a stance, we may nevertheless concede that there are some things it makes invisible and incomprehensible. If we meet a friend with suspicion, secrets that would be made open to the sympathetic listener are closed to us, though we might mark things sympathy would have missed. 'Every human creature resembles ourselves, and by that means has an advantage above any other object, in operating on the imagination', Hume reminds us.[16] Similarity gives us privileged access to the productions of human thought, a specifically inside view that is quite distinct from the objective attention we can bestow on other objects. Sympathy does not imply approval, however often it may lead to it; what it does imply is real, personal, human engagement – intellectual give and take. It is this engagement that much politicized literary criticism of the novel lacks.

Eagleton's digest of Eliot's literary project as a concerted effort to 'resolve a structural conflict between two forms of mid-Victorian ideology: between progressively muted Romantic individualism, concerned with the untramelled evolution of the "free spirit", and certain "higher", corporate ideological modes …(essentially Feuerbachian humanism and scientific rationalism)', is useful and accurate in its own way, but it rather lacks sympathetic imagination.[17] A too eager and facile taxonomizing of the politics of a novel is belittling and, in its rejection and reification of the mobile and imaginative politics of fiction, hostilely pre-emptive of serious intellectual engagement. George Eliot seems to anticipate just such a treatment when she has Dorothea exclaim against the theoretical reduction of her world-view: '"Please not to call it by any name … You will say it is Persian, or something else geographical. It is my life."' The cool allotment of labels, no matter how astutely assorted, can no more capture the spirit and significance of a great novel than it can that of a life, and this is true even, and perhaps particularly, if our interest is in political significance. Hume

---

16   Hume, *Treatise*, II.5.359.
17   Terry Eagleton, *Criticism and Ideology* (London: Verso, 1978), p.111.

speaks of sympathy as a movement in which 'the idea is presently converted
into an impression', a movement made possible because 'as in strings
equally wound up, the motion of one communicates itself to the rest; so all
the affections readily pass from one person to another, and beget
correspondent movements in every human creature'.[18] Modifying but
echoing his terms and elaborating on his theory, Eliot speaks of a
sympathetic discernment that is 'but a hand playing with finely-ordered
variety on the chords of emotion – a soul in which knowledge passes
instantaneously into feeling, and feeling flashes back as a new organ of
knowledge'.[19] Sympathetic understanding is a matter not of objective
examination but of subjective participation. An appreciation of the dynamic
behind an idea, of the passion with which it is felt and the imagination
which keeps it in motion, is no more accessible to 'powerfully distancing'
theories than the beauty of a view is accessible to a blind scientist with a
theoretically comprehensive knowledge of the workings of human sight. The
imaginative endeavours of times past are evidence of human soul-searchings
that we may understand and feel from the inside, as well as coldly and
objectively from the outside. The similarity between our condition and that
of our literary subjects, not only as fellow human beings but also as
conscientious fellow wrestlers with political problems, and many of the same
problems at that, provides us the only access we need.

From such a perspective, if we can no longer deconstruct and deflate, we
can fill in the blanks where we find incoherence teetering on the brink of
lucidity. A sympathetic consideration of the problems faced in fiction as well
as of the objects fallen short of makes it less tempting to judge according to
pre-established, fixed rules that are devised to consolidate the self-
complacence of the critic at the expense of his object. Sympathetic reading is
reading with the grain, polishing up a glow that can illumine our own
thinking. Elbow grease is not wasted in this endeavour. We have not
exhausted the promise of the sympathetic critical attitude – it may well be
impossible ever to do so.

My project of tracing some of the invocations of sympathy in the novel,
on the one hand, and my enthusiasm for sympathy, on the other, may seem
incompatible, rendering my project 'biased', an instance of the reading
practice which Catherine Belsey has long been suspicious of, because it
'manifests a prior commitment in its reproduction of the values and

---

[18]   Hume, *Treatise*, I.XI.317, III.I.376, II:XXII.
[19]   George Eliot, *Middlemarch* (1872), ed. David Carroll (Oxford and New York:
Clarendon Press, 1986), II:xxii:218, IV:xxxix:382.

strategies of the text it undertakes to judge'.[20] There are good reasons, however, to reject this objection. Politicized criticism already implies prior commitments, and Belsey's own practice manifests the converse priority of rejecting the values and strategies of the past's texts. Besides, any protest on this score begs the question against my sympathetic project, for the sympathy I try to exercise, and that I trace in the novels, has nothing to do with impartial observation. It is precisely to assumed critical impartiality – to spurious pretensions of objectivity or scientific immunity from the temptations and quagmires of all embedded perspectives – to which my use of sympathy is opposed. In her chapter in *The Cambridge Companion to the Victorian Novel* (2001), Linda M Shires tells us that Victorian realism is ideologically suspect because it 'supposes a privileged epistemological point of view from which both knowledge and judgement can be truthfully and precisely issued to establish consensus among implied author ...and reader'.[21] The fact that she can miss the application of these words to her own theorizing is a symptom of a lack of critical distance from her own conceptions in proportion to the vast gap she establishes between herself and Victorian fiction. A truly successful sympathetic reading, on the contrary, brings us close to the text but gives us an outside perspective on our own assumptions.

All this is not to say that I don't think what I have to say is true – like George Eliot, I would insist that sympathy is an indispensable mode of understanding, not a form of irrational subjectivism. Paradoxically, leaving ourselves open to the elements of truth in alien systems of thought places our own truth-claims on a firmer basis. Sympathetic attention to the intellectual struggles of the past gives us the hope of opening new perspectives, establishing vibrant and dynamic relations with those perspectives, and letting the passion and commitment and restlessness that shape them flow into us. It helps us to resist the Lytton Strachey-like smugness that so destructively permeates the still essentially modernist critical dogma of our culture.

The biggest threat to political insight and passion is stasis and complacency, and a continual mechanical 'exposure' of the 'ideologies' of literary texts has substantially served such complacency. Such acts of exposure require no real analysis of political goals and strategies, and no

---

[20] Catherine Belsey, 'ReReading the Great Tradition', in Peter Widdowson (ed), *ReReading English*, (London and New York: Methuen, 1982), pp.121–35, p.122.

[21] Linda M Shires, 'The Aesthetics of the Victorian Novel: Form, Subjectivity, Ideology', in *The Cambridge Companion to the Victorian Novel*, ed. Deirdre David (Cambridge: Cambridge University Press, 2001), p.63.

positive commitment to any ideals at all; they simply provide a cheap glow of action and virtue by comparison. The construction of a theory of literature, especially a political theory of literature, is such an ambitious and challenging endeavour that any readiness to accept as complete its conclusions and boundaries must be complacency. I make some attempt here to extend the theory of fiction in the kind of unexpected directions suggested by sympathetic readings of Victorian novels. The consequences of sympathy are always unexpected. Dissolving the boundaries between subject and object, sympathy prevents us from simply repeating ourselves.

My main object here is to re-frame the debate over the fundamental politics of the Victorian novel sympathetically; to show that it is possible to argue with all the rigour and novelty to which theory aspires that the novel as a genre is quite as capable of incisive political and ethical critique as it is of ideological consolidation. In this book sympathy is both a recurring object of attention, intricately connected to the insights I attribute to the novels, and a guiding critical principle. Each chapter draws out, through sympathetic attention to the texts in hand, a distinct formal or thematic mobilization of sympathy – sympathy as a weapon, pitted against individualism, victimization and inequality, and as a force capable of imagining and realising a better future. The chapters will build up a fuller picture of what precisely I make, and what a number of representative Victorian novels made, of that subtle and humane concept.

iii. Reaction?

It would be easy to assume that I differ from the political critics with whom I find fault for the simple reason that our basic political objectives are different. I doubt that this is the case, and I hope that my arguments throughout will serve to expose the fallacy of any such assumption. However, a profound difficulty in finally settling the question of the connection between political objectives and critical-theoretical commitments arises from the taboo against the explicit voicing of any positive political statements, even in criticism where negative statements abound. This taboo has made my argument on behalf of Victorian fiction more difficult. Because the positive political standards of the criticism that arraigns Victorian fiction remain elusive, it is only fiction's innocence as charged that is open to explicit demonstration; its positive merit according to those standards remains a cloudy question.

The critics I am arguing with might also object that defending the novel's politics on the grounds of its advocacy of sympathy is a tactic bound to fail because sympathy is not political but rather a matter of personal ethics. Those inclined to pose such an objection will already have been nodding to themselves knowingly as, by my bracketing together of the moral and the political, I confirm their worst suspicions as to my confusion and naivety. I have clearly failed to grasp, they inwardly remark, that fundamental premise of politicised criticism: namely, that morality and ethics serve precisely to displace politics. Sympathy is either an unnecessary supplement to politics, or a hypocritical and manipulative bourgeois fantasy.

Novels cannot organise trade unions or any other political associations, cannot orchestrate strikes or build arsenals in preparation for the revolution. Novels operate on individuals and their beliefs and inclinations, and often primarily (in the nineteenth century anyway) on middle-class or déclassé readers. They advocate and forward the adoption of sympathy, first and foremost (if not only), by individuals. These fundamental facts are the bedrock of most politicized critiques of the novel, and the conclusions to which the elaborate arguments and demonstrations of such criticism lead are often more or less already comprehended in judgements based on these facts.

The lack of any positive values on which to found a political critique, and the dismissal of the novel as a 'private' realm of discourse, both follow from one popular structuralist version of Marxism, which distinguishes itself from 'idealist' utopian socialism by adopting the guise of a science. Theory, in this tradition, sets itself up not as a statement of political ideals or objectives, nor as an argument designed to persuade its hearers to adopt those ideals and objectives, but rather as a subjectless scientific insight into the way things are and will be.

EP Thompson has long since exploded this reading of Marx. He argues, on the evidence of the highly moral and emotional tone of much of Marx's writing, that when the latter appeared to be rejecting ethical or moral discourse in favour of a pared-down, objective economism he was, in fact, 'writing with his tongue firmly in his cheek, and striking a pre-emptive blow against his critics by borrowing the rhetoric closest to the hearts of every exploiter who could exonerate himself as being the *träger* of economic "laws"'.[22] The idea that moral judgements, personal feeling, responsibility and will on the one hand, and economic and political reality on the other, do not mix, originates in political economy, and not in Marx. And even if

---

[22]   Thompson, p.340, in sidelong allusion to the theoretical elimination of human subjects from the process of history that Louis Althusser proposes through his notion of 'interpellation' and his concept of subject-positions as no more than vectors or '*träger*' within the social system.

this idea were authentically Marxian, we would have to get rid of it. After all, Marx wrote with the expectation of particular economic developments. Given this expectation, he was able to set aside (some of the time), for the sake of parsimony, the utopian socialist's invocations of ideals, and faith in the potential of social regeneration before or independent of material development. But Marx's predictions have failed, and will fail, at least for the foreseeable future, to fulfil themselves. If a proletarian revolution were still possible, without that inexhaustible abundance of resources predicted by Marx there would be no necessary reason for it to extend equality to the world's worst off, who are now not proletarians. We can no longer conceive any way in which an egalitarian world-order could be created as a mechanical result of material pressure and its issue in class/self-interested self-assertion: the most effectively 'exploited' and the worst off are no longer the same people, and so strength and suffering come apart, and the suffering of some must rely for remedy upon the strength of others.

In any case, effective collective action has always been dependent upon group feelings of solidarity. Individuals must not only recognize the alignment of their interests with those of a certain group, they must also feel a selfless commitment to that group's interest. They must be spurred to action by understanding and feeling the suffering of others – by what I will be calling 'sympathy'. To posit such a sense as (potentially) central to human nature and human society is no more essentialist than to give rational self- or group-interest that pride of place. And if there are reasons for insisting that such a sense must always be discretely contained within classes until after the revolution, those reasons entail far more than a simple deduction from materialist principles. Even a picture of man as a cog in a material mechanism must make certain assumptions about the shape of that cog; that is, about human subjectivity.

As GA Cohen puts it, 'we can no longer believe the factual premises of [Marxist] conclusions ...cannot share Marx's optimism about material possibility, but we therefore also cannot share his pessimism about social possibility if we wish to sustain a socialist commitment'.[23] It is because of a failure to confront this notion that much contemporary politicized literary criticism is characterized not only by complacency but also by despair. These are not contradictory but rather complementary attitudes. It is easy to feel confident that you are doing all you should when you believe there is nothing to be done: you have nothing better to do than critique those less

---

[23]   GA Cohen, *If You're an Egalitarian, How Come You're So Rich?* (London and Cambridge Mass: Harvard University Press, 2001), p.115.

disillusioned. Nancy Armstrong's statement of the highest aspirations of her criticism is a good illustration – 'to use my power as a woman of the dominant class and as a middle-class intellectual to name what power I use as a form of power rather than to disguise it as the powerlessness of others' – at once lofty and tragically absurd.[24]

Marx and Engels were surely right to criticize utopian socialism for its failure to found its projections for the future on an analysis of present economic and social conditions. But utopian confidence in the human power to choose the forms that history will take, and to exercise that power through rational and emotional persuasion, should not be dispensed with as unnecessary or idealist. Realist fiction has a solid claim to found itself precisely on the analysis of present conditions that Marx and Engels found lacking in utopian socialism. We should not automatically suspect its self-conscious harnessing of this analysis to a persuasive, prescriptive, normative and sympathetic discourse. Marx himself made use of such discourse, albeit sometimes rather surreptitiously.

To strike the balance between the useless abstraction of utopian socialism and classical Marxism's defeatist pessimism about the possibility of any social change not wholly subservient to material change, we need to adopt a distinctive perspective. Sympathy may offer the key to both our hopes for and our understanding of social possibility. Sympathy, as we shall see, is never just a mode of understanding; it is, by definition, a spur to action. Sympathy allows us to consider material conditions from a human perspective, through the lens of human feeling, self-consciousness and social awareness, even as that lens is trained always on determinate material circumstances. That perspective tells us about and allows us to *feel* constraints, needs and potentials all at once.

The question of the political status of sympathy is, in the end, however, like most questions of politics, hard to address in the abstract. The chapters that follow provide a more concrete (though, for that very reason also more oblique) consideration of the question.

Apart from the objections to the fundamental premises of my study which might be anticipated from the quarter of mainstream theory, I can also imagine one major objection from another quarter. There is still a large body of criticism, some (if not much) of it politicized criticism, that goes about its business of research, reading and argument without wasting its time thinking about the sillinesses of theory. Why have I allowed myself to

---

[24] Nancy Armstrong, *Desire and Domestic Fiction* (Oxford: Oxford University Press, 1987), p.26

be diverted from my engagement with this serious, responsible criticism by indulging in this skirmish with absurdity? This question does worry me, because I respect this sort of criticism and in many ways would like to get on with it myself. But not quite yet.

In the year I was born, EP Thompson prefaced *The Poverty of Theory* (1978), his prescient broadside against the dangers and fallacies within the rising tide of structuralist political thought, with an epigraph from Marx: 'To leave error unrefuted is to encourage intellectual immorality'. More than 25 years later, many 'politicized' critics working with a theoretical model which has proved far more contagious than even Thompson ever dreamed, are either unaware of or ignore the critique of structuralist premises that he voiced. As a consequence, I feel it a matter of responsibility to renew the critique; to formulate some of the various objections which crowd into the mind on reading so much contemporary politicized criticism. This book is not an exercise in pure political or historiographic theory, and many of the abstract political arguments that it forwards with regard to particular novels are given much more elaborate and comprehensive exposition elsewhere by political thinkers to whose work I refer. I share with Thompson, however, a conviction that certain premises of theory are manifestly and dangerously hollow, and need to be challenged.

iv. The chapters

This book is structured by the several primary angles from which the Victorian novel has been theorized as socially conservative: new-historicist and post-colonial criticism (Chapter One), Barthesian semiotics (Chapter Two), and anti-humanist, feminist, and what has conventionally passed as 'Marxist' criticism (Chapters Three, Four and Five). I suggest, in each case, the limitations of the politically hostile assessments that have been made of Victorian fiction, and demonstrate how the latter, in its turn, suggests gaps in the very theories that have been used to dismiss it.

Political criticism of Victorian fiction has clustered around two issues in particular. First, the political effects and implications of 'fictional realism' as a representational form have fallen under the deepest suspicion. Secondly, the 'subject-centred' focus of Victorian fiction and the 'humanism' of its value system have been impugned. The novel is accused, on both these counts, of making what is really 'political' seem 'natural', what is really a matter of the structures of historical process and language seem 'human', and of concealing and contributing to the manipulations of power. The two charges are intimately related, and my focus in this book shifts gradually from a consideration of the first to a consideration of the second.

Chapter One develops the argument initiated here: that sympathetic attention to the intuitions of the past as they are manifest in fiction is at once a valuable opportunity and an imperative duty for contemporary criticism. In particular, I equate the violent misreading of the past that has been so self-consciously embraced by new-historicism with the cultural arrogance and violence of imperialism. A close reading of Dickens' *Dombey and Son,* in conjunction with his account in *All the year Round* of the mid-nineteenth century's most dreadful shipwreck, reminds us of the importance of historical witness and of sympathetic dialogue across time. Dickens and his contemporaries were much more aware of the impossibility of absolute objectivity in writing history, of the amorphousness of events, and of the selectivity of language and narrative, than recent political criticism has allowed. However, the figurative structures of Dickens's novel provide powerful imaginative warnings of the nihilism implicit in any abandonment of the responsibilities we owe to history. They suggest that all humanity – past, present and future – is united in the struggle to preserve meaning and value against the titanic force of historical change, and that a trans-historical dialogue, characterized by sympathy and forgiveness, should be constructed upon the consciousness of this unstable common ground.

Chapter Two argues that the kind of sympathetic engagement with fiction argued for in the previous chapter is not as dangerous or as illusory as many literary critics have thought. I address the argument that literary realism, of which Barthes voiced such influential suspicion, is not only philosophically naïve, but also politically conservative in its reification of the status quo. Barthes, Miller, Davis, Crosby, Gallagher and many others argue that fictional realism constructs a 'world of significance', in which material reality is reduced to grand ideological structures of meaning. Critics of this persuasion consider the details enumerated by such fiction as no more than a kind of secondary camouflage designed to disguise its signifying 'interpellating' function. This conclusion, I argue, is itself no more than a tautological restatement of the partiality of the radically anti-empiricist premises of this mode of criticism, superficially disguised as historical critique. My alternative suggestion is that these details in what I call (after the Victorian association of women with what is material, immediate and particular) 'feminine' fiction, are basically *insignificant,* and only sometimes and secondarily do they serve as vehicles for carrying the 'meaning' of the work as a whole. Their role is to incite us to imagine, sensuously and emotionally, an experience not our own. Such imagining is conducted through the diversity of subjective positions that these fictions allow us to inhabit. These novels thus cultivate and extend our powers of sympathetic imaginative projection. Rather than teaching the exclusive 'facts' of History, they train us in the historical and political virtue of sympathy.

The idea of sympathy has become associated, to its discredit, with Victorian personal and family values. The representation of family in Victorian fiction is seen by much recent literary criticism as monolithically ideological: anti-feminist, anti-egalitarian, pro-capitalist and, worst of all, disseminative of 'humanism' and 'essentialism'. I take these last two words to stand, roughly, for the idea, presumed to be motivated by opposition to social change, that certain attributes and behaviour are 'naturally' human, and differentially distributed among men and women in accordance with their sex, and that their practicability and value adheres in naturalness. The essentialism of domestic fiction is perceived as facilitating an evasion, or false reconciliation, of political contradictions, and the prioritization of sympathy is taken as part of this exercise. The second half of this book shows that this is a distortion, in several ways. The domestic focus in fiction, and, indeed, the focus on the 'natural', is neither inherently conservative, apolitical, nor merely a lower case or allegorical reflection of public politics, but rather the site of a naked struggle between rival conceptions of human nature, society and the proper scope of sympathy – the basic components of Victorian ideological conflict. The separation of personal and moral from the social and political is precisely what is at stake at the heart of domestic fiction, and the battle is hotly fought out.

Victorian fiction show us that the proof that family life gives us of human interdependence and natural capacity for mutuality and cooperation is a resource that political theory neglects at its peril. What has often been viewed as a conservative, anti-feminist emphasis on traditional family values is at least as much a radical rejection of the rising politics of self-ownership and the de-moralization of wider social relations.

Chapter Five argues that the gender, family and social politics of Eliot's *The Mill on the Floss* must be understood in this context. The novel constitutes perhaps the most radical critique ever of the whole notion of the adequacy of individual rights to human well-being. In rejecting Stephen, Maggie rejects the containment of sympathy within the freely-chosen conjugal bond; a forced contraction of social instinct at the root of the public/private, goods/rights divides. Maggie's history is an engagement with historical circumstance in the struggle for a new kind of non-alienated, altruistic and sympathetic relation that can expand the restrictions and exclusions of the family and operate in and on the modern world. Eliot provides an imaginative argument for the idea that the good should be conceived not as an abstract law but rather as the sympathetic potential of an essentially communal mankind. The novel is a powerful plea against the judging, rewarding, and punishing of human beings (or, by extension, of the novels in which they express their weakness, their struggles and their desires) according to an objective, rigid and unforgiving rationale, and for the widest and most active possible mobilization of sympathy.

Domestic fiction's detailed and affective pictures of the diurnal patterns of family life provide a unique insight into some of the central problems of moral and political philosophy. Domestic habits profoundly circumscribe and condition social, economic and political action. As the most far-reaching ideological intervention in this arena ever, domestic fiction demonstrates the complex range of senses in which the family, and the sympathetic attitudes we associate with it, were, and are, political.

For me, perhaps the greatest contribution of Victorian fiction comes from its investment in and explorations of sympathy. I hope this study of a few great novels will suggest just how important sympathy is – not only for the investigation and understanding of the past, but also for the shaping of the future.

CHAPTER 1

Charles Dickens, Uncommercial Space-Time Traveller:
Dombey and Son and the Ethics of History

As the abyss of time widens between judges and defendants, it is always a lesser experience judging a greater ... If the spirit of the trial succeeds nothing will remain of us but a memory of ...atrocities sung by a chorus of children ... Man proceeds in the fog. But when he looks back to judge people of the past, he sees no fog in their path. From his present, which was for them the faraway future, their path looks perfectly clear ...he sees their mistakes but not the fog ...forget[s] what man is ...what we ourselves are.

MILAN KUNDERA, *Testaments Betrayed*

i. Victorian and postmodern collisions

For the central currents of post-colonial and new-historicist criticism, 'history', as it is usually thought of, is in every sense the History of the West. As Robert Young puts it, 'History, with a capital H ...cannot tolerate otherness or leave it outside its economy of inclusion. The appropriation of the other as a form of knowledge within a totalising system can thus be set alongside the history (if not the project) of European imperialism'.[1] Young argues that History's linear narrative of logical cause and effect, teleologically tending towards totality, rhetorically occludes other 'histories', and rhetorically legitimates the subjugation of other peoples in the cause of ascendant western man's supposedly preordained mission to unite the globe under his rule of enlightenment.[2]

---

[1] Robert Young, *White Mythology* (London: Routledge, 1990), p.4.

[2] The proliferation of capital letters in the prose of the exponents of this view is meant

The oppressive power of History has been detected not only in history writing itself, but also in related forms of writing, and particularly in the novel. In Edward Said's words, 'If we study the impulses giving rise to [the novel] we shall see the far from accidental convergence between the patterns of narrative authority constitutive of the novel on the one hand, and, on the other, a complex ideological configuration underlying the tendency to imperialism'.[3] Said is far from alone in seeing the entire novel genre as not only inherently related to, but as absolutely constituted by, the imperialist impulse. Much recent criticism of Dickens's *Dombey and Son* – notably, that of Said himself, of Deirdre David and of Suvendrini Perera – is influenced by such a view of history and the novel's relation to it.[4]

Implicit in the tone of Young, Said, and much of the criticism influenced by them is the assumption that an awareness of the tensions and illusions behind 'History' as a grand narrative is something that has only recently become available. The polemical force of their approach would be undermined by the acknowledgment that Empire-building mid-nineteenth-European century culture was already deeply marked by such an awareness. We need to remember that Dickens, along with many of his contemporaries, had a very sophisticated conception of the complex relation between history as it happens, narrative, and power. The conscientiousness of his negotiation of this problem not only pre-empts the arguments of contemporary postcolonial and new historicist theory; in some respects, as I will argue, it offers them a lot to learn. In this chapter I will examine the ethical implications of current strategies for reading the culture of the past, and seek in Victorian texts themselves alternative negotiations of the responsibilities demanded by history.

I will focus here on *Dombey and Son* and one of Dickens's journalistic offerings to *All the Year Round*. Both are products of a particular sense of history and of an attitude to remembrance that can be observed elsewhere in the culture of the period – in newspaper reactions to the incident at the centre of Dickens's article, in the explicit statements of nineteenth-century philosophers of history, and in the Victorian preoccupation with

---

to express, I take it, the rhetorical elevation of the contingent and particular into the absolute and universal – my own discussion of this perspective necessarily follows this typographical convention, inseparable as it has become from the sense expressed, notwithstanding its now rather jarring voguishness.

[3] Edward Said, *Culture and Imperialism* (London: Chatto and Windus, 1993), p.82.

[4] Deirdre David, *Rule Britannia* (Ithaca and London: Cornell University Press, 1995); Suvendrini Perera, 'Empire and the Family Business in *Dombey and Son*', *Victorian Studies* 33:4 (1990), 603–20.

memorialization and sentimental nostalgia. The incident that is recorded in Dickens's journal article starkly illuminates problems of historicity that are at the heart of *Dombey*, as well as of the practice of literary criticism. The juxtaposed texts highlight Dickens's powerful acknowledgement of the stubbornness of these problems and the subtlety of his exploration of them.

ii. 1859 – History on the rocks

In 1859, Dickens published the first of a series of reports written in the persona of the 'Uncommercial Traveller' for *All the Year Round*. Opening with a focus on the orderly passage of time, so easily chronicled and captured by the dates and methods of historians and journalists, the report purports to be an account of a similarly orderly, teleological universe in which details range themselves in regular and predictable sequence:

> Never had I seen a year going out, or going on, under quieter circumstances. Eighteen hundred and fifty-nine had but another day to live, and truly its end was Peace on that sea-shore that morning. So settled and orderly was everything …in the bright light of the sun and under the transparent shadows of the clouds, that it was hard to imagine the bay otherwise, for some years past or to come … The Tug-steamer lying a little off the shore, the Lighter lying still nearer to the shore, the boat alongside the Lighter, the regularly-turning windlass aboard the Lighter, the methodical figures at work, all slowly and regularly heaving up and down with the breathing of the sea, all seemed as much a part of the nature of the place as the tide itself …. So orderly, so quiet, so regular – the rising and falling of the Tug-steamer, the Lighter, and the boat – the turning of the windlass – the coming of the tide.[5]

The very identity of the moment is inextricably linked with its date, 'eighteen hundred and fifty-nine', which seems to cement it in a historical narrative as 'settled and orderly' as the prospect itself. The pulsing rhythm of the prose, with its composed, monotonous repetitions and syntactical structures, suggests a perfect fit between the medium of description and the scene described. Nothing can be lost on, or to, the reporter — what goes around comes around, like the 'regularly turning windlass', which the

---

[5]   Charles Dickens, 'The Shipwreck' in Michael Slater and John Drew (eds), *The Uncommercial Traveller and Other Papers, 1859–70* (London: JM Dent, 2000), p.29. Hereafter *UT*.

passage brings around in good order before our eyes twice, along with the Tug-steamer, the Lighter, the boat, and the words that cement our assurance – 'quieter ...shore ...settled ...orderly ...lying ...shore ...lying ...shore ...regularly ...regularly ...orderly ...quiet ...regular'. The breathing sea is a reassuring presence, validating the parallel rhythms of human activity. The slight ambiguity flickering about the conception of the year as at once 'going out' and 'going on', the mutation of the 'going' into 'the coming of the tide', and the almost oxymoronic constructions 'regularly-turning', 'regularly heaving', 'transparent shadows', seems lulled away by the pervading tranquillity, as the language itself appears to embody a reconciliation between change and permanence, the immanence of the present moment and the intransience of writing. The scene, and the language in which it is captured, seems as 'transparent' as the shadows of the clouds, 'for the moment nothing was so calmly and monotonously real under the sunlight as the gentle rising and falling of the water ...and the slight obstruction so very near my feet' (*UT*, p.29).

However, such a sense of stability is only 'for the moment', the opaque sea only seems still, while beneath it is constantly in flux: 'the tide was on the flow'. The radical instability and discontinuity implicit in the dying of the old year are shown to be a corollary undercurrent of the onward flow of time:

> There was some slight obstruction in the sea within a few yards of my feet: as if the stump of a tree, with earth enough about it to keep it from lying horizontally on the water, had slipped a little from the land – and as I stood upon the beach and observed it dimpling the light swell that was coming in, I cast a stone over it. (*UT*, p.29)

This ambiguous ripple in the smooth regularity of empirical detail is the trace of the instability of time – of its inherent disruptiveness, discontinuity and chaos. Do what he will to master the scene through concrete description, to toss a rhetorical pebble over it by comparing it with familiar sights, the journalist cannot trace any common cause for the ripple. In fact it is the sign of a rupture and a displacement greater than that of a tree from land to sea, for

> that slight obstruction was the uppermost fragment of the Wreck of the *Royal Charter*, Australian Trader and passenger ship, homeward bound, that struck here on the terrible morning of the twenty-sixth of this October ...went down with her treasure of at least five hundred human

lives, and has never stirred since! From which point, or from which, she drove ashore, stern foremost; on which side, or on which, she passed the little Island in the bay, for ages henceforth to be aground ...these are rendered bootless questions by the darkness of that night and the darkness of death. (*UT*, pp.29–30)

Nevertheless, even the sight of the exposed twisted metal of the wreck cannot shatter the 'prevailing air the whole scene wore, of having been exactly the same for years'. The moment refuses to spell out its own history – 'bootless' are attempts to make it speak. Reflection and memory seem 'to glide down into the placid sea, with other chafe and trouble'. In self-conscious use of the journalist's jargon of 'transparent' reportage – 'Australian Trader and passenger ship, homeward bound ...morning of the twenty-sixth of this October ...at least five hundred human lives' – Dickens conjures the disaster as an official 'event', but recognises nonetheless the inadequacy of such an account. His writing struggles to capture change, which is so 'hard to imagine'.

The *Royal Charter* foundered off Anglesey in a freak hurricane, a 'complete horizontal cyclone', which raged over Britain, killing 800 people, and destroying factories, piers, and railway lines as it went; it reached 12 on the Beaufort Scale. Force 11 is described as '64–75 mph, very rarely experienced; accompanied by widespread damage'. Force 12 is not described; it lies beyond the controlling resources of classification, the narratives of science.

The traditional rhetorical use of an anthropomorphized nature as legitimating model for an organic, harmonious, God-given history of society, predictable according to laws as inevitable as those of Newtonian physics, is inverted by such an unpredictable natural catastrophe. The wreck of the *Royal Charter*, as Dickens presents it, embodies both the sheer randomness of history and the difficulty of capturing, narrating and remembering such randomness. It is this difficulty, made urgent and anxious by a haunting sense of the immanence of past and future time, that haunts Dickens's first non-fictional contribution to the journal he originally considered naming 'Change', or 'Time and Tide'.[6]

Dickens visited the church where the drowned were buried:

It is a little church of great antiquity; there is reason to believe that some church has occupied the spot, these thousand years or more

---

6   John Forster, *The Life of Charles Dickens*, 3 vols (London: Chapman and Hall, 1872–4), III, p.214.

...things usually belonging to the church were gone, owing to its living congregation having ...yielded it up to the dead. The very Commandments had been shouldered out of their places ...on the stone pavement...were the marks and stains where the drowned had been laid down. The eye, with little or no aid from the imagination, could yet see how the bodies had been turned, and where the head had been and where the feet. Some faded traces of the Australian ship may be discernible on the stone pavement of this little church, hundreds of years hence, when the digging for gold in Australia shall have long and long ceased. (*UT*, p.32)

Dickens's attention is riveted by a sense of time, an awesome sense of interminable transience, of perpetual displacement, where everything must be shouldered out or must yield. The place, in its changes and its permanence, is a symbol of past, present and future – Dickens's mind races back a thousand years or more, and forward hundreds, 'long and long'. A succession of churches in the place establish a continuum, while each buries and obliterates its predecessor – there is reason to believe there has always been 'some' church on 'the spot' – memory and history conjoin uncertainty and exactitude. Wishfully effacing the enormity of his own memorializing endeavour (change is so 'hard to imagine'), Dickens fancies that the event may leave material traces of its own that will speak with 'no aid from the imagination', but his framing of the suggestion only emphasizes its hopelessness. When I visited the church I found the pavement buried under a glossy pine floor.

Dickens' attention is transfixed by a consciousness of the historicity of his own account. The wreck and his record of it are suspended together in the invisible web of time and change. The bodies, he tells us, had papers in their pockets, which 'carefully unwrinkled and dried, were little less fresh in appearance that day, than the present page will be under ordinary circumstances, after having been opened three or four times' (*UT*, p.33). A levelling bond of mutability and mortality establishes an intimacy between Dickens and the dead, whose very breast pockets are open to his inspection. Through the indexical – 'the present page' – and the paper on which his account is and will be written – at once under his hand, and under that of his reader in future years, or future centuries – he links himself and us to the corpses with a double implication: all may be either lost 'at sea' or, through the redeeming force of an intimate, sympathetic memory, saved from the engulfing tide of time. 'The present page' transcends time, even through its vulnerability to its ravages.

Dickens, in this article, seems inspired by a conception like Carlyle's, of historical witness as an 'unspeakably precious' 'Letter of Instruction...the only *articulate* communication ...which the Past can have with the Present, the Distant with what is Here, [which] comes to us in the saddest state; falsified, blotted out, torn, lost and but a shred of it in existence; this too so difficult to read'.[7]

> I thought of the many people, inhabitants of this mother country, who would make a pilgrimage to the little churchyard in years to come ...of the many people in Australia, who would have an interest in such a shipwreck ...I thought of the writers of all the wreck of letters I had left upon the table; and I resolved to place this little record where it stands. (*UT*, p.40)

His account, with its transcription of letters from relatives of the drowned, some quoting the words of the drowned, mingles the voices of the living and the dead. Some of the relatives of the dead to whom he refers rationalise their loss as the will of God, but Dickens himself gives no assent to this attribution of purpose to the chance event. He sees fit, nevertheless, destined though his account may be to become just another 'wreck of letters', to memorialize both the disaster and the local rector, Stephen Roose Hughes, who 'most tenderly and thoroughly devoted himself to the dead' (*UT*, p.31). Dickens makes of the whole incident, whose very randomness makes it seem almost insignificant, beyond the call of the historian[8], a symbol of the difficulty and the importance of writing and of memory.

Roose Hughes spent months identifying the bodies of the drowned,

---

[7]   Thomas Carlyle, 'On History Again', in *Critical and Miscellaneous Essays*, 5 vols (London: Chapman and Hall, 1899), III, pp.167–8.

[8]   The wreck has not received much attention from historians. The only secondary accounts of the wreck are given by local historians A McKee (*The Golden Wreck* (London: Souvenir Press, 1961)) and R Williams ('Anglesey and the Loss of the "*Royal Charter*"', *Transactions of the Anglesey Antiquarian Society and Field Club* (1959), 21–43). These two accounts often conflict, and neither deals with the contemporary reaction in any detail. Many of the particulars of the disaster are here reconstructed from the sometimes contradictory accounts of local and national newspapers, and from the sermons of the local rector. The perceived magnitude and significance of the disaster at the time are reflected in the density of news coverage. Not only local papers, but also *The Times* and the other nationals, carried an update on the situation in almost every issue throughout the final months of 1859 and into 1860. In 1860, relatives of the drowned, 'BA & J K' published an account, *Wreck of the 'Royal Charter', Steam Clipper, on her Passage from Australia to Liverpool* (Dublin: Glashan and Gill), few copies of which survive today.

burying them decently, and writing upward of 1,075 letters to their relatives. He is Dickens's emblem for the preservation of memory in the face of time:[9] 'I read more ...in the fresh frank face going up the village beside me, in five minutes, than I have read in anathematizing discourses (albeit put to press with enormous flourishing of trumpets), in all my life' (*UT*, p.32). The rector's efforts are placed in opposition to the exclusiveness of institutional religious memorialization: 'Convocations, Conferences, Diocesan Epistles, and the like ...will [never] do ...half so well ...as the Heavens have seen it done in this bleak spot upon the rugged coast of Wales' (*UT*, p.40). More vivid and immediate signs of mortality supplant the conventional forms of religious ceremony; not only have the 'Commandments ...been shouldered out of their places', but 'Hard by the Communion-Table, were some boots that had been taken off the drowned and preserved – a gold-digger's boot, cut down the leg for its removal – a trodden-down man's ankle-boot with a buff cloth top – and others – soaked and sandy, weedy and salt' (*UT*, p.33). Dickens dwells on the way in which Hughes patiently examined the bodies, and other wreckage, 'cutting off buttons, hair, marks from linen, anything that might lead to subsequent identification, studying faces, looking for a scar, a bent finger, a crooked toe, comparing letters sent to him with the ruin about him' (*UT*, pp.32–3).

Among the most useful identifying marks were the details of each sailor's tattoos: 'This tattooing was found still plain, below the discoloured outer surface of a mutilated arm ...carefully scraped away ... It is not improbable that the perpetuation of this marking custom among seamen, may be referred back to their desire to be identified, if drowned' (*UT*, pp.39–40). The significance of the tattoo, a seemingly gratuitous inscription on the body, is thus realized retrospectively, through painstaking discovery and search for a particular answer. Foucault uses such a concept of the retroactive attribution of meaning as the basis of his genealogical method, so reconciling the generality of significance with the particularity and incidentality of the event, the textuality of history with its reference to something extra-textual. He observes that significance is accorded to events through a conjunction of the questions posed by the historian and 'their correlation with other previous or simultaneous events'.[10] He sees this

---

9   Roose Hughes's tomb stone in Llanallgo records 'his humble and disinterested exertions on the memorable occasion of the wreck of the *Royal Charter*', and states that 'the subsequent effects of those exertions proved too much for him and suddenly brought him to an early grave.'

10   Michel Foucault, 'Politics and the Study of Discourse', *Ideology and Consciousness* 3 (London: Routledge, 1978), p.14.

conceptualization as engaging with 'the event (assimilated in a concept, from which we vainly attempted to extract it in the form of a *fact*, verifying a proposition, of *actual experience* ...the empirical content of history); and the phantasm (reduced in the name of reality and situated at the extremity ...of a normative sequence: perception-image-memory-illusion)'.[11]

As Young interprets it, Foucault's phantasm, 'rather than constituting the event, hovers over its surface like a cloud, as an effect of meaning...repeating the (non) event, as an event' without seeking 'to lay claim to "the real" or Truth as such'.[12] As Young points out, Foucault draws on Deleuze who, in *The Logic of Sense*, asks 'Where is the battle?' He might, however, have looked to Dickens's contemporary, de Tocqueville, who, in *Democracy in America*, pre-empted this question (and a famous one of Baudrillard's) with his own 'Did the American Revolution really happen?'[13] Dickens's focus on the tattoos suggests that he, too, has little to learn from postmodern theory. If we are to seek to track down the dawn of historiographic conscience and self-awareness as either event or as phantasm, we will need to do our hovering in the nineteenth century or earlier, not in the twentieth.

The history of the tattoo is an interesting illustration of the slippery twists of history and of cultural significance. Captain Cook introduced the word 'tattoo' to Europe, but the tattoo had long been used not only by the Romans but also by tribes in many parts of the world to mark slaves. British army deserters and American slaves were tattooed. However, in the nineteenth century tattooing came into fashion amongst the English upper classes. Perhaps with reference to this conflicted history, the protagonist of a *Punch* sketch sending up an *Edinburgh Review* article about the Graffiti of Pompeii (printed in the month of the wreck), is named 'Sir Cannibal Tattoo'. The article invokes Macaulay's powerful post-colonial image of the New Zealander of the future who, 'in the midst of a vast solitude, takes his stand on a broken arch of London Bridge to sketch the ruins of St. Paul's' while musing on '"the decline and fall of the British Empire"'.[14] 'When that

---

[11] Foucault, *Language, Counter-Memory, Practice*, ed. Donald F Bouchard, trans. Donald F Bouchard and Sherry Simon (Oxford: Blackwell, 1977), p.180.

[12] Young, pp.82–3.

[13] Gilles Deleuze, *Logic of Sense*, trans. Mark Lester, ed. Constantin V. Boundas (London and New York: Athlone, 1990); Alexis de Tocqueville, *Democracy in America* (1835), trans. Henry Reeve, ed. Phillip Bradley (New York: Vintage Books, 1945). This is one of the themes of the book.

[14] Thomas Babington Macaulay, 'Von Ranke' (1840), in *Macaulay's Essays for the Edinburgh Review* (London, Glasgow and New York: Routledge, 1887), pp.571–93,

eternal New Zealander of Lord Macaulay's', Punch writes, 'gets off the broken arch of London Bridge, pockets his sketches, and comes pottering about the abandoned metropolis, Sir Cannibal Tattoo ...will discover in extinct London much the same sort of mural annotations as Mr Punch...found in Pompeii'. This 'indefatigable traveller and antiquary' and contributor to *The Polygamic Review*, 'will ponder over the London Graffiti much as Mr Punch has done over those of the buried city'.[15] *Punch* gives examples of the amusing misinterpretations Sir Cannibal will put upon these scraps of writing, whose original, familiar, contemporary meaning has been utterly obscured by time, radical cultural difference and, presumably, a history of imperial fall on the one hand and of extension on the other. The racist clichés invoked here are self-ironising, as *Punch* takes a peep into the chasms of cultural and historical relativity suggested by the experience of an imperial era.[16] The consciousness of the levelling might of historical change produces a disturbing flight of sympathetic imagination.

But can we really trace in such preoccupations the significance of Dickens's 200-mile journey to witness the scene of a wreck? Other publications were vaguely suspicious of his deed of commemoration; the *Saturday Review* considered it 'questionable taste' in the Uncommercial Traveller to have 'placarded ...the virtues of a Welsh clergyman'.[17] Why might this have been? In a letter to Roose Hughes, Dickens claimed to 'have written [the article] out of the honest convictions of my heart, and in the hope that it will at least soften the distress of many'.[18] Was this the case, or did he travel as a professional journalist to feed the voyeuristic appetite of the public?

In fact, Dickens resisted the account of events that grabbed the popular imagination. The enormous *Royal Charter* was one of the first ships made of that particularly English resource, iron, which, through its use in rail tracks and engines, played so large a part in the expansion of Empire. Fitted with auxiliary steam power, she also embodied a significant step in the transition

---

p.572. This image became deeply embedded in the Victorian imagination. It is casually alluded to, in a manner that assumes it to be widely recognisable, by all kinds of writers from 1840 until the end of the century.

[15] *Punch*, vols 36–7, 29 October 1859, p.174.

[16] I was visiting the ruins of the Roman Forum when momentous news broke on 11 September 2001. No later image resonated so strongly with the moment as that conjured by Macaulay.

[17] *Saturday Review*, 23 February 1861, p.195.

[18] Charles Dickens to S. Roose Hughes, in *The Letters of Charles Dickens*, ed. Madeline House, Graham Storey, Kathleen Tillotson, et al. (Oxford: Clarendon Press, 1965–2003), IX, pp.196–7.

from sail to steam. Her accommodation, suitably, was exceptionally luxurious. Like the later *Titanic*, she was a symbol of progress and national pride.

She was built to cater for the huge outflow of 100,000 English emigrants to Australia prompted by the 1850s gold rush.[19] The gold fields seemed an uncanny literalisation of the colonial economic dream: gold, nobody's property, was available to anyone willing to make the journey and to work for it. The dream realised, the *Royal Charter* was set to bring back home £400,000 worth of the precious metal on a return passage whose speed would break all records.

News of the wreck of this particular ship was, naturally then, a terrible deflation of nationalist rhetoric. While the gold rush represented the role of chance in capitalist endeavour in its positive aspect, the wreck seemed a hideous metaphor for the unpredictability of economic crash. Thousands of pounds simply 'went under'.

The details of the disaster, in so far as they emerged, were equally embarrassing. A Maltese – termed in the newspapers variously as, 'black', 'negro', and 'coloured' – swam ashore from the wreck with a line from which a boatswain's chair was swung.[20] Many might have been rescued by this means, but the women, whom the crew deemed should go first, would not countenance the immodesty of the vehicle. A lengthy argument ensuing, the opportunity of saving lives was lost. Narratives of female modesty – a legitimating moral touchstone of Empire – were made to look tragically ridiculous. Worse still, many passengers were drowned by the freight of gold they attempted to take with them.[21]

As Williams records, 'at a moment when the perils of a long voyage from Australia were supposed to have been surmounted ...the tragedy appeared inexplicable to the shocked public and uncanny in its circumstances'.[22] The *Daily News* made explicit the profound effect of the wreck, which it regarded as

---

[19] R. Williams, 'Anglesey and the Loss of the *"Royal Charter"*', *Transactions of the Anglesey Antiquarian Society and Field Club* (1959), 21–43, pp.26–40.

[20] *Daily Telegraph*, 29 October 1859, p.3; *Daily News*, 28 October 1859, p.5; *Illustrated London News*, 29 October 1859, p.2.

[21] Various accounts of the hesitancy of the women were given in the papers throughout November 1859. The *Daily Telegraph* (29 October 1859, p.4) carried an account of the gold carried about the passengers, presumably derived from the same report as that given in the local papers: 'a gentleman ...tied two black canvas bags around his neck: he was lost ...other persons fastened money about their persons; all were lost' (*Caernarfon and Denbigh Herald*, 5 November 1859, p.2).

[22] Williams, p.21.

one of those terrible calamities which are remembered for centuries ...
If what is called 'progress' be truly defined as an increasing domination
over time and space, then England, marching in the van, atones for her
pre-eminence with many a hostage ...every now and then we offer up
costly sacrifices to avenge our triumphs, and correct our pride ...it
would be easy for some glib interpreter of Providence to pronounce
homilies on the fate of a ship laden with the Root of all Evil ...but this
catastrophe may point [a] more serviceable moral ...human destinies
are ...a chaos, and it is not for ...wisdom to presume to fabricate out of
inexplicable chances a providential order of its own.[23]

The *Daily News*, however, could not sustain this depressing profundity of
reflection. There was irresistible temptation to look for a scapegoat, some
way of glossing this demoralising breakdown in the narrative of colonial
success. Chauvinism was the ready resort: wild rumours circulated that the
Welsh had ignored the ship's signals for help 'as no one who knows Welsh
pilots will be surprised to hear', had drawn her into danger and 'plundered'
and mutilated drowned bodies.[24] The *Daily Telegraph* precipitated the
scandal:

> We believe that there are yet cannibals in some holes and corners of
> the globe. We know that wretches exist who earn a hideous livelihood
> by the systematic destruction of infant life. We have heard legends of
> bygone barbarians ...affiliated and akin to these miscreants – the scum
> and refuse of humanity, [are the] Welsh wretches inhabiting the shore
> contiguous to the wreck, who, with true Cambro-British greed, have
> been employing themselves not in offering assistance ...but in
> plundering the wreck ...gangs of wreckers have swooped down ...
> Averse as we are to needless bloodshed, there are circumstances under
> which it behoves every honest man to cry 'Mort aux voleurs'; and it
> would be with very little sorrow we should hear that some of the
> rapacious brutes ...had been shot by the military.[25]

23 *Daily News*, 29 October 1859, p.4.

24 *Daily News*, 29 October, 1859, p.4; 28 October 1859, p.5; *Guardian* 2 November
1859, p.3. Fables of fisherwomen hiding gold in their kettles beneath periwinkles are
still current, and the purchase of a flashy car by a man from Moelfre may even
today be sometimes darkly accounted for on Anglesey by the hint that he inherited
the remains of a fortune found on the wreck.

25 *Daily Telegraph*, 29 October 1859, p.4.

The Welsh were spoken of in terms connecting them with remoter colonized peoples – 'childish', 'disgracefully incompetent'; their land depicted as an uncivilized region befitting such barbarians – an 'inhospitable-looking district, where the population is thin, and the houses ...mere huts'.[26] *The Times* also carried tales of 'plunderers of the wreck', 'horrible pilferers of corpses'.[27] It was 'general belief that the inhabitants of that coast were so avaricious that it would scarcely be safe to go amongst them'.[28] The depth of the racial suspicion of the Welsh is apparent in the 'suggestions' referred to by the coroner, of 'putting some English gentlemen on the jury'.[29]

The extremely hazardous part played by the locals in the rescue of 39 passengers was neglected, and the role of the Maltese, Joie Rodrigues (referred to in all accounts, even twentieth-century, as 'Joseph Rodgers/Rogerson') glorified instead. In patriotic language, the papers recalled how 'the noble fellow gallantly dropped overboard and breasted the waves with the resolution of a British Sailor'.[30] He was awarded a medal and praised for his resolution in accomplishing a feat which would be 'ever remembered by every true British seaman' – the accommodation of one cultural Other thus facilitating the exclusion of another.[31]

It is not surprising that visiting journalists were struck by the 'primitive' life of the islanders. The living conditions of this remote part of Wales were a world away not only from those of London but also from those of the rural south-east. The villagers along the coast, mainly without ownership of boats, often subsisted by a form of fishing with stone pens or traps, and by the collection of tiny shellfish. Even at the parsonage the visitor could not find true nineteenth-century British civilisation – the rector's wife and daughters, like others of their class in this part of the country, were illiterate. As the *Daily Telegraph* jeered, with only a little xenophobic exaggeration, 'Welsh Squires ...are unable, when in love, to write letters to their inamoratas'.[32] Wales represented for the English not only the colonial periphery brought

[26] *Liverpool Courier*, 29 October 1859.
[27] *The Times*, 5 November 1859.
[28] Letter from William Marshal, *Herald*, 17 December 1859, p.6. Marshal writes to the local paper to express his gratitude to the people whose country he had entered with extreme trepidation.
[29] Report of Inquest, *Herald*, 5 November 1859, p.2
[30] *Herald*, 5 November 1859, p.2.
[31] *Herald*, 5 November 1859, p.2, and letter from William Gilmour, *Herald*, 26 November 1859, p.2. Rodrigues's written statement that he owed his own life to the daring of the villagers (transcribed in local papers) was taken no notice of nationally.
[32] *Daily Telegraph*, 29 October 1859, p.4.

close to home, but also the past; Mrs Gaskell commented that 'Welsh people …are what I suppose we English were a century ago'.[33] Despite the poverty, however, and the 'miserable accommodation which Moilfre afforded', survivors and relatives of the drowned alike wrote of inhabitants 'remarkable for their kindness of heart and simplicity of character', 'the very reverse' of what they were described to be in the papers; 'I never experienced anything but the greatest kindness from every person'.[34]

Dickens alone amongst the London journalists whitewashes the story, refusing even to acknowledge the currency of the anti-Welsh scandals, and yet refraining from any framing of their kindness in 'noble savage' terms. He simply remarks upon 'courteous peasants well to do, driving fat pigs and cattle to market …neat and thrifty dwellings, with their unusual quantity of clean white linen, drying on the bushes'. The locals 'had done very well, and assisted readily … The people were none the richer for the wreck, for it was the season of the herring shoal – and who could cast nets for fish, and find dead men and women in the draught?' (*UT*, pp.29, 32).

The Uncommercial Traveller refuses to trade on the racist angle. His deferential treatment of the people of Anglesey is part of his scrupulous concern for the claims of the past, and the duty of the historian. Travelling 'for the great house of Human Interest Brothers' with 'rather a large connection in the fancy goods way', he resists the urge to give shape and meaning to the narrative through construction of a demonized Other, but lets the event retain instead its power as symbol both of sheer historical contingency, and of the difficulty and necessity of writing such contingency into history.[35]

iii. Postmodernism reading the past: Pilot or wrecker?

Dombey and Son makes interesting reading alongside Dickens's account of the shipwreck. Both texts are intimately related to a questioning of the nature of history and of historiography – ground they share with current new historicist and post-colonial theorization of the novel. But such criticism responds to *Dombey and Son*, for the most part, with none of the sympathy

---

[33] Elizabeth Gaskell, 'The Well of Pen-Morfa', in *The Works of Mrs Gaskell* (London: Smith, Elder and Co., 1906), II, pp.242–66, p.243.

[34] 'B & J K', pp.90, 87, and letters from William Marshal, relative, and John Foster, survivor, *Herald*, 17 December 1859, p.6.

[35] Charles Dickens, 'His General Line of Business', in Michael Slater and John Drew (eds), *The Uncommercial Traveller and Other Papers, 1859–70* (London: JM Dent, 2000), p.28.

that one might have expected from this overlap of interest.

Perera points out that 'as the repressed second half of the title makes clear, *Dealings with the firm of Dombey and Son, Wholesale, Retail and for Exportation* is Dickens's parable of mercantile capitalism; it is also inherently and immediately a narrative predicated on an economy of empire'.[36] She sees the novel's critique as directed exclusively at free trade, its attitude to monopoly trade remaining entirely uncritical. She discusses the novel's treatment of colonialism with regard to the 'dark servant of the Major's'. Although the Major's abuse of his servant is clearly an allusion to the violence of Empire, Perera maintains that 'the power relations governing *Dombey and Son* are laid bare in the text's assumption of "the Native's" unrepresentability in human terms; in its confidence that "the Native's" predicament is comic, and *can* only be represented humorously'. The point of the novel, for Perera, is to reconcile imperial trade with the stability of the mid-Victorian family.[37]

Deirdre David concurs in negatively evaluating the politics of the novel, arguing that while

> the ending ...forgive[s] Dombey for striking his daughter, the novel never really forgives Major Bagstock for hitting his native servant ...it sees no moral need to do so. The configuration of race and gender politics in which it is explicitly not acceptable for a British father to hit his middle-class daughter but implicitly acceptable for a retired Indian army officer to beat his dark servant, speaks directly to Dickens's complex and unhappy view of empire ...the beating of Florence, the punishment delivered to her father, and the forgiveness he is granted, imaginatively overshadow ...Bagstock's brutalisation of his servant ...leaving unmolested the political institutions of empire that have ...created his suffering.[38]

According to this view, not only are the satire of Tox's racism and the criticism of the Major's violence absolutely negated by the plot's treatment of Florence, but the depictions of patriarchal injustice are no more than acts of ideological containment, because the novel 'declines ...to attack directly the financial institutions with which Dombey is affiliated'. With historical hindsight, the novel can be forced to disclose what it attempts to conceal, 'the dark servant ...is a visible product of empire that Victorian

---

[36] Perera, p.605.
[37] Perera, p.612.
[38] David, pp.66–67.

writing...cannot erase but must represent ...in the formal cause of social realism'.[39]

This familiar mode of reading equates one rhetorical movement with another in ways not immediately suggested by the novel. Plot is considered from an exclusively teleological point of view – Walter's engagement in trade at the end of the novel is read as negating the novel's critique of capitalism. Proof of one inadvertent collusion in ideological evasion is taken to constitute the whole novel as an evasive exercise. But this totalising approach seems in contradiction with the critique of western History of which post-colonial criticism forms a part. Such a contradiction could only be justified if it could be shown that the text itself proclaims the coherence of history, the comprehensive transparency of its own historiography, and demands to be read as a totality. Dickens's text does no such thing.

As long as they acknowledge their own status as phantasmic projections of meaning incapable of capturing any essence of the text, such post-colonial readings are relatively uncontentious. However, a more objective status is often implicitly claimed: take for example Said's influential assertion that to write criticism of the Victorian novel without paying attention to its colonial context is to become complicit with imperialist ideology; a conclusion following from his notion that the novel's 'main [or elsewhere, 'principal'] purpose' is to 'keep the empire ...in place'. Said, along with others such as Brantlinger and Azim, constructs a totalizing history of the genre: 'the history of the novel [has] the coherence of a continuous enterprise'.[40]

The elegant simplicity of this kind of approach is unfortunately unable to accommodate the complexity and scope of what David off-handedly refers to as 'the formal cause of social realism'. Contrary to her suggestion, there is surely no straightforwardly aesthetic reason why Dickens is obliged, despite his deepest ideologically conditioned wishes, to represent Bagstock as colonial or his servant as 'Native'. *Dombey* would be coherent and plausible without these details. But the novel's realism is an ethical and historiographic commitment as well as a formal one – or rather, it is an ethically determined choice of historiographic form. Dickens's vision of the nature of history and of historiography, as we shall see, commits him to relating more than he can narrativize; to non-teleological, incidental sallies of social record and critique which are self-validating even as they are rolled into the onward thrust of the narrative which embodies the blind ongoing of

[39]   David, pp.73, 72.

[40]   Patrick Brantlinger, *Rule of Darkness* (Ithaca and London: Cornell University Press, 1988); Firdous Azim, *The Colonial Rise of the Novel* (London and New York: Routledge. 1993); Said, pp.88, 90.

time. As John Forster remarked, 'The didactic in Dickens ...derived its strength from being merely incidental'.[41]

To establish a critical position from which Dickens's ends and means may be justly analysed and evaluated in turn requires some vigorous wrestling with the ethics of history. Post-colonial and new historicist critics have grasped this nettle bravely, though perhaps sometimes rather roughly. For instance, Perera argues that 'the "ideological presumptions" underlying a text are revealed ...by the question ..."whose view is *not* expressed"', and Said proclaims that 'in reading a text, one must open it out ...to what its author excluded'.[42] This exorbitant supplementary project implies an absolute rejection of such 'knowledge' as novels do offer, including contestations of imperialism and other dimensions of their social world. Readings 'against the grain' disregard on principle what the author wants to convey, 'voudrait dire', as they say. Catherine Belsey's formulation is paradigmatic of certain historicist readings: 'a form of criticism which rejects the pseudo-knowledge offered by the text provides a real knowledge of the work of literature'.[43]

The question is: from what privileged position is such a rejection made? Paradoxically, it is precisely the same tools of 'Othering' instrumental in imperialism that nurture the illusion of special moral and epistemological privilege vis-à-vis the past now. Unable to cope patiently with the fact that bad things happen in history, and suspicious of cultural difference, critics, like the Victorian newspaper journalist, are desperate to find somebody to blame, with or without good evidence. Multi-vocal history is too often, in consequence, made subservient to a grand, albeit counter, narrative.

If the past, not only of the colonized but also of the colonizer, is another country, intercourse with it is ethically complicated by cultural difference. Earlier historicist critics like Kathleen Tillotson grappled with history's distance. They saw the task of the literary critic as a strenuous application of historical evidence for the elucidation of the literary text. For much recent historicist criticism however, the task is not to complete the hermeneutic circle of (ideological) 'understanding', but to disillusion through misunderstanding. While it recognizes the urgency and difficulty of hearing the voices of history's silenced Others, it underestimates the alienness of those voices which, even as they appear to address us more directly, are nevertheless also fragile and liable to slip into incomprehensible silence. The

---

[41]   Forster, III, p.23.
[42]   Perera, p.612; Said, p.79.
[43]   Catherine Belsey, *Critical Practice* (London: Routledge, 1980), p.129.

binary oppositions of self/other (where 'self' is immediately accessible, and 'other' the object of reconstruction) and of victor/victim structure such criticism, which introduces a parallel (and covert) opposition of guilt/innocence to serve as a moral pivot privileging it to punish and silence one side of the opposition at the expense of the other. However, the idea of the absolute guilt or innocence, power or impotence of the actors of history – the 'sovereign model' that suggests that such a structure can simply be reversed – is, as Foucault himself has argued, a hangover of the subject-centred, metaphysical notion of history that new historicism attacks as totalitarian.[44]

In Victorian studies in particular, it is often assumed that the 'dominant' voices of the period are so audible as to be virtually our own; no special sympathetic effort should be needed to see Dickens's perspective. But as Tillotson points out, in an observation which is surely even more pertinent now than it was in the 1950s, the Victorian age is for most people a confused 'phantasmagoria of stage-coaches, Barsetshire, women in white, and Hugh Thomson illustrations; and a class of undergraduate students, invited to expose their knowledge of the field, will begin by happily hazarding Jane Austen', (or, in my more recent experience, Wilfred Owen and the war poets).[45] Furthermore, the typical reaction of the modern general reader or undergraduate student to a nineteenth-century novel, far from exhibiting the dangerous sympathy that new historicism so fears, is to condemn it for being sexist, racist and so on (by our standards). Such popular criticisms may be founded. But do they provide ethical justification for the rejection of texts from the past as no more than fodder for misreading?

New historicist criticism often acknowledges the historicity of its own account. Bruce Robbins suggests that its 'ethical imperative is ...necessarily tolerant ...full of loopholes ...must always relativise itself – and must recognise full "political correctness" as by definition unattainable'.[46]

---

[44] The colonial contexts of the wreck of the *Royal Charter* demonstrate the fluidity of power: returning colonialists, 'comprising some of the most wealthy in the colony', many descended from ex-convicts, returned to a country that had previously consigned them to abjection but now, with their new-found wealth, guaranteed them a fêted arrival. Wrecked off the coast of Wales, another colony of sorts, a few senseless bodies were perhaps robbed by starving people. Some locals were tried and became convicts themselves, the remainder branded as criminal and, for their pains, taxed twice the usual rate to pay for local burial of the drowned, to which the Board of Trade made no contribution ('BA & J K', p.5; Williams, 31, 34–5).

[45] Kathleen Tillotson, *Novels of the Eighteen Forties* (Oxford: Clarendon Press, 1954), p.1.

[46] Bruce Robbins, 'Colonial Discourse: A Paradigm and its Discontents', *Victorian*

Levinson acknowledges new historicism's 'failure ...to objectify our own subjectivity ...to articulate the subject-object, present-past, criticism-poetry polarities as a mode of relation ... We seem determined *not* to make anything of the historical differentials precipitated by our criticism'. In expiation, she confesses, in terms of violence and rapine, the exploitation of the texts of the past by new historicists, whose 'critical ravishing' 'redeems to murder'. This 'aggressive re-enactment of the past' is justified by an attitude of abjection before the future; 'we *invite* the generations that succeed us to tread us down: totalize our phrases and violate our knowledge'.[47] The other main players in new historicism, Catherine Gallagher and Stephen Greenblatt, agree that there is no getting around the abusive violence of every political reading: 'any attempt at interpretation, as distinct from worship, bears a certain inescapable tinge of aggression'.[48] Really? I could have sworn I try to understand people every day, without any hint of aggression entering into my attitude towards them. A more positive ethical relation between past and present should not, I think, be abandoned as a hopeless project.

The questioning of metaphysical foundations (or rather of the lack of them), which raises these particular problems, is not a new phenomenon. The very rapidity of social change in the nineteenth century made the determining power of material history on constructions of meaning and value starkly manifest. Contrapuntal colonial cultural contact served a similar revelatory purpose – demonstrating also the potential violence involved in the contact of different schemes of thought. *Dombey and Son* investigates this determining power – the chaos of historical events and the consequent relative contingency of every account of the world – and boldly seeks to draw from the chaos a positive and sympathetic historiographic ethic.

iv. 'Chaos of being': *Dombey and Son* and the squalls of history

In an oft-cited passage, Carlyle wrote that 'in our age of Down-pulling and Disbelief, the very Devil has been pulled down ...the Universe ...all void of

---

Studies 35 (1992) 212.

[47] Marjorie Levinson, 'The New Historicism: Back to the Future', in Marjorie Levinson et al. (eds), *Rethinking Historicism* (Oxford: Blackwell, 1989), pp.20, 53, 49, 54, 51.

[48] Catherine Gallagher and Stephen Greenblatt, *Practising New Historicism* (Chicago and London: University of Chicago Press, 2001) p.8.

Life, of Purpose, of Volition, even of Hostility: it was one huge, dead, immeasurable Steam-engine, rolling on, in its dead indifference, to grind me limb from limb'.[49] *Dombey* reads like an elaboration of this thought and its figurative embodiment. It is saturated with passages suggestive of the chaotic character of history, and the difficulty of salvaging meaning and value in the face of it. Such passages constellate around the train, 'the power that forced itself upon its iron way − its own − defiant of all paths and roads …dragging living creatures of all classes, ages, and degrees behind it'.

> The first shock of a great earthquake had, just at that period, rent the whole neighbourhood to its centre …streets broken through and stopped …buildings that were undermined and shaking, propped by great beams of wood …a chaos of carts, overthrown and jumbled together, lay topsy-turvy at the bottom of a steep unnatural hill …confused treasures of iron soaked and rusted in something that had accidentally become a pond. Everywhere were bridges that led nowhere; thoroughfares that were wholly impassable; Babel towers of chimneys …temporary wooden houses and enclosures …fragments of unfinished walls and arches, and piles of scaffolding, and wildernesses of bricks, and giant forms of cranes, and tripods straddling above nothing. There were a hundred thousand shapes and substances of incompleteness, wildly mingled out of their places, upside down, burrowing in the earth, aspiring in the air, mouldering in the water, and unintelligible as any dream. Hot springs and fiery eruptions, the usual attendants upon earthquakes, lent their contributions of confusion to the scene. Boiling water hissed and heaved within dilapidated walls; whence, also, the glare and roar of flames came issuing forth; and mounds of ashes blocked up rights of way, and wholly changed the law and custom of the neighbourhood.
>
> In short, the yet unfinished and unopened Railroad was in progress; and, from the very core of all this dire disorder, trailed smoothly away, upon its mighty course of civilisation and improvement.[50]

Here, the grand narrative of History, 'progress', 'civilisation and improvement' is ironically contrasted with the manifest disorder and contingency of reality. Arguments about whether Dickens thought the railway was a good or a bad thing miss the point − he represents it primarily

---

[49]   Carlyle, *Sartor Resartus* (London: Chapman and Hall, 1896), II:vii:133.

[50]   Dickens, *Dombey and Son* (1848), ed. Alan Horseman (Oxford: Clarendon Press, 1974), ch.6, p.65. Hereafter, *DS*.

as a brute and amoral historical eruption.[51] The equation of the railroad with natural forces alludes to the ironic fact that what man sees as his evolving 'control' over nature through civilisation produces a force every bit as savage and blind, its 'red eyes, bleared and dim' (*DS*, ch.55, p.743).

Like the hurricane of 1859, earthquakes manifest a chaotic dimension of nature, which science cannot predict or explain. Dickens's extension of the notion of material determinism to man and his society suggests, in this light, not predictability and evolution but rather seemingly meaningless catastrophe. Social history, like natural history, in the relentless independence of its force, destroys all confidence of control or meaning. Society's projected schemes are provisional, aimless and subject to sudden rupture, 'temporary ...enclosures', 'bridges [leading] nowhere', culture and meaning are mere contingencies without metaphysical foundation, 'Babel towers ...tripods straddling above nothing'; the railroad 'wholly changed the law and custom of the neighbourhood'. No narrative can arrest or freeze meaning in the face of such protean energy. The resonance between the scene painted by Dickens and the inscrutable ruins of future London viewed by Sir Cannibal Tattoo reveals a common preoccupation. Time proves all cultural certainties constructions upon chaos.

Solomon Gills's instruments for 'the working of a ship's course, or the keeping of a ship's reckoning, or the prosecuting of a ship's discoveries', 'chronometers, barometers, telescopes', are useless in this world of chaos. The only people to enter his shop are a woman who asks the way to Mile-End Turnpike, and a man who asks *change* for a sovereign.[52] In the ever-turning, ever-changing modern world of commerce, Gills's measurements of space and time are behind the times; 'discovery' has been replaced by 'new invention, new invention – alteration, alteration – the world's gone past me. I hardly know where I am' (*DS*, ch.4, pp.36, 41).

A preoccupation with time as solvent of meaning and stability, the very element of chaos, recurs throughout the novel. Captain Cuttle changes his clock to suit himself, Gills is paradoxically kept 'behind the times' by the punctuality of his own. Clocks tick menacingly in each crucial passage of the

---

51 Steven Marcus sums up the argument over whether Dickens is 'for' or 'against' the railway in his book, *Dickens: From Pickwick to Dombey* (London: Chatto and Windus, 1965).

52 The *Royal Charter* was instrumental in proving that such traditional implements were indeed becoming outmoded. She was used in an experiment that showed that the magnetism of the new iron ships cast compasses out and, as it turned out, she was finally wrecked by a storm which no barometer could have predicted (Williams, 38, 40).

novel, witnessing Mrs Dombey's death, Paul's enslavement to books, his
death, and Florence's rejection by her father. A Tiresian voice perpetually
warns that 'time is flitting by; the hour is coming with an angry tread' (DS,
ch.43, p.583). There is a sense that, as Hayden White puts it, 'Men are
awash in a historical sea more threatening than [the] natural world'.[53]

The voice of the waters forewarns 'old-fashioned' Paul that there is no
place for him in the grand narrative of Dombey and Son:

> His fancy had a tendency to wander to the river, which he knew was
> flowing through the great city; and now he thought how black it was,
> and how deep it would look, reflecting the hosts of stars – and more
> than all, how steadily it rolled away to meet the sea ... He felt forced,
> sometimes, to try to stop it – to stem it with his childish hands, or choke
> its way with sand – and when he saw it coming on, resistless, he cried
> out! ... 'Why will it never stop ...? it is bearing me away, I think!' (DS,
> ch.16, p.221)

As in his record of the shipwreck, Dickens here shows himself, like Paul,
mesmerized, horrified, by time and change – by the black, opaque depths,
and the ceaseless flow of history as it happens, resistant to all attempts to
check or fix it. The shipwreck is the novel's paradigmatic historical event,
unpredictable and often, as in the case of the *Royal Charter*, inexplicable, an
irrecoverable assigning of human life to the depths, in which natural and
historical chaos combine. Not only is *Son and Heir*, the ship on which Walter
travels, lost, and Solomon Gills feared drowned at sea, but Florence in her
trouble feels like 'the sole survivor on a lonely shore from the wreck of a
great vessel'. The life of the modern city in which she exists is compared
with the ungovernable force of water: 'a stream ...flowing, indifferently, past
marts and mansions, prisons, churches, marketplaces, wealth, poverty, good
and evil, like the broad river ...awakened from its dreams of rushes, willows,
and green moss, and rolling on, turbid and troubled, among the works and
cares of men, to the deep sea' (DS, ch.48, pp.638–9). Trade itself is subject to
the tides, which are associated with the cycles of the capitalist economy:

> The sea had ebbed and flowed, through a whole year. Through a
> whole year, the winds and clouds had come and gone; the ceaseless
> work of Time had been performed, in storm and sunshine. Through a
> whole year, the tides of human chance and change had set in their

---

[53] Hayden White, *Metahistory* (Baltimore and London: Johns Hopkins Press, 1973),
     p.145.

allotted courses. Through a whole year, the famous House of Dombey and Son had fought for life, against the cross of accidents, doubtful rumours, unsuccessful ventures, unpropitious times …the ship …strained so hard against the storm, was weak, and could not bear it. (*DS*, ch.58, p.773)

In the sea's depth lies not just death, but utter annihilation. Not only is material change inevitable, but the cultural change that accompanies it may result in every significant trace of people and events being swept away, just as Stagg's Gardens disappears and is forgotten by the cab driver. Forms of life as well as individuals become extinct. With no meaning 'out there' to be somehow realized in history, structures of cultural signification have no extra-temporal anchorage, no legitimation that can withstand the 'indifferent' sweepings away of time. So we see the hopes of Captain Cuttle swept away with his song; 'almost the whole world of Captain Cuttle had been drowned …he thought …of Lovely Peg, that teak-built and trim ballad …gone ashore upon a rock, and split into mere planks and beams of rhyme. The Captain sat in the dark shop thinking of these things …looking with sad eyes upon the ground, as if in contemplation of their actual fragments, as they floated past him' (*DS*, ch.32, pp.452–3).

The novel's use of the shipwreck both as literal cause of loss of life and as poetic symbol of loss of significance, of ways of life, is symptomatic of the dual objectives of realist fiction. Evoking the individual moment in all its immediate physicality on the one hand whilst, on the other, also straining to give significance to contemporary experience through metaphoric structures and narrative devices, the novel serves to immortalize both the brute facts and the human meanings of its historical moment. *Dombey* strikingly manifests this dual-aspect witness-bearing. Dickens's plans for the separate numbers in which the novel was first issued, written in advance, display the way he mixes the incidental and the significant in his construction of the narrative, his interweaving of over-determined systems of significance with the mutable world of objects. Alongside his indications of the main bones of the plot are interspersed references to some of the small material details he intends to include, their significance speaking for itself, or not, as the case may be: 'Mirrors – hearth-rugs', 'floor cloth – clock', 'Captain Cuttle's big watch'.[54] Here and there a twist in the plot is captured wholly figuratively, as if incapable of abstraction from its material conceptualisation: 'forcing system', 'as if he had taken life unfurnished and the upholsterers were never

---

[54]   Appendix B, *Dombey and Son*, pp.836, 838, 840.

coming', 'breasting the window like a little bird', 'daughter …like a horse for sale'.[55] The indivisibility of material history and cultural significance are the very touchstone of Dickens's compositional practice.

The sea, like the train, is just such a complex real-life emblem of the levelling oblivion of time. The symbol is of an emptiness; as the signifier equally of peace and regularity and of chaos and disjunction, it is a cancelling out, a blank. We are never told what the waves, at once threatening and soothing, are saying. The sea will not reassure us that our own perspective is a truth that will last forever.

The chief object of satire in the novel is the hubristic unconsciousness of the relativity of every perspective, of every account of the shape of history:

> The earth was made for Dombey and Son to trade in, and the sun and moon were made to give them light. Rivers and seas were formed to float their ships; rainbows gave them promise of fair weather; winds blew for or against their enterprises; stars and planets circled in their orbits, to preserve inviolate a system of which they were the centre …A D …stood for anno Dombei – and Son. (*DS*, ch.1, p.2)

The whole of western History, structured by 'A D', is implicated in the satire. The reference to ships targets the obliviousness of trade and Empire to the relativity of their own cultural values; that to the sun and planets brings to mind the astronomical discoveries of the Renaissance that initiated the train of modern thought that began in casting out God and eventually left man in a mechanistic world oblivious of him and his meanings. *Pace* Said's assertion to the contrary, this passage seems to me absolutely central to the spirit of the novel. It seems almost on its own to provide positive proof that *Dombey* is not guilty as charged of supine complicity with the colonial project. Said's remark that this passage 'recalls, mocks, *yet ultimately depends on* the tried and true discourse of imperial free trade …its sense of all but unlimited opportunities for commercial advancement abroad' is rather baffling.[56] It seems strange to speak of satire as 'depending on' the discourse it attacks, and attach to that dependence the kind of implication of complicity that is the force of Said's qualification. *Dombey* is very much about how to cope with time and change without depending on teleological narratives of progress and providence.

If history is chance, narratives are constructions that are partly a product of that chance. Every future narrative of history will share the relativity and

---

55   Appendix B, pp.838, 836, 841.
56   Said, p.14.

provisional status of the rest of its cultural moment. Carlyle voices the thought:

> it is not in acted, as it is in written History ...every single event is the offspring not of one, but of all other events, prior or contemporaneous, and it will in its turn combine with all others to give birth to new: it is an ever-living, ever-working Chaos of Being ...this Chaos, boundless as the habitation and duration of man, unfathomable as the soul and destiny of man, is what the historian will depict, and scientifically gauge ...by threading it with single lines of a few ells in length![57]

Dickens's novel *enacts* the thematised difficulty of recording and narrating history. It is the very pulse of the accounts of Dombey's train ride, of Paul's final illness, of Carker's final journey, in their bewildering enumeration of detail and stylised repetition of phrase:

> through the rushing landscape, and hurried headlong ... The very speed at which the train was whirled along ...was a type of the triumphant monster, Death.
>
> Away, with a shriek, and a roar, and a rattle, from the town, burrowing among the dwellings of men ...among objects close at hand and almost in the grasp, ever flying from the traveller, and a deceitful distance ever moving slowly within him: like as in the track of the remorseless monster, Death!
>
> ...where the mill is going, where the barge is floating, where the dead are lying, where the factory is smoking, where the stream is running ...away, with a shriek, and a roar, and a rattle, and no trace to leave behind but dust and vapour: like as in the track of the remorseless monster, Death!
>
> ... Away, and still away, onward and onward ever: glimpses of cottage-homes, of houses, mansions, rich estates ...of old roads and paths that look deserted, small, and insignificant as they are left behind: and so they do, and what else is there but such glimpses, in the track of the indomitable monster, Death!
>
> Away, with a shriek, and a roar, and a rattle ...working on in such a storm of energy and perseverance, that amidst the darkness and whirlwind the motion seems reversed, and to tend furiously backward ...Away once more ...with a shrill yell of exultation ...tearing on,

---

[57] Carlyle, 'On History', in *Critical and Miscellaneous Essays*, II, pp.83–95, 88.

spurning everything ...sometimes pausing for a minute where a crowd
of faces are, that in a minute more are not ...it comes tearing on
resistless ...its way, still like the way of Death, is strewn with ashes
thickly. (*DS*, ch.20, p.275–6)

As in the description of the wreck of the charter, such passages suggest, in
their form, the contradictory character of time and history – a medium at
once of loss and of persistence – as key phrases come back to us again and
again, not exactly repeated but never entirely changed. In such moments,
Dickens resigns the clarity and order of the realist novelist's perspective, as
Dombey senior resigns his conceptual command over his world, to immerse
himself in a storm of language electrified by the terrifying sense of time.

The death of the eponymous son half way through the novel,
confounding both father's and reader's plans for his advancement, mimes
history's aimlessness. I have suggested already that to read the significance
of a novel as being refracted through its conclusion is to beg questions about
the teleology of narrative. The conclusion of *Dombey* is peculiarly
uncompelling. Toots and Susan are married off without explanation or
emotional justification; Alice is despatched in a brief and conventionalized
repentance chapter dominated by the inconsequential ramblings of the
irrelevant Wickham; Edith disappears, and Walter and Florence's union is
overshadowed by the antics of Toots. The six marriages seem to parody the
conventional 'happy ending', some being so predictable as hardly to figure
as events at all, and all the rest so unpredictable that they bear no
significance whatever. The endings seem selected almost at random from
amongst innumerable other possibilities. Indeed, such appears to be the case
from Dickens's plans, which are full of sudden alterations and indecisions.
'Uncle Sol to die? – No', 'Carker and family – Mr. Morfin. No'.[58] As Forster
points out, the novel 'was to do with Pride what its predecessor had done
with Selfishness. But this limit [was] soon overpassed; and the succession of
independent groups of character, surprising for the variety of their forms
and handling ...went far beyond the range of the passion of Mr Dombey
and Mr Dombey's second wife'.[59] In no way is the totality of the narrative
entailed by its founding premises – it is arrived at serendipitously. The
substance of the novel is heterogeneous and extraneous, the plot being,
Dickens held, '"the stock of the soup". All kind of things will be added to
it'.[60] The form and significance of narrative is made gratuitous by the realist-

---

[58]   Appendix B, pp.842, 847
[59]   Forster, II, p.309.
[60]   *Letters*, IV, p.590.

empiricist premises of the novel, even as the realist-empirical details are gratuitous in terms of the construction of plot. The product is an excess which Dickens himself recognized. 'I ...have ...to be constantly requiring to restrain myself from launching into extravagance'.[61] Realist fiction opens the joins between the roles of theory and of empirical fact in our construction of the world, and then stitches them up with a double seam into a stronger understanding. The fact that as regards Walter, ultimately the hero of the novel, Dickens originally considered that 'it would be a good thing to disappoint all the expectations [raised] of his happy connection with the story and the heroine, and to show him gradually and naturally trailing away ...to ruin', is indicative of the scant degree to which the novel relies on teleological narrative, or upon the self-sufficient and organic human subject and its corollary, exclusively subject-centred historiography.[62]

Foucault observes that 'making historical analysis the discourse of the continuous and making human consciousness the original subject of all historical development and all action are the two sides of the same system of thought'.[63] Already aware of the sleight of hand embodied in subject-centred views of history, Dickens demonstrates the determining power of history over human consciousness. Carlyle wrote with a similar emphasis: 'the conscious or half-conscious aim of mankind, so far as men are not mere digesting machines, is the same in no two ages'.[64] Something like a material version of Carlyle's time-spirits seems to animate Dickens's characters:

> Was Mr. Dombey's master-vice, that ruled him so inexorably, an unnatural characteristic? It might be worth while ...to inquire what Nature is, and how men work to change her, and whether, in the enforced distortions so produced, it is not natural to be unnatural ...bind the prisoner to one idea ...and what is Nature to the willing captive ...hear the magistrate or judge admonish the unnatural outcasts of society; unnatural in brutal habits, unnatural in want of decency, unnatural in losing and confounding all distinctions between good and evil; unnatural in ignorance, in vice ...in mind, in looks, in everything. (*DS*, ch.47, p.619)

It is a critical commonplace that Dickens's characterization is not rounded,

---

[61] *Letters*, IV, p.612.

[62] Quoted in Forster, II, pp.312–13.

[63] Foucault, *Archaeology of Knowledge*, trans. Alan Sheridan (London: Routledge, 1989), p.12.

[64] Carlyle, 'On History', II, p.86.

that his characters seem to have no interior world. When we are given insights into their psychology, we see there the determining force of history. As Raymond Williams says of *Dombey*, 'general vices ...general virtues ...are seen as being created, in all their generality, by the pressures, the relationships, the governing character of a history and a society', 'society is the creator of virtues and vices; its active relationships and institutions at once generating and controlling, or failing to control, what in the earlier mode of analysis could be seen as faults of the soul'.[65] The fates of the various characters are circumscribed by their historical positioning. So, in the passage above, Dickens's picture is of man as much a 'willing captive' to social codes as was ever envisaged by Nietzsche or Althusser. He elaborates on it in Morfin's stress on the force of habit, which 'confirms some of us in villainy − more of us in indifference − that hardens us ...and leaves us as susceptible as images to new impressions and convictions ...quite content ...to let everything ...go on, day by day, unquestioned, like a great machine − that was its habit and mine − and to take it all for granted and consider it all right ...because I was used to it' (*DS*, ch.53, p.711). 'When ...called upon to plead to my conscience, on my death bed', he says he will answer, 'I was deaf, dumb, blind, and paralytic, to a million things, from habit' (*DS*, ch.33, p.459). Linda Shires and Catherine Gallagher have noted the Victorian novel's preoccupation with the 'constructivism/ voluntarism' debate.[66] *Dombey* shows clear evidence that the theory that society shapes individuals as mere cogs of a giant deterministic machine had indeed begun to infringe (not for the first time) upon traditional ideas of 'conscience', guilt and innocence; as Carlyle put it, the Devil himself was being pulled down.

For instance, Edith and Alice, who might as prostitutes have been expected to serve as symbols of guilt, are instead presented as arguments for the extenuation of guilt by circumstance. Even their mothers serve only as instruments of their 'corruption' − in each case the primary cause is poverty and a society that treats women as chattels, 'steeled ...offered and rejected, put up and appraised ...paraded and vended to enhance [their] value' (*DS*, ch.54, p.724). Edith proclaims, 'I was a woman ...laying snares for men − before I knew myself ...or even understood the base and wretched aim of every new display I learnt' (*DS*, ch.27, p.381). Alice sees her present in her past; she speaks of herself and her life in the third person, signalling her

---

[65] Raymond Williams, Introduction to *Dombey and Son* (Harmondsworth: Penguin, 1970), p.16.

[66] Linda Shires, 'Afterword', in *Rewriting the Victorians* (New York and London: Routledge, 1992), p.187; Catherine Gallagher, *The Industrial Reformation of English Fiction, 1832–1867* (Chicago and London: University of Chicago Press, 1985).

paucity of control over her own being, throwing out her own name again and again as if to mock the notion of individuality it represents:

> 'There was a child called Alice Marwood', said the daughter ...looking down in terrible derision of herself, 'born among poverty and neglect, and nursed in it ... She lived in homes like this, and in the streets, with a crowd of little wretches like herself ... There was a girl called Alice Marwood. She was handsome ... What came to that girl, comes to thousands every year. It was only ruin, and she was born to it'.
>
> ... 'There was a criminal called Alice Marwood ...she was tried, and she was sentenced ...how grave the judge was, on her duty, and on her having perverted the gifts of nature – as if he didn't know better than anybody there that they had been made curses to her! – and how he preached about the strong arm of the Law – so very strong to save her, when she was an innocent and helpless little wretch!
>
> ... 'So Alice Marwood was transported ...was sent to learn her duty, where there was twenty times less duty, and more wickedness, and wrong, and infamy, than here. And Alice Marwood is come back a woman. Such a woman as she ought to be, after all this. In good time, there will be more solemnity, and more fine talk, and more strong arm ...and there will be an end of her; but the gentlemen needn't be afraid of being thrown out of work. There's crowds of little wretches, boy and girl, growing up in any of the streets they live in, that'll keep them to it till they've made their fortunes'. (*DS*, Ch.34, pp.468–9)

In line with this stress on the importance of social circumstance in determining individual lives, Dombey's reformation is not represented as being achieved by Florence's marriage, nor by spontaneous inward revelation, nor by any other such 'personal' matter. It takes his firm's collapse, his social fall, to effect the revolution in his character. Even Morfin's extraordinary sympathy with the Carkers seems reduced when the prosaic cause turns out to be the thin walls of his office. He makes clear his awareness of the difficulty of bootstrapping himself out of his 'narrow' habits of thought. 'We are so d – d business like ... One don't see anything, one don't hear anything, one don't know anything ...even that doubt may be habit' (*DS*, ch.33, pp.459–61).

The treatment of 'the Native' self-consciously enacts this point. Abiding by the novel's realist conventions, recording incidental details of the social world he inhabits, Dickens is drawn to depict a denizen of a radically other culture, for whom he can command from within his own cultural resources sympathy, but not understanding. Dickens and his reader are divided from the cultural context of the Native not by a thin wall but an ocean, by complex layers of political intricacies and cultural disjunction. India is figured as impossibly removed from England; 'If you were in India, I should die', Paul tells Florence; Bitherstone's plans of returning to it by land are hopeless – a sea journey of mortal danger lies between the two locations. When Dickens adopts Tox's ironized habit of calling the servant 'native' 'without connecting him with any geographical idea whatever', the irony extends to include the relativity and superficiality of the author's own treatment of him (*DS,* ch.7, p.86). 'Native' implies a missing context, conjured only to convey its incredible difference and dislocation from English culture – the 'foreigner' is 'currently believed to be a prince in his own country' (*DS,* ch.20, p.272). To attempt to represent him comprehensively without knowing or describing such a context would be to extend Tox's naivety. The character cannot but remain a marvellous enigma. Brian Cheadle draws attention to Jameson's insistence 'that within the asymmetrical world system of nineteenth-century mercantile and industrial capitalism, any resistance could be only partial, in that the racist inequities of the colonial periphery were inaccessible to metropolitan experience'.[67] In this context we may recalls Esther's Summerson's observation of the culture gap between gentlewomen and brick makers in *Bleak House.* She becomes 'painfully sensible that between us and these people there was an iron barrier, which could not be removed …by whom, or how, it could be removed we did not know, but we knew that'.[68] Whereas his acquaintance with the social conditions and culture of the English working class permits Dickens some scope for their depiction, when it comes to Britain's colonized peoples, he has not even that scant knowledge. Caught up in the gratuitous excesses of fictional realism, any totalising endeavour is predestined to fail. Dickens's philosophy of history constrains him to acknowledge the limits of his knowing.

v. Relativism and absolutism: Navigating Scylla and Charybdis

What I am saying may seem to point towards Robbins's argument that 'Dickens's critique of institutional modernity …is wary of such humanist

---

[67] Brian Cheadle, 'Despatched to the Periphery', in Anny Sadrin (ed.), *Dickens, Europe and the New Worlds* (London: Macmillan, 1999), p.103.

[68] Dickens, *Bleak House* (1852–3), (Oxford: Oxford University Press, 1948), p.108.

values as responsibility, which it shows to be produced by the system ... Dickens, like Althusser, proposed a vision of history as process without a subject'.[69] Wary though he may be of traditional conceptions of blame, however, Dickens is wisely reluctant to reject responsibility *per se*, and to abandon the subjective dimension of history. The effect of Alice's account of the determining force of material conditions upon her is not to make us view her scientifically, as a mere excrescence of historical mechanism, but rather to feel with her all the more, to make our sympathy with her all the more authentic. Her speech expresses a subjective experience of the coercive power of history; the gap between the speaking voice and the 'Alice Marwood' of whom she speaks is dense with feeling, and in this expression of her own fractured history, as sophisticated, controlled and analytic as it is passionate, Alice claims her place in the novel as a full, if splintered person, no mere passive side effect or victim of history. History, for Dickens, still has suffering subjects: the point in his materialism is to bring us all the closer to their perspectives, and to regard them with all the more humanity as limited, struggling mortals.

The rapid and convulsive changes of the 1840s exposed not just the relativity of social forms, but also the barbarism of existing conditions; it must have seemed crucial to avoid the pitfalls attending the de-subjectivisation of history – the undermining of working notions of morality and epistemology. Outrage against the barbarity of history is always founded on the sense that even if history is not the untainted product of individual human centres of consciousness, such palpitating nodes of life are the registers of real pain and real need and should be attended to.

And because Dickens shows that in the context of history there is no absolute innocence or absolute guilt, he is able to suggest that historical circumstances, by their nature extenuating, supply grounds for sympathy and forgiveness – a central and distinctive theme throughout nineteenth-century fiction. Thus we pardon Edward Rochester, sympathise with the blunders and egoism of Dorothea Brooke, and pity Anna Karenina. So, in *Dombey*, Edith and Alice forgive their mothers, and the reader, at the climax of the novel, is called on to forgive Dombey.

Through humanism, and a sympathy founded on the acknowledgment of the pressure of circumstances, Dickens attempts to evade either the strong containment argument or the depressing sense of alienated nihilism that is so often drawn from Foucault and Althussers's premises. Nevertheless, to

---

[69]   Bruce Robbins, 'Telescopic Philanthropy', in Homi Bhabha (ed.), *Nation and Narration* (London and New York: Routledge 1990), p.220.

retain the ethical underpinning of social life, the idea of guilt must be maintained. Accordingly, abandoning realism, Dickens constructs a mythically guilty character whose consciousness is limited neither by history nor its histories.

Carker is this representation of absolute guilt – he knows too much, more than any historical character. He embraces the guilt of knowing. He is a watcher, an observer, somehow outside the action; he seems to operate beyond the natural schema of time, space and deductive knowledge (like the most predatory postmodern critic): 'Mr. Carker cantered behind the carriage ...watched ...as if he were a cat, and its four occupants, mice ...a gallop across a field, enabled him to anticipate the carriage coming by the road, and to be standing ready, at the journey's end' (*DS*, ch.27, p.375). While the other characters are constrained by the rules of one game – their own individual historical moment – and have limited appreciation of the repercussions of their moves, 'Carker plays at all games'; 'I have sometimes played, and won a game – it's a mere trick – without seeing the board' (*DS*, ch.26, pp.367–8). He uses the history of others against them; thus, for example, playing upon the power of Dombey and the helpless shame of Edith. He never sleeps: 'the mirror ...showed ...the image of a man, who saw ...a crowd of people slumbering on the ground at his feet, like the poor native at his master's door: who picked his way among them, looking down maliciously enough, but trod upon no upturned face – as yet' (*DS*, ch.26, p.368). In the face of a pitiless omniscience that exploits the history of others while defying history's claim upon itself, all human beings are historical victims. The bond of vulnerability that unites the strongest and the weakest in the face of such a power is movingly represented by the levelling comparison with the native.

Only at the moment of retribution does Carker's preternatural omniscience desert him. Like Levinson, he foresees the retributive violence of history, but he learns that it is something to be dreaded. Pursued by history along an 'open road, which seemed to glide away along the dark plain, like a stream ...whither did it flow?', he is terrified by the collapse of his assumed omniscience and immunity to time – 'the clocks were faintly striking two' (*DS*, ch.55, p.732). History, 'impetuous and resistless', gains upon him, limiting, blinding and crippling as it advances in all its ineluctable contingency. In this powerful expressionist passage, Dickens conjures the overwhelming dread of history for those whose historical guilt is unredeemed by any sense of the saving power of sympathetic human memory:

long roads, that stretched away to an horizon, always receding and never gained ...faces came to dark doors and ill-glazed windows ...rows of mud bespattered cows and oxen were tied up for sale in the long narrow streets ...receiving blows on their blunt heads from bludgeons that might have beaten them in ...bridges, crosses, churches, postyards, new horses being put in against their wills, and the horses of the last stage reeking, panting, and laying their drooping heads ...little cemeteries with black crosses settled sideways in the graves, and withered wreaths upon them dropping away ...long roads, dragging themselves out, up hill and down, to the treacherous horizon.

...a host of beggars – blind men with quivering eyelids, led by old women holding candles to their faces; idiot girls; the lame, the epileptic, and the palsied ...passing through the clamour, and looking from his seat at the upturned countenances and out-stretched hands, with a hurried dread of recognising some pursuer pressing forward ...

It was a fevered vision of things past and present all confounded together ... Of being madly hurried somewhere, whither he must go ... A vision of change upon change ...and no rest ...unable ...to comprehend the points of time and place in his journey ...the turbid river held its swift course undisturbed, between two brawling streams of life and motion ...great crowds of people, soldiers, coaches, military drums, arcades ...at length lost in the universal din and uproar ...and no rest. (*DS*, ch.55, pp.737–8)

This is, I think, an unrivalled expression of the terrific force of time and change – of the obscurity of our view of the past and the future, our blindness or view through 'dark doors and ill-glazed windows'; of our vulnerable, idiotic, blunt-headed incapacity to comprehend the violent forces of change, which seems to us little more than a string of unconnected images; of the way in which those forces harness us against our wills, and the way in which the effort to play our part leaves us panting; of the fragility of the traces we leave behind – 'black crosses settled sideways, and withered wreaths upon them drooping away' (like writing?) – and, most of all, of the terror of an unsympathetic, pursuing future 'pressing forward'.

By representing absolute guilt in Carker, a figure outside the historical forces of the novel, Dickens maintains it as part of a framework within which there are gradations of culpability. Power and knowledge open the way to grander guilt, and within the limits imposed by a collective consciousness groups and individuals behave more or less scrupulously. The most 'innocent' characters derive their innocence from their lack of knowledge and lack of power, their lack of proactive engagement with history. Florence, Gills, Cuttle and Toots are utterly powerless, ignorant and unquestioning, without power to do wrong or scope to think it; they are characterized by boundless personal humility in the face of the changing world. Gills sees himself as behind the times, Cuttle vests an unquestioning confidence in the oracular Bunsby's ability to understand and predict the world around him which, in the light of Bunsby's portentous and incoherent answers, is a parody of man's unreasonable faith in a significant universe. Cuttle and Florence share a 'simple innocence of the world's ways and the world's perplexities and dangers ... No child could have surpassed Captain Cuttle in inexperience of everything but ...an odd sort of romance, perfectly unimaginative, yet perfectly unreal, and subject to no considerations of worldly prudence or practicability'. In their innocence, they have only a tenuous relation to the historical forces of the novel, being represented comparatively timelessly as 'a wandering princess and a good monster in a story-book' (*DS*, ch.49, pp.652–3). Theirs is a blameless naivety in which every well-intentioned character in history to some extent participates.

However, such passive innocence is incapable of maintaining itself – it relies for survival upon action and judgement. The ignorant Florence is not a model of historical responsibility, but a representative of the vulnerability that must be protected by a responsible ethics of history. Just as ultimate evil stems from Carker's misuse of omniscience, so from omniscience alone could stem the ultimate good:

> Oh for a good spirit who would take the house-tops off ...one night's view of ...the scenes of our too-long neglect ...the tremendous social retributions ...[and] men, delayed no more by stumbling-blocks of their own making ...would then apply themselves, like creatures of one common origin ...tending to one common end, to make the world a better place! Not the less bright and blest would that day be for rousing some who never have looked out upon the world of human life around them, to a knowledge of their own relation to it, and for making them acquainted with a perversion ...in their own contracted sympathies ...as great, and yet as natural in its development when once begun, as the lowest degradation known. (*DS*, ch.48, p.620)

Total knowledge is demonstrably impossible, as the extravagance of the image implies. But Dickens insists on maintaining rational consciousness and reflection, the proper helpmates of sympathy, as values. Limited historical beings, Dickens suggests, need to combine humility in the face of the historical contingency of ethical judgements with a daring bravery in attempting to overcome it; what Schumpeter describes as the will to 'realise the relative validity of one's convictions and yet stand for them unflinchingly'.[70] This effort is essential, even though some degree of guilt is always incurred in the very act of engaging with the dirty medium of history.

Without such active faith, when efforts at knowledge resign their teleological justification – their metaphysical claims to be the reflection of The Truth – there is little between them and despair, as Dickens's contemporary Benjamin Constant realized, in a passage which resonates closely with Dickens's more figurative invocations of the passage of time:

> Man, victor of the fights he has engaged in, looks at a world depopulated by protective powers, and is astonished at his victory ... His imagination, idle now and solitary, turns upon itself ...generations follow each other, transitory, fortuitous, isolated, they appear, they suffer, they die ... No voice of the races that are no more is prolonged into the life of the races still living, and the voice of the living races must soon be engulfed by the same eternal silence. What shall man do, without memory, *without hope, between the past which abandons him and the future which is closed before him?*[71]

For such a philosophy, tomorrow is a source of dread, as it is for Dombey in his despair of communication with, and forgiveness by, his daughter: suicide beckons. But Florence, taught to do so, as she says, by her child, her future, returns to her father.

If there is no meaning *behind* history from which to seek legitimation, legitimation must be granted *by* history, through the community of time-dwellers. With such a trans-historic community in view, the perspective of the present is to be recorded for its own sake, in all its particularity. Assuming no absolute legitimacy of its own, the present relies upon a reciprocating future, in like modesty, not to exclude its voices. That all meaning suddenly rides on our own histories makes their construction the more urgent. Though confessedly partial, these narratives open communication with the future. Within the realist form, Dickens captures the suffering and experience of the spoilt child, the beggar, the ex-convict,

---

[70] Joseph Schumpeter, *Capitalism, Socialism and Democracy* (London: Allen and Unwin, 1943), p.243.

[71] Benjamin Constant, from *De la religion dans sa source, ses formes et ses développements*, quoted by Georges Poulet, *Studies in Human Time* (Baltimore: Johns Hopkins Press, 1956) p.212.

the pauper, refracted through his own fragmented understanding of contemporary experience; these glimpses of alien life are conveyed to the future unsubsumed by any finished story. That the specific integrities of such passages of witness are as worthy of a sympathetic hearing as the contradictions between them is an ethical suggestion criticism might hear from the novel.

The solution Dickens proposes to the problem voiced by Constant is an attentive listening between the ages of history. To avoid relativist nihilism in the present, it is necessary to believe that the ethical meaning of our time and our deeds will not be twisted or obliterated by the future – that although not metaphysically validated, they can be redeemed in a conversation between past and present that brings meaning to both sides. Entering into a responsible and reciprocal relation with the past and the future is a crucial spur to attempts at understanding and criticizing the present. It provides us with an ethical defence against the worst excesses of opportunism and bad faith. This agenda, established in the nineteenth century, remains a tacit premise of modern journalism and historiography. Habermas makes it explicit: a claim 'is made by the dead on the amnesic power of living generations ...we have the weak power of an atoning remembrance ...[which] can generate a reflexive distance from our own traditions, a sensitivity to the profound ambivalences of the tradition which have formed our own identity'.[72]

Dickens explicitly makes the link between historical amnesia and an abandonment of values in the present. Witness the unhistorical and fanciful Victorian medievalism of the deeply corrupted Mrs Skewton – 'Those darling bygone times ...their dear dungeons, and their delightful places of torture ...everything that makes life truly charming! ...dear old Priests ...the most warlike of men ...the days of that inestimable Queen Bess ...so extremely golden ... She was all heart!' (*DS,* ch.27, pp.375–6). Demonstrating such scant responsibility to the past, she herself can expect none from the future; dead, she 'lies unmentioned of her dear friends, who are deaf to the waves that are hoarse with repetition of their mystery, and blind to the dust that is piled upon the shore, and the white arms that are beckoning ...all goes on, as it was wont, upon the margins of the unknown sea' (*DS,* ch.41, p.563).

On the other hand, to be conscious of history is to keep our own practice open to ethical dialogue with other voices. So history (in a passage

---

[72]   Jurgen Habermas, 'The Limits of Neo Historicism', *Autonomy and Solidarity* (London: Verso, 1992), p.242.

highlighted in Dickens's plans) seems to condemn the sale of Edith to Dombey:

> the pictures on the walls ...observed ... Grim knights and warriors looked scowling ... A churchman, with his hand upraised, denounced the mockery of such a couple coming to God's altar ... Ruins cried, 'Look here, and see what We are, wedded to uncongenial Time!' ... Loves and Cupids took to flight afraid, and Martyrdom had no such torment in its painted history of suffering. (*DS*, ch.27, p.376)

Dickens replaces the trope of truth and value as a privileged monologue with one of meaningful dialogue – where ethical and truth-values are produced in the act of dialogue itself, as it orients towards, circles around truth. Such democratic dialogue is implied also by Carlyle's model of the urge to document the present; 'the Celt and the Copt, the Red man as well as the White ...warring against Oblivion ...would feign unite himself in clear conscious relation ...with the whole Future, and the whole Past'.[73]

If committed engagement in this dialogue involves contamination by the guilt of history, value must needs be ascribable to perspectives implicated in that guilt; while being acknowledged, it must also be redeemed – its subjects saved from silenced moral otherness. The dialogue Dickens envisages relies upon redemption in the form of sympathy and forgiveness of the past by the present. Such a notion may be applied to our reading of Dickens himself. To say that they were a product of their time is not to condone his attitudes to race, to class or to gender. But such a disagreement does not absolve us from the duty of seeking not only to engage with these attitudes but also to give a sympathetic hearing to his investigations of other issues on which we share common ground, and can have a meaningful conversation. As Carlyle observes of the 'palimpsest' manuscript of the past, 'some words ...may be deciphered; and if no complete Philosophy, here and there an intelligible precept, available in practice [may] be gathered ...well understanding ...that History ...can be fully interpreted by no man'.[74]

This is a communal gesture, a bond of conversation forged between past, present and future on the basis of their mutual contingency and culpability. As Edith expresses it in her forgiveness of Dombey: 'dead as we are to one another ...I will be repentant too ...when I thought so much of all the causes that had made me what I was, I needed to have allowed more for the causes that had made him what he was. I will try, then, to forgive him his

---

[73] Carlyle, 'On History', *Critical and Miscellaneous Essays*, II, p.83.
[74] Carlyle, 'On History', p.89.

share of the blame. Let him try to forgive mine' (*DS*, ch.61, p.827). Forgiving Dombey with her, we are not asked to reinstate the morally absolute law-giving Father, but to accept the humility of a chastened representative of historicity. Finally, Dombey needs Florence and her offspring – the future – more than they need him. Florence learns to replace the legitimation of paternal love with the contingency of the kindness of others, like the orphan at the Skettles's who proclaims herself content without parents. From Florence's position of power over Dombey, even the gratuity of her pleading forgiveness *of him* is consistent with this allegorisation of the necessity of humility, kindness and sympathy on the part of the present when confronted with the helpless past.

Dickens's novel, like his essay on the shipwreck, is a piece of witness-bearing that not only speaks to his contemporaries of their own moment of history, but also asks us to engage it in ethical trans-historical conversation. Foucault claims the nineteenth century saw 'in the immense domain of practice only the epiphany of a triumphant reason ...only the historico-transcendental destination of the West'.[75] *Dombey and Son* displays no such dogma, but rather suggests an incidental view of history, and a historiographic ethic adapted to it; a sympathetic listening that redeems shattered meanings as it transmutes them, through the sea change of dialogue, into the strange language of a future they never dreamed of, blending the specificity and mutability of each moment of history into a unified infinity. The novel's concluding vision of generations united in kindness by the sea is an emblem of solidarity in the face of time. The dead participate in the significance of the relationships of the living. Paul has that place in memory that he so anxiously sought; with the novelist himself also bearing lasting witness to such victims of history, his dying confidence is justified:

> the present and the absent; what was then and what had been – were blended like the colours in the rainbow, or in the plumage of rich birds when the sun is shining on them, or in the softening sky when the same sun is setting. A solitary window, gazed through years ago, looked out upon an ocean, miles and miles away; upon its waters ...the same mysterious murmur he had wondered at ...he thought he heard sounding through his sister's song, and through the hum of voices, and the tread of feet ...Through the universal kindness he still thought he heard it, speaking to him. (*DS*, ch.14, p.200)

---

[75]   Foucault, 'Politics and the Study of Discourse', p.24.

CHAPTER 2

Other People's Shoes:
Realism, Imagination and Sympathy

With this sense of the splendour of our experience and of its awful brevity, gathering all we are into one desperate effort to see and touch, we shall hardly have time to make theories about the things we see and touch. What we have to do is to be for ever ...courting new impressions, never acquiescing in a facile orthodoxy of Comte, or of Hegel, or of our own.

WALTER PATER, *The Renaissance*

Dombey and Son takes the chaos of history as its structuring theme. However, the very use of 'theme', or the combination of realism (fiction presenting what seems like a picture of the familiar world of experience) with the organised, overarching significance and unity of plot, has been interpreted as in some way already a concession to an imperio-historical conception of history as a unified, significant and teleological progress. Lennard Davis, for instance, suggests that 'plot in narratives, and most particularly novels, helps readers to believe that there is an order in the world', so that 'we might say that the idea of plot is part of an idea of history – that history and novels share a certain faith in plot'.[1] Needless to say, for the reasons suggested at the start of the last chapter, this is a very *bad thing* as far as Davis and like-minded critics are concerned.

I have suggested that there are elements in *Dombey* that resist being subsumed by the progression of plot and its structured import. However, the argument of the last section relies upon the assumption that many events and scenes in the novel have a deep and generalisable thematic and narrative significance – that scenes and events 'mean' something in the wider context of the novel as a whole, over and above their simple, 'literal' presence as part of the fiction. In *Dombey*, I have argued, many of the events

---

[1]   Davis, pp.212, 213.

and scenes enact, employ and implicitly argue for a particular ethic of history. In this chapter, I will use the word 'Significance', with a capital 'S', to refer to this type of secondary, generalizing meaning that lies behind the superficial details of fiction.

I hope I have already shown that Significant realism can disrupt the exclusivity of history as well as consolidate it. The novel's conjunction of realism (a relatively new kind of writing) with Significant narrative (an old and ubiquitous one) is easily explained as a chance of literary development, rather than as an ideological symptom. Furthermore, the argument for the complicity of Significant plotting in historical violence can hardly be held from collapsing into the argument that any attempt to speak, to mean, should be held accountable for such violence – which seems an untenable position. Language just *is* exclusive and simplifying, but that does not mean that we cannot use it to express an ideal of inclusiveness and complexity.

However, there are texts that seek to delay and supplement the simplifying process involved in human sense-making. I turn now to part of the novel tradition that does as much as one can imagine to evade the difference-cancelling constructions of Significance.

i. Feminine fiction

It was a Victorian commonplace that female minds, and female novelists, have a peculiar affinity for recording, with little striving after generalization, the superficial appearances and sensations of material experience, and for chronicling the personal and emotional. Sarah Ellis, for example, remarked that 'to women belongs the minute and particular observance of all those trifles which fill up the sum of human happiness or misery', and Emily Davies alluded to the consensual opinion that 'woman has a loving care for the individual; the man an unimpassioned reverence for the general and universal'.[2] Women were widely considered to be exclusively concerned with immediate perception and material detail.

> They care to conquer each point as they reach it, but not to understand its exact bearing on the last, and those before it. They are not eager to *map* or *plan* their world of thought. With men, the pleasure of understanding clearly how different facts are related, is often greater

2   Sarah Ellis, *The Women of England* (London: Fisher, Son and Co., 1839), pp.38–9; Emily Davies, 'The Influence of University Degrees on the Education of Women', *The Victorian Magazine*, June 1863, reprinted in C.A. Lacey (ed) *Barbara Leigh Smith Bodichon and the Langham Place Group* (London: Routledge, 1987), pp.415–27, p.420.

than the pleasure of studying any of them individually; with women it is the reverse.[3]

For RH Hutton, these feminine characteristics were seen as both the greatest strengths and the greatest weaknesses of women when it came to writing fiction:

> Feminine perceptions are finer, subtler, quicker than men's; again, their delicacy and skill in delineation is greater; but what they lack is an eye for universality, a power of seeing the broad representative element in any individual fact or scene, which connects it with other facts and scenes beyond itself …[women have rarely] devoted a really scientific study to special classes of scenes, or forms, or expressions.[4]

This notion was closely connected to a biological scheme that placed emotional and particular observation lower in a hierarchy of faculties than abstract reasoning, and placed women lower on the evolutionary scheme than men. For Herbert Spencer, women were connected with children and the lower races, in whom we 'see an absorption in special facts' and by whom 'generalities' are 'scarcely recognized'.[5]

Gaye Tuchman suggests that 'the details of personal, emotional, and everyday life', were 'the least admired aspects of novels' in the nineteenth century.[6] Her impression is borne out by Hutton's remarks. For Hutton, the general and universal is the backbone of success in art. Particularity is but a means to the illustration of the general:

> [Male art goes] to the heart of a *large class of scenes* …It is grasp, comprehensiveness, a kind of *generality and universality* of treatment, which distinguishes masculine from feminine art …the success of the greater artists …concentrates the fruits of a whole world of meditations and observation on general types of things, bringing out with vivid effect in a particular case, a profound insight into general relations or

---

3   RH Hutton, *The Relative Value of Studies and Accomplishments in the Education of Women* (London, 1862), p.19.

4   Hutton, *Relative Value*, p.20.

5   Herbert Spencer, 'The Comparative Psychology of Man', in *Essays Scientific, Political and Speculative*, 3 vols (London: Williams and Norgate, 1891), I, pp.351–70, p.354.

6   Gaye Tuchman, 'When the Prevalent Don't Prevail: Male Hegemony and the Victorian Novel,' in Walter W. Powell and Richard Robbins (eds), *Conflicts and Consensus* (New York: Free Press, 1984), pp.139–58, p.154.

laws ... Almost every picture that solicits attention, does so on the
grounds of mastering some *class* of fact which goes quite beyond the
individual subject painted.[7]

I will be seeking to contest a continuing marginalization in contemporary
criticism of what Hutton designates as 'feminine' characteristics; a
marginalization now manifested in the insistence that, deep down, all novels
are about general, abstract ideas, and that what look like incidental details
and particulars in narrative are somehow secondary, ancillary functions of
general, universal, abstract Significance. Many critics now believe, and
many more behave as though they believe, that all fiction is Significant; that
there is no such thing as 'feminine' fiction, in Hutton's sense.

From this idea, in large part, has issued the political critique of the novel,
for contemporary criticism has not retained Hutton's esteem for the
universal. There is a current suspicion that a prioritizing of the general and
universal reflects and encourages patriarchy, bourgeois hegemony, and
imperialism. Hutton's remarks alone would be enough to prompt such
misgivings. He associates abstract habits of thought and 'general principles',
as embodied in masculine art, with

> delight in extensive *power*, that pleasure in a wide grasp of detail, in
> moving men and things *by masses and collectively* – that delight which the
> merchant feels at the transactions which he regulates by the stroke of a
> pen, which the politician experiences in dealing with nations as if they
> were individuals. Women have little of this delight in moving for
> themselves armies of facts or persons; their interests are individual alike
> in dealing with men or things.[8]

Cristina Crosby argues that *all* novels, whether by men or women, are
generalizing and abstract, and she takes the possibility that this aesthetic
practice might have political corollaries very seriously. She suggests that
Victorian fiction generally, and that of Eliot, Dickens, and Charlotte Brontë
in particular, is an instantiation of the fact that 'in the nineteenth century
"history" is produced as man's truth, the truth of a necessarily historical
Humanity'. She is one of many who have argued that Victorian history,
and, by extension, Victorian fiction, is the history of man transcendentally
conceived, a History from which female experience, along with non-white,
non-male experience, is doubly excluded: '"man" can emerge as an

[7] Hutton, *Renlative Value*, pp.21–2.
[8] Hutton, *Relative Value*, pp.17–18.

abstraction ...only if there is something other than history, something intrinsically unhistorical ..."woman"'.[9] She makes explicit an assumption that lies behind much contemporary criticism: that both history and fiction are in the violent and political business of reducing heterogeneous materiality and diversity to a single narrative, making all experience point in one, ideologically-determined, direction – and that both history and the novel can be read only from a metaphysical and male subject position.[10]

Although Crosby recognises the Victorian identification of 'woman' as a category 'with the immediacy and intimacy of social life', she nevertheless insists that 'personal' narratives about women turn out to be no more than oblique affirmations of male Historical Reality.[11] Hutton lists Charlotte Brontë, Elizabeth Gaskell, Charlotte Yonge, Elizabeth Sewell and Dinah Craik as thoroughly feminine writers, and George Eliot as less thoroughly so. For Crosby, on the other hand, the guilt of novels that she thinks *pretend* to be about the immediate and particular is simply double-dyed. Brontë, Eliot, and all apparently 'feminine' novelists, are also – albeit covertly – guilty of complicity with the political impulses that Hutton attributes to the generalizing artist.

I will argue, against Crosby, that Hutton really hit on something: there *is* such a thing as a feminine imaginative perspective as he describes it, an art 'not *separable*, as it were ...from the visible surface and form of human experience', though such art may be produced by men as well as women. [12] Despite the sexual stereotypes to which his critical distinction might seem to be related, this perceptive Victorian critic did not himself biologize the difference between masculine and feminine practices of fiction, attributing it rather to social placing and expectations, educational regimes, and individual temperament, and arguing, for instance, that 'the type of Dickens' genius is, in many respects, feminine'. This inclusion of *the* major male novelist of the period in the 'feminine' category suggests that Hutton's insight is really into a characteristic of mid-Victorian realist fiction in general.[13]

Women, of course, have had greater influence on the novel than on any

---

[9]   Cristina Crosby, *The Ends of History: Victorians and 'The Woman Question'* (New York and London: Routledge, 1991), p.1.

[10] One of the central arguments of post-colonial literary criticism runs the same way. See Edward Said, *Culture and Imperialism* (London: Chatto and Windus, 1993).

[11] Crosby, p.2.

[12] Hutton, 'Novels by the Authoress of "John Halifax"', *North British Review* XXIX (Nov. 1858), 466–81, 467.

[13] Hutton, 'Authoress of "John Halifax"', p.469.

other genre, in both its production and reception. Excluded as they were from the world of business, and attributed with a nature directly opposed to the realms of History – intellectual, political and economic progress – it would have been strange if a female-dominated genre had not sought to investigate, for its own sake, experience outside Significant plot structures. This chapter focuses on 'feminine' texts that manifestly contravene the 'devotion to consistency and the subsuming of events under a more totalizing structure' that Davis, Crosby, and so many others diagnose as a pernicious characteristic of the novel.[14] I want to explore the particular characteristics, function, and appeal of such fiction.

My argument will be in direct opposition to Crosby's assertion that in the descriptions of daily life that one finds in the narratives of Eliot and others writing in the same genre, 'the objects of ...investigation are stripped, exposed, discarded in a thoroughly objectifying operation' as the novelist 'strips away the specificity of that figure, of that historical time' so that 'every fact is only the means to an end', the construction of a teleological History of man, of a humanism 'which will do whatever is necessary to consolidate one norm, one standard, one reality, the humanity of western white bourgeois man'.[15] The texts I will examine clearly do not, as Crosby says of Eliot's whole oeuvre, *subsume* the 'individual' to the 'collective', the 'empirical' to the 'ideal', the 'psychological' to the 'philosophic', and the 'particular' to the 'world-historical' in their portrayal of experience.[16] I will focus on texts by some of the novelists dealt with by Hutton: Elizabeth Sewell's *The Experience of Life*, Elizabeth Gaskell's *Mary Barton* and 'Half a Lifetime Ago', Charlotte Brontë's *Shirley* and George Eliot's *Scenes of Clerical Life* (and, briefly, *The Mill on the Floss*). My argument, however, applies equally to innumerable other nineteenth-century texts, not least to many novels written by men.

The 'unselfconscious' realism of these texts (unselfconscious, at least, in the areas that interest Crosby, though conscious enough in those that interest me) is, I will argue, as much a mode of 'feminized history' as the more playful self-referentiality of Thackeray's *Henry Esmond* – a text of which Crosby approves. They also have a claim to contesting 'disciplined history by focusing precisely on what the latter must eliminate', as she says of *Esmond*.[17] But their energy is manifest not in the negative and abstract sallies against the unreality of History that Crosby attributes to Thackeray, but instead in vibrant affirmations of the reality of the extra-Historical.

---

[14]   Davis, p.202.
[15]   Crosby, pp.15, 16, 42.
[16]   Crosby, p.13.
[17]   Crosby, p.60.

My most ambitious claim will be that, rather than merely addressing abstract questions of 'the instability of identity, of subject and object, of time itself',[18] feminine fiction participates in, as well as treats of, the non-abstract, the particular, the sensual – that is, the experiential – and so transcends these abstract categories and oppositions.

ii. 'The nothingness of this life and the desirability of cut glass'

As Elizabeth Deeds Ermarth and many others have pointed out, in the early novel, as represented by the work of Defoe, the action of the plots is interpretable, made Significant, in the light of the progress not of historical man but of the individual soul. If Crusoe's story is one of imperialism, it is imperialism justified by divine and spiritual, rather than historical, transcendence; as a man alone on the island, his soul faces God without social intermediary. And yet, his story is without doubt materialist; the symbols of eternity, in the Calvinist tradition, are read off from the worldly record of a struggle for bourgeois advancement. Watt observes in Defoe's novels the 'confusion of religious and material values to which the Puritan gospel of the dignity of labour was peculiarly liable'. As he says, 'the heritage of Puritanism is demonstrably too weak to supply a continuous and controlling pattern for the hero's experience'.[19] In its subsequent development, the novel attempted to incorporate into its realism Fielding's objection to the fictional illustration of the agreeable idea that 'Virtue is the certain Road to Happiness, and Vice to Misery', 'namely, that it is not true'.[20] By the 1870s, George Eliot could bring into sharp focus the naivety of an earlier time's reconciliation of its dual investment in 'piety and worldliness, the nothingness of this life and the desirability of cut glass'.[21]

To suggest that, facing this contradiction, the nineteenth century performed an immediate volte-face, and transferred its faith all at once from religious to historical transcendence, would be, as Ermarth points out, a distortion.[22] In fact, many novelists of the mid-century cling with considerable tenacity to the idea of a divine order. However, unlike Defoe,

---

[18] Crosby, p.47.

[19] Ian Watt, *The Rise of the Novel* (London: Penguin, 1979), pp.81, 89.

[20] Henry Fielding, *Tom Jones* (1749), ed. Martin Battestin and Fredson Bowers (Oxford: Clarendon Press, 1974), XV, I, p.783.

[21] George Eliot, *Middlemarch*, III, XXVII, p.263.

[22] Elizabeth Deeds Ermarth, *The Novel in History* (London and New York: Routledge, 1997), Ch.1.

they often treat the divine as *completely*, unknowably transcendent, rather than as something that confers Significance on material existence. The superfluity of schemes of worldly order, given the nothingness of this world, is made a focus; the workings of providence are entirely inscrutable, the distribution of worldly success is to human perceptions entirely arbitrary. Order exists in heaven, and makes no contact with worldly experience beyond giving the faithful the strongest impression of the meaninglessness and inSignificance of experience, of history as it appears to man. In the face of the seemingly chaotic break-up of traditional society brought about by the industrial revolution, the novels of Victorian religious revival often promise to conduce not so much to a perception of the workings of divine order in the world, but rather to epistemological resignation with regards to experience below in the faith of order above.

We find a prime example of this novelistic solution in the fiction of Elizabeth Sewell, a relatively prolific and popular mid-century novelist, who has received little critical attention. The pervasive religiosity of novels such as *The Experience of Life* does nothing to explain or structure the diurnal experiences they describe (with a detailed materialism that rivals that of Defoe). *The Experience of Life* manifests a marked departure from the Significant plot structures associated with the novel, as the narrator points out:

> I am not going to write a tale, not at least what is usually so called. A tale is, for the most part, only a vignette, a portion of the great picture of life, having no definite limit, yet containing one prominent object, in which all the interest is concentrated. But this is not a true representation of human existence. For one person whose life has been marked by some very striking event, there are hundreds who pass to their graves with nothing to distinguish the different periods of their probation, but the changes which steal upon them so naturally as scarcely to occasion a momentary surprise. They hope and enjoy, they are disappointed and sad, but none points to the history of their lives, as containing warning or example ...[I write] less with the view of exciting great interest, than with the desire of describing what must be a lot of hundreds similarly placed.[23]

The novel indeed contains little striking incident, hardly any incident at all beyond ordinary deaths and unpredictable changes of fortune. It is a

---

[23]   Elizabeth Sewell, *The Experience of Life* (1853) (London: Longman, Brown, Green, 1859), p.1. Hereafter, *EL.*

detailed record of the experience of such changes, accompanied by a religious commentary on the total obscurity of the Significance of their disorder. One of the first passages chronicles the effort of the narrator, on the day of her confirmation, to maintain a faith in divine order in the face of worldly disorder, through thinking of God to the *exclusion* of the worldly incidents of which the narrative is a tissue: 'I remember listening to …the raised voices, the clatter of trays and glasses and plates, the roll of the carriages driving into town, and feeling very disturbed and uncomfortable …the world was …in a tangle …whatever the state of the world might be, there was no doubt that my first duty was order in my own mind' (*EL*, p.23). It is in exactly this sort of resigned but determined spirit that Sewell applies herself to the daunting task of writing a novel centred upon a heroine who is repelled by and opposed to the very sounds and sights that define the genre in which she finds herself.

The plot chronicles the fluctuations of the wealth of the narrator and her family, the only explanation for which lies in the vague malevolence of a worldly uncle and a distant cousin. Incidents include the marriage of some of the members of the family, the professional success or failure of others, and the death of several; the narrator's confirmation, bouts of illness, assumption of household and charitable duties, formation of friendships, purchase of dresses, fright and bravery in the face of unsteady horses/cattle, and achievement of maidenly resignation in the face of the noisy chaos, hardship and injustice of the world. The novel's paradoxical project seems to be to capture experience precisely in order to show that it holds no interest. The single life is valued over marriage, as 'the unmarried woman careth only for the things of the Lord, that she may be holy both in body and spirit; but she that is married careth for the things of the world' (*EL*, p.139). Marriage would only link the narrator more strongly to the experience of this world, the pleasurable or painful experiences of which, though they are 'atoms only in the immensity of an eternal happiness' on which it is 'vain to spend a thought', form, nevertheless, the substance of the novel (*EL*, p.324). Each meticulous record of pain or pleasure is soon qualified with an annihilating gesture beyond the earthly:

Vistas of green lawn, smooth as velvet, lost beneath the shade of a solitary spreading beech or chestnut; gravel walks winding amongst thickets of delicate shrubs; bright colours fixing the eye on the precise spot where colour was most needed, or leading it on to some beautiful point at a distance, some glimpse of the blue sheet of water, or some opening in the woods …bright, yet withal sad and restless, as all beauty must be, since it is mourning for and seeking after perfection. (*EL*, p.75)

Strangely, *The Experience of Life*, despite the lack of incident, and the pointed inSignificance of its detail, is, in its own way, a page-turner. However, unless the reader can share the narrator's indifference to the quality of all experience in the awesome face of eternity, it is hard not to object to what the contemporary reviewers might have called the 'painfulness' of the reading experience. Events are denied metaphysical Significance, while at the same time the reader seems forbidden the 'worldly' interest of pleasure in detail for its own sake. The unbelieving reader is pushed towards the state of nihilistic doubt and self-disgust in which the heroine finds herself at the start of the novel.

Clearly, abandonment of Defoe's conception of a divinely ordered material history for the sake of a dualistic world-view in which meaning, Significance and value are in heaven while experience is on earth is not unproblematic in its novelistic results. But many of Sewell's contemporaries avoided Defoe's paradox neither by writing self-negating novels like hers, in which the materialist experiential narrative is negated by the spiritual moral, *nor*, as in the established account espoused by Crosby, by shifting the locus of transcendent Significance from heaven to history. Though abandoning, like Sewell, the project of finding Significance in the material world, they chose, unlike her, to uphold raw experience itself as an object of irreducible interest and value, without regard to its 'meaning' as part of any metaphysical or historical grand narrative.

As we shall see, substantial parts of the narratives dealt with here either dispose of or marginalize transcendent Significance. Any 'message' is swamped under a plethora of details of daily life endowed with so much inherent interest that it is the passages of Significant incident or apostrophe, and not of description, that the reader is inclined to skip. Such narratives seem designed to cater for readers like Mrs Linnet, in George Eliot's short story 'Janet's Repentance' (from *Scenes of Clerical Life*), who

On taking up the biography of a celebrated preacher ...immediately turned to the end to see what disease he died of, and if his legs swelled, as her own occasionally did, she felt a stronger interest in ascertaining any facts in the history of the dropsical divine – whether he had ever fallen off a stage coach, whether he had married more than one wife, and, in general, any adventures or repartees recorded on him previous to the epoch of his conversion. She then glanced over the letters and diary, and wherever there was a predominance of Zion, the River of

Life, and notes of exclamation, she turned over to the next page; but any passage in which she saw such promising nouns as 'small-pox', 'pony', or 'boots and shoes', at once arrested her.[24]

iii. 'Small feminine ambitions': Getting a feel for feminine fiction

Eliot's *Scenes of Clerical Life* privileges incidental description over progressive plot. In 'The Sad Fortunes of the Reverend Amos Barton' the events are no more than a structure on which to hang the experiences of Amos and his neighbours, and above all, the hidden experience and humdrum details of his wife's life and death. Eliot observes that a 'woman's world lies within the four walls of her own home; and it is only through her husband that she is in any electric communication with the world beyond' (*SCL*, p.61). Mrs Barton's tale has no connection with the forward march of History. 'Janet's Repentance' chronicles the paradigmatically un-witnessed, unacknowledged, yet common experiences of fatuous domestic violence and addiction.

If marriage is the telos of much fiction, serving to drive and complete narrative, as DA Miller suggests, then disappointed love is a paradigmatic subject of non-teleological, inSignificant fiction. Like *The Experience of Life*, two out of the three *Scenes of Clerical Life* – 'Janet's Repentance' and 'Mr Gilfil's Love-Story' – also frustrate romantic teleology. In her introduction to *Scenes of Clerical Life*, Jennifer Gribble finds the depiction of the latter story's heroine, Tina, a 'confirmation of cultural stereotypes associated with ...European revolutionary ardour'.[25] Certainly, the story makes allusions to the revolution in France:

> In that summer [of 1788], we know, the great nation of France was agitated by conflicting thoughts and passions, which were but the beginning of sorrows. And in our Caterina's little breast, too, there were terrible struggles. (*SCL*, p.105)

But the relation of the story to the History of European revolutionary ardour is not, in fact, one of synecdoche, but rather of ironic contrast. The narrator comments:

---

24 George Eliot, *Scenes of Clerical Life* (1857) (London: Penguin, 1998), pp.218 –109. Hereafter, *SCL*.

25 Jennifer Gribble, Introduction, *Scenes of Clerical Life*, xxvi.

While this poor little heart was being bruised ... Nature was holding on her calm inexorable way ...the sun was making brilliant day to busy nations on the other side of the swift earth. The stream of human thought and deed was hurrying and broadening onward ...the toiling eagerness of commerce, the fierce spirit of revolution, were only ebbing in brief rest; and sleepless statesmen were dreading the possible crisis of the morrow. What were our Tina and her trouble in this mighty torrent, rushing from one awful unknown to another? Lighter than the smallest centre of quivering life in the water-drop, hidden and un-cared for as the pulse of anguish in the breast of the tiniest bird. (*SCL*, p.132)

The refusal of the universe to validate human experience is emphasized, and the contrasts between the 'history' of Tina and the 'History' of revolution are everywhere highlighted.

In contrast with *public* 'History', that of Tina is deeply concealed, requiring special narrative manoeuvres to bring it out. The story begins with no mention of Tina, but ostensibly relates to the life of an obscure and long dead clergyman, Mr Gilfil. His house is like that of an unmarried man, as we might first imagine him to be; it 'seemed to tell a story of wifeless existence that was contradicted by no portrait, no piece of embroidery, no faded bit of pretty triviality, hinting of taper fingers and small feminine ambitions' (*SCL*, p.88).

However, we cannot trust the story told by these appearances; we cannot so easily assign Gilfil to the general 'class' of bachelor. The narrator, equating himself with Mrs Patten, a village gossip, in a 'taste for personal narrative' and in communicativeness, steps in to relate a different kind of tale (*SCL*, pp.88, 89). The narrative itself is ironically presented as a piece of small feminine ambition, a faded bit of triviality, an embroidered portrait, which has nothing to do with the grand Significance of masculine History, whose furthest outposts are represented in the Vicar's sitting room, where the smell of tobacco, the horse-hair chairs, and the Turkey carpets hint at a comically tenuous relation to trade, war and Empire.

Tina's former room in Gilfil's house is locked, but all the daily articles in it have been preserved. A dressing-table, a looking-glass with bits of wax-candle still remaining in its sockets, a scent-bottle, a fan, a dressing-box, a work-basket, slippers, an unfinished baby-cap. Each article vividly signals its daily function, or imaginatively conjures a living 'history' of the daily actions of the woman whose portrait hangs on the wall; but this history seems inaccessibly lost in time, like the 'fashion long forgotten' of her preserved gowns, or the rusted pins which cannot be pulled back through the fine fabric of the pincushion in which they are buried. Mrs Gilfil's life is shut off from History, just as the room is locked and kept separate from the changes of the world. We are told that even during Gilfil's time as clergyman in the town, no one but Martha knew much more about his wife than that she sang well and died. The distance of Mrs Gilfil's history is further highlighted by the dawning awareness that in the previous *Scene*, 'Amos Barton', the narrator brought us into that very same room without any mention of Mrs Gilfil; by the period of that earlier tale even the smallest tokens of her existence had been swept away; it is another woman who dies in the room. This unmentioned palimpsest of events deftly gestures towards the reality of an infinity of hidden lives that rely on no transcendent unity of narrative Significance for validation. The revelation that the narrator is in fact 'much better informed' than the citizens of Shepperton, and can tell Tina's story, seems a miracle beyond historical law. The narrative is hardly a narrative at all, its conclusion is known at the beginning as a dead end, a locked room. And yet it is happy to rest in this contingency, to make it the structure for a relation of the most minute details of an experience of emotional turmoil. Clearly even the telling of insignificant stories is worthwhile; the epithet is no longer value-laden.

Eliot's first story, 'Amos Barton', is set a long time after the second, 'Mr Gilfil's Love-Story', but it begins with a description of the church as it was in the old age of Gilfil, comparing it with the church as it is in the present day, which is further compared to the bald head of Barton, who himself has been gone a couple of decades. The narrative proper starts neither in the present time nor in that of Gilfil – the narrator insistently resists telling *his* story – but twenty or so years back. 'Mr Gilfil's Love-Story' similarly starts with a backward glance of thirty years to the death of Gilfil, before taking us back to the incidents of his mature years, and then right back to his youth, and then even further back to the infancy of Tina. If this all sounds confusing, that's because it is. This messy and incidental interrelation between the characters and time-frames of the different scenes, this looking back and forward, and back and back, creates a vertiginous sense of existences intransigent to monolithic plotting, of time as a process of compound forgetting, rather than of unfolding narrative.

Gaskell's short story 'Half a Lifetime Ago' begins with a similar convolution of time-sequence, with similar effect. [26] A certain house, we

---

[26]   The link, that will be built upon here, between the realism of Gaskell and that of Eliot was acknowledged by Eliot herself; 'I was conscious, while the question of my power was still undecided for me, that my feeling towards Life and Art had some affinity with the feeling which had inspired *Cranford* and the earlier chapters of *Mary*

learn, is 'no specimen, at the present day, of what it was in the lifetime of Susan Dixon. Then, every small diamond pane in the windows glittered with cleanliness. You might have eaten off the floor; you could see yourself in the pewter plates and polished oaken awmry, or dresser, of the state kitchen into which you entered. Few strangers penetrated further than this room'.[27] Tourists, even at the time long past to which the narrator initially refers, could see no further into the deeper history of Susan than their own reflections in the polished surfaces. Susan would not talk, the servants, even those who knew her story, would not speak of it. The reader is at a double distance; even these opaque traces are now themselves gone. The narrative 'miraculously' uncovers the experience of Susan – her devotion to her idiot brother, and her desertion by her lover to which it leads. Susan's story is presented through detailed accounts of her diurnal experience. When her separation from her lover is made final, she sets out to make clap-bread, 'one of the hardest and hottest domestic tasks of a Daleswoman'. As she 'beat her cakes thin ...she was surprised by a touch on her mouth of something – what she did not see at first. It was a cup of tea, delicately sweetened and cooled, held to her lips, when exactly ready ... "Lass! ...it is not long to bide, and then the end will come"'.[28] Here, sensuous vehicles are inseparable from the fundamental emotions they embody. Life is reduced to a flux of experience, a sensuous interval between birth and death. As Terence Wright observes, 'Gaskell is not the woman to see life as something simply to be transcended ...the very brevity of the moment, the transience of the world, means that they take on an absoluteness of their own'.[29]

iv. Significant or sensuous reading?

What do such large loose baggy monsters, with their queer elements of the accidental and the arbitrary, artistically *mean*?   HENRY JAMES

Barton.' Letter to Mrs Gaskell, 11 November 1859, in *The George Eliot Letters*, ed. Gordon S. Haight, 9 vols. (New Haven: Yale University Press, 1954–1978), III, p.198.

[27] Elizabeth Gaskell, 'Half a Lifetime Ago' (first published in *Household Words*, XII, 6–20 October 1855), in *The Manchester Marriage, and Other Stories* (Stroud, Gloucestershire: Alan Sutton, 1990), pp.89–90.

[28] Gaskell, 'Half a Lifetime Ago', p.118.

[29] Terence Wright, *Elizabeth Gaskell 'We are not Angels': Realism, Gender, Value* (Houndsmills, Basingstoke, Hampshire and New York: Macmillan Press, 1995), p.27.

Realism has nothing to do with detail for its own sake.

ELIZABETH DEEDS ERMARTH

Hitherto I have largely been speaking of the attitude to, the statements about, extra-Historical, inSignificant reality that are suggested by what I refer to as feminine fiction. What my argument amounts to so far is, in effect, that the significance of these narratives lies in their validation of inSignificance. I want now to move beyond this paradoxical claim, to a consideration of the functions of feminine fiction that lie altogether outside the realm of narrative Significance.

If, as Crosby says, 'history is the Word, promising that the sensible will be intelligible in the fullness of time', I am claiming that feminine fictions are not historical in this sense, because they refuse to privilege the Significant.[30] The sensible, as they present it, does not become intelligible – it is not made to *mean* anything, but 'speaks' for itself. The illustration of this idea demands a more explicit account of the way such texts might operate upon their readers.

Such an account cannot be given without straying from the standard literary-theoretical approach to the function of language in fiction, typically exemplified in its contemporary form by Crosby and Davis. It is worth unpicking these critics' basic assumptions, for not only are their accounts of fictional language radically incomplete, but this inadequacy means that their shared argument about the politico-historical function of the novel is in fact circular, their conclusions necessitated by the partiality of the terms in which their premises are framed. This circularity decisively invalidates the application of their analysis to particular rhetorical forms considered as the expression of particular political interests.

The background to Crosby's argument is Roland Barthes' influential theory that in classic realist fiction there is a single message, or at most a 'limited plural' of messages behind the text, which it is the reader's role to attain.[31] The text leads the reader into a position from which the text's meaning, its overarching Significance, may be grasped, that position being the unitary and unified perspective of Western Man, from which vantage a world of experience can be reduced to a single abstract Significance.[32]

---

[30]   Crosby, p.145.

[31]   Roland Barthes, *S/Z*, trans. Richard Miller (New York: Hill and Wang, 1985), p.8.

[32]   Some version of this argument is a background assumption behind a great many recent theoretical studies of realist fiction. Other notable expressions of it can be found in stock inclusions in undergraduate reading lists such as: DA Miller, *The Novel and the Police*, Colin MacCabe *James Joyce and the Revolution of the Word* (London:

Crosby and Davis, along with innumerable others, follow Barthes's argument that *all* that seemingly 'irrelevant' inSignificant details do is say, '*we are the real*; it is the category of "the real" (and not its contingent contents) which is then signified ...the reality effect is produced'.[33] It is, in other words, precisely by seeming to evade the conceptual structures of Significance behind the work, by seeming to have no 'signified', that these details connote, indirectly signify, the notion that the novel in question is an objective picture of the real. As Davis puts it, 'Characters in novels ...live in a "world of relevancy", and even when the irrelevant occurs in the novel it serves "the interest of provoking secondary illusions"'.[34]

This is really little more than a systematic and politicized formulation of the standard assumptions of un-Theoretical literary criticism. Barbara Hardy, for example, contends that a detailed description of a scene in a novel serves 'the double purpose of narrative and theme ...domestic scenes which are not ...essential to the development of plot [are] there ...in all successful novels, to give the essential illusion that the action is rooted in normal space and time'.[35] This reality effect is, these days, considered a means to the beguiling transmission of the ideological message of the novel, embodied in the (thus disguised) value-laden presentation of its events. Material details vanish and an 'interpellating' ideology remains. Thus Davis argues that 'novels are pre-organized systems of experience in which characters, actions, and objects *have to mean something* in relation to the system of each novel itself, in relation to the culture in which the novel is written ... When we "see" a house in a novel, there is nothing "there", and worse, there is really no "there" for a "there" to be. The house we "see" in our mind is largely a cultural artefact. It must be described as a cultural phenomenon with recognizable signs to tell us what kind of a house, what

Macmillan, 1979), and Catherine Belsey *Critical Practice* (London: Routledge, 1980). Eliot and Brontë are always prime targets. In arguing against this view, I commonly encounter one of two responses. Most of those working within the field cannot believe its basic terms are open to challenge, and those working outside it cannot believe the view is worth challenging, or that anyone could really hold it. These responses make critical engagement with the question seem as pressing as it is generally thankless.

[33] Barthes, *The Rustle of Language*, trans. Richard Howard (Oxford: Blackwell, 1986), p.48.

[34] Davis, p.113, in turn citing Karlheinz Stierle, 'The reading of fictional texts', in Susan R Suleiman and Inge Crosman (eds.), *The Reader in the Text* (Princeton: Princeton University Press, 1980), p.98.

[35] Barbara Hardy, *The Novels of George Eliot* (London: Athlone Press, 1963), p.185.

class, whose taste, and so on'.[36]

My central argument runs directly against the categorical implications of Davis's generalization. His use of 'largely' in 'largely a cultural artefact' does a great deal of rather illegitimate work. It allows him to use the force of the obvious observation that to 'imagine' a house is not to have physically in one's head an individual house as it objectively exists independent of any human observer or community, to advance the much more contentious claim that such an imagining is nothing in excess of the webs of Significance which create and circumscribe it – that the imagining of a house, in other words, has *nothing whatever to do* with sensuous and concrete encounters with real material houses (if even those are possible).

It is worth considering, at this point, whether Davis believes that a non-fictional description of a house is any more or less a cultural artefact than a fictional one. After all, Barthes applied his approach to non-fictional cultural discourses. Davis's argument is lent plausibility by its relation to a widespread critical preoccupation with the arbitrary and differential construction of linguistic meaning in general. This preoccupation finds resolution in a number of different stances, ranging from an uncontroversial (and again trivial) acknowledgement of the fact that the abstraction of linguistic systems radically shapes our interaction with the material world, to much more controversial claims about our radical entrapment within language. Whether or not Davis and Crosby accept the extremity of the latter view (presumably Davis holds that we are 'largely' shut off from the material world by language), their arguments are parasitic upon it. Neither does anything to show why theirs is an accurate account of the function of fictional language in particular, as distinct from language *tout court*. As we will see, only a radically anti-empiricist conception of representation *in general* can fill the gaps they leave in their argument without weakening it to triviality.

And yet Davis and Crosby et al. charge novels *in particular* with implying that the material universe is a vast structured web of objective transcendental meaning called History that denudes material reality of all its sensuous particularity. They do so without regard to the fact that, given their understanding of the function of fictional language, there is simply nothing else that the details (or any other features) in any text (of any period, bourgeois or not) could be doing if not being Significant in this grand, over-arching, Historical way, and so, by analytical extension, being what such critics define as imperially and patriarchally Historicist (this is the first flaw

---

[36] Davis p.24, my italics.

in their position, which renders it question-begging.) According to their premises, this is necessarily true, but it has to do with the general nature of fiction (and language generally) and not with a particular ideology of history.

The only alternative account of the function of fictional representation open to these critics is one of 'subversive' deformation of the norms that they claim to have exhaustively described. The Thackeray novels that Crosby approves do not abandon Signification but, she claims, self-consciously Signify its impossibility, and subversively draw attention to the norms that she claims to have comprehensively fathomed. A small task for massive novels full of detailed descriptions, to embody a deconstructive message that Crosby can communicate in a couple of paragraphs! Most Victorian novels are indeed unpardonably long and baggy if this is all they are up to. (This is the second flaw in Crosby and Davis's position, which renders it implausible.)

There are two ways out of this doubly unsatisfactory critical position. To get rid of the first problem we will want to abandon the equation of the construction of Significant narratives as such with either the conviction that the universe is objectively meaningful, or with imperialism and patriarchy. There is, after all, an inescapable need for the shaping and ordering of language *and* narrative in any human grappling with the world.

However, in abandoning this strong claim about the political evil of Significant narrative, we may want to retain a weaker version of Crosby and Davis's argument, which will actually help us get over the second absurdity, and understand why Victorian novels are, from a Significance-orientated perspective, so long and baggy.

The critique of 'identity thinking' has a long and sensible history. Our constructions of Significance *do* always leave something out, make something disappear, place materiality at something of a remove. And some linguistic constructions are more abstract, place sensuous reality at a greater remove, than others – it is one thing to come across a real manor house and categorize it mentally as 'a manor house', in a manner that somewhat obscures our sense of the material presence and particularities of that specific house, and another to read about a 'manor-house' in a text in which we understand that we must take the words as no more than code for 'upper class', which can in turn only be understood as one component in a wider ideological message of the text. One experience involves sensuous perception, the other is an extremely roundabout way of making a very general and mediated statement about the way things are, or perhaps, some might argue, for interpellating us as obedient subjects within a particular ideology.

Where, then, do novels lie on the scale of abstraction – what, in comparison to other instances of language use, is their relation to sensuous reality? And do all novels occupy the same place on the scale? Such questions, strictly ignored by Davis and Crosby, will lead us to a better understanding, as well as to a distinctive political defence, of the baggy Victorian novel. Of course reading a novel is a more abstract activity than eating a peach. But, I will argue, it is often nowhere near as abstract an activity as Davis and Crosby suggest – it is often, indeed, in a special sense less abstract than reading a text that is intended primarily to convey real facts to its reader. The novel may not be so deeply and thoroughly immersed in the higher order abstraction of Significance as we imagine. The mid-Victorian novel is in fact, I will argue, politically exceptional precisely because it is exceptional in the degree to which it strives to undercut that abstraction, and to relate, *through its very fictitiousness*, as closely as possible to the sensuousness of material experience.

The appreciation of this dimension of the novel is beyond the Barthesians because of the partiality of the terms within which they operate – terms determined by the structuralist movement's roots in linguistics, from which the post-structuralist rebels have not broken free. What they see in fiction are structures of detail-transcendent Significance, of over-arching meaning, because that is all structuralism has taught them to look for there. Their criticism is directed not at the novel *per se*, but at the novel *à la* Structuralism.[37]

In his introduction to Tzvetan Todorov's seminal work, *The Poetics of Prose*, Jonathan Culler describes the structuralist project, the prospective heir to traditional literary criticism, as an attempt to create 'a systematic theory of literature', that is, 'an account of the modes of literary discourse and of the various conventions and types of organization which produce meaning in literature' (let us call this point (**a**)). This conception of the task of criticism is radical, because 'speakers of a language are, of course, primarily concerned with the meanings of the sentences they hear or utter, just as readers are primarily concerned with the meanings of literary works' (**b**). The role of poetics is to show us 'the problems which literature encounters as it tries to organize and give meaning to human experience' (**c**).[38] If we consider these

---

[37] The novel has repeatedly fallen victim to this kind of transference of guilt. In Barthes' *S/Z* it is often very hard to tell whether the 'culprits' responsible for the passivity and political domination involved in a 'readerly' reading experience are the 'literary institutions' (p.4) and the 'philologists' (p.7), or the classic texts themselves.

[38] Jonathan Culler, Introduction to Tzvetan Todorov, *The Poetics of Prose*, below, pp.8, 13.

three statements about fiction together, and add another (**d**) in Todorov's own words, we can see how the unquestioned premises of structuralist criticism guarantee a condemnation of the novel according to Davis and Crosby's lights:

(**a**) An account of the *systematic production of literary meaning* will constitute a complete theory of 'literature'.

(**b**) Readers of literature are concerned with *the meanings* of literary works.

(**c**) The function of literature is *to organize and give meaning* to human experience.

(**d**) The distinctive thing about *meaning* in literature is that 'whereas in speech, the integration of units does not exceed the level of the sentence, in literature the sentences are once again integrated into utterances and the utterances are once again integrated into utterances of larger dimensions, until we reach the work as a whole'.[39]

If we take these statements in conjunction, we can see just how contentious they are. Consider (**b**) in the light of (**d**). Of course when we read we need to know the primary sense of the words we encounter, but when we read as ordinary readers and not as critics, is it true that our primary concern is always the sense or meaning, in the strong sense of (**d**), of the work as a whole? Post-structuralism has contested the fragile distinction between literature and ordinary speech set up in (**d**) on the grounds that normal communications may also form part of wider systems of meanings, and that the systems of meaning inside the literary work cannot be isolated from those outside it. We could also make the contrary objection that when we are reading literature unprofessionally we are no more inclined to refer each primary sense to one on a higher level than we are when asked to switch the kettle on (though the reason for our neglect is distinctively different in the two cases).

If we entertain doubts about the conjunction of (**b**) and (**d**), we have no reason to accept (**c**) – if readers *do not* try first and foremost to squeeze meaning out of fiction, then it is not obvious that fiction's main function is to organize and give meaning to their experience.

To move beyond this negative critique we will need to reject (**a**). An account of the production of literary meaning, as defined in (**d**), adds up to less than a complete theory of literature. For, from the very start, it excludes an assessment of the *scope* of the extraction of Significance in reading fiction.

---

[39]   Tzvetan Todorov, *The Poetics of Prose* (Oxford: Blackwell, 1977), p.24.

It just assumes that extraction of Significance is all that is going on.

In outlining his project, Todorov refers to Gottlob Frege's discussion of the question of meaning or Significance, so 'long neglected' by linguistics. Frege posits a model of language as follows: Attached to any utterance is both a *Sinn* [what Todorov calls 'meaning', now usually translated as 'sense'] and a *Bedeutung* [referent].[40] Sense is expressed by, or associated with, the words and sentences of language by convention. The referent – the object to which the words refer – is determined by the sense. However, as Frege says, the '*Bedeutung* and sense of a sign are to be distinguished from the associated idea [*Vorstellung*]. If the *Bedeutung* of a sign is an object perceivable by sense, my idea of it is an internal image, arising from memories of sense impressions which I have had and acts, both internal and external, which I have performed'.[41]

As Todorov rightly points out, 'only the meaning [*Sinn*] can be apprehended with the help of rigorous linguistic methods'.[42] Poetics must therefore isolate *Sinn* as its only object. However, by ignoring the relations of *Sinn* to *Bedeutung* and *Vorstellung*, structuralism shuts off the possibility of discussing what is most obviously distinctive about fiction (for illustration of this notion, see Figure 1 on page 84 and its text). Frege points out that fictional statements are, in fact, highly distinctive in that *reference* is not part of their primary function – usually there is no referent. They do not even try to refer to anything. 'In hearing an epic poem ...apart from the euphony of the language we are interested only in the sense of the sentences and the images and feelings thereby aroused. The question of truth would cause us to abandon aesthetic delight for an attitude of scientific investigation. Hence it is a matter of no concern to us whether the name "Odysseus" for instance, has a *Bedeutung*, so long as we accept the poem as a work of art. It is a striving for truth that drives us always to advance from the sense to the *Bedeutung*'.[43]

Most communication is an effort to achieve reference – to communicate about the world, to tell the truth or to tell lies about the state of affairs. We hope our listener will learn something, or be misled about something, by the meaning (or *Sinn*) of our words. Fictional statements, on the other hand, do

---

[40]   Whether *Bedeutung* is better translated as 'reference' or 'meaning' is a contentious issue (see Mike Beaney's Introduction to *The Frege Reader*, as below).

[41]   Gottlob Frege, *On* Sinn *and* Bedeutung (1892), in *The Frege Reader*, trans. Max Black, ed. Michael Beaney, (Oxford: Oxford University Press, 1997), pp.151–71, pp.152, 154.

[42]   Todorov, p.24.

[43]   Frege, p.157.

not have referents, or (*necessarily*) tell us anything, even indirectly or by implication. While *The Mill on the Floss* suggests, or even explicitly makes, a wide range of statements about the real world (such as, for example, 'women's education in the early nineteenth century was radically inadequate'), 'Maggie shook her heavy hair back and looked up eagerly' is in itself no such statement, however we may feel it feeds into such statements indirectly as a Significant detail. We can imagine a fiction that made no Significant statements about the real world whatsoever.

I have suggested that if, in feminine fiction, irrelevant details function as camouflage, and the Significant details are the ideological fighters, then each fighter must be weighed down by ten times his own weight in netting and burnt cork. But the 'ideological camouflage' explanation for inSignificant fictional detail is not only superficially implausible, it also depends on a cripplingly partial account of the function of fictional language. It is my contention that the primary *raison d'être* of the nineteenth-century novel's reams of detail lies in the fact that in fiction words can play quite another function instead of, or as well as, contributing to true or false statements. Giving this last idea bolder outlines will help us account for the sheer volume of seemingly 'irrelevant' descriptive detail that we associate with Victorian fiction, the sort of detail that is dismissed by Barthes as 'only a sort of setting meant to receive the jewel of a number of rare metaphors, the neutral, prosaic excipient which swathes the precious symbolic substance'.[44]

v. Stories as 'props'

Not to understand the distinction between an untrue sentence and one that, like most fiction, elicits not an inference about a state of affairs but an *imagining* of the things it tells of, is to miss an important distinction. If we fail to note this distinction we will find ourselves, like Davis, amazed at our frequent engagement in 'the rather startling (upon examination) action of believing that inside the novel is not only a three-dimensional space but a person with some kind of physical and psychological depth and contour as well'.[45] We don't *believe* anything of the kind – even temporarily – but rather imagine it. To confound believing with imagining is not – crucially – to make a mistake as to the degree of conviction involved. Imagining the heat of the sun on your back is about as different an activity as can be from believing that tomorrow it will be sunny. One experience is all but sensual, the other wholly abstract. When we tell a story, although we may hope also

---

[44]   Barthes, *S/Z*, p.144.
[45]   Davis, p.103.

to teach a lesson, our primary objective is to produce an imaginative experience – even an autobiographical novel with real referents does not have as its primary function the communication of information. Most factual statements, on the other hand, do not incite us to imagine them – the point in them is to shape our beliefs and future conduct in the absence of direct experience. We can, however, imagine treating a non-fictionally intended statement as though it were fictional – 'never mind whether it really happened, just imagine it' – or treating a fictional scenario as though it were factual – 'you will best understand this situation if I tell you that the people of Iraq have been living under the eye of Big Brother'.

Kendall Walton suggests that the essence of what is thought of as 'representational' fiction is that it is used by a society as a prop in games of make believe.[46] We use fictional detail in much the same way as we might use a tree when pretending to climb a mast – certain constraints are imposed, but the active transformative effort is all ours to make. Walton sees the activity of reading fiction as a structured daydream. In daydreams, we do not seem simply to go through a string of abstract thoughts – unless, perhaps, we are dreaming about giving a lecture or writing a novel. Rather, we entertain something like the sense-experience of the things we dream of, and the mental reaction that accompanies such experiences. This is not, as I have suggested, all we do in reading fiction, but I want to explore and illustrate this dimension of the experience before returning to this important qualification in (**vii**).

Barthes seems to be partly aware of language's potential for such conjurings of imaginary experience. He speaks of the Alexandrian craze for '*ecphrasis*, the detachable set piece ...whose object was to describe places, times, people or works of art' without reference to any particular persuasive goal, and reminds us that 'classical rhetoric ...institutionalized the fantasmatic as a specific figure, *hypotyposis*, whose function was to "put things before the hearer's eyes"'.[47] He insists however that this function of literature had died out by the nineteenth century. He does so partly in deference to the intuitions of structuralism, partly because of a number of characteristics of the Flaubert passage he analyses (it describes a real place, is shaped by the rules of *le beau style*, and compares Rouen to a painting), and partly because of the 'realist' conventions of nineteenth-century fiction. However, if we do not share his deference for the structuralist precedents, there seems no good reason to accept his cursory reading of

---

46   Kendall L Walton, *Mimesis as Make-Believe: On the Foundations of the Representational Arts* (Cambridge, Massachusetts and London: Harvard University Press, 1990), Ch.I.

47   Barthes, *Rustle*, pp.143, 145, 147.

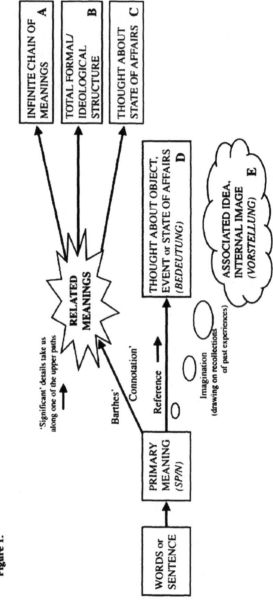

Figure 1.

Consider a sentence taken from a novel, such as 'On a grey but dry November morning Dorothea drove to Lowick in company with her uncle and Celia'. In this case it is not an option to follow the middle path – there is no (real) state of affairs to which the sentence might refer, which it could give us true or false information about. We can choose whether to follow one of the upper paths or to follow the bottom path. As in most fictional statements, we are given special provisions for taking one or other of these paths. 'Grey' and 'dry' link up with and fit into larger structures of meaning as regards the relation between Dorothea and Casaubon; these structures in turn contribute, on the one hand, to the formal unity of the novel, and, on the other, to those statements about the real state of social affairs as regards marriage and so on that the novel as a whole adds up to. However, 'grey' and 'dry' also help us along the bottom path, allowing us to form an imaginative impression of Dorothea's journey in sensuous terms, recalling our own experiences of grey days, etc.

The nub of my argument is that the detailed descriptions of feminine fiction characteristically encourage us to take the bottom path, before we explore any of the others. It is for this reason that structuralist and post-structuralist accounts of the function of such details are so radically inadequate. Furthermore, as the bottom path is a likely choice in reading any fiction (or indeed poetry) whatever, a consideration of what it means to take the bottom path should throw light on aspects of other reading experience that are ruled out of consideration by structuralist and poststructuralist approaches.

This diagram gives a rough indication of some of the mental paths we might take from a written or spoken sentence, according to Frege, Todorov, Barthes and others (it is designed to illustrate possible occurrent processes, not the structure which provides the necessary conditions for such processes). Of course, the diagram greatly simplifies the experience of reading – it ought to be marked by various arrows looping backwards and forwards between stages and paths. But, nevertheless, it brings out some important distinctions. Notice that structuralism and post-structuralism are concerned only with the structures and mechanisms that allow us to follow the paths to the two upper-most destinations, A and B. Both exclude any consideration of possible journeys along the middle or bottom paths. But if we neglect the important choice taken at the cross-roads at the centre of the diagram, we block our understanding of the difference between fictional and non-fictional language. For this difference lies primarily in the fact that when we come across non-fictional sentences we habitually travel first and foremost along the middle path, but because this is blocked in reading fiction we have to choose among the upper and lower paths.

We can see why Davis would be concerned about the abstraction of fictional language – in his scheme, we can only refer to anything non-abstract via a long chain of related meanings, if then. But he neither makes nor draws on any argument that explains why we must always take the upper paths. He writes as though it were fiction that forced us to do so, whereas is it his own theoretical apparatus which blinds him to the other possibilities – as though a man using a geiger counter were to complain that all he ever detects is radioactivity, never any shapes or colours.

one French 'realist' novelist (if Flaubert is, indeed, a realist in the sense that Gaskell and Eliot are, and not rather a naturalist) as representative of realism in general. Furthermore, it is not at all clear why the description of familiar, common and representative scenes characteristic of fictional realism – quite as much as accounts of fantastic scenarios such as 'lions or olive trees in a northern country' that are shaped by what Barthes calls 'the luster of desire' – cannot put things before the reader's eyes.

Barthes makes an entirely unwarranted leap of inference from a partially accurate intuition that the descriptions of realism have little to do with the 'aesthetic finality of language', either in its self-conception or its practice, to the idea that the extra-aesthetic function of language must have something to do with Significance, or some sort of charade of positivistic truth-telling. He insists that while 'the motto implicit on the threshold of all classical discourse …is: *Esto (let there be, suppose …)*' the novel 'renounces this implicit introduction'.[1] Feminine fiction, however, shows no signs of such renunciation.

Think, for example, of the famous beginning of *Adam Bede*: 'With a single drop of ink for a mirror, the Egyptian sorcerer undertakes to reveal …far reaching visions … This is what I undertake to do … I will show you the roomy workshop of Mr Jonathan Burge'. Surely Eliot chooses the figure of the Egyptian sorcerer to suggest that her art is in the business not of objective historiography but rather of imaginative, fantastic and – from a positivistic scientific point of view – highly suspect, artifice. Images of phantasmal conjuring or imagining frame the descriptive passages of feminine fiction with sufficient frequency to suggest that even where they are explicitly absent we are still implicitly involved in such a trope. Barthes assumes that where a passage is, or purports, to be about a real event, person or place – such as Rouen – it is no longer designed to 'put things before the reader's eyes'. There is no reason to come to this conclusion. Daydreams, fantasies, can be about either real *or* imaginary places – it just does not matter. As Frege says, the question of truth or falsity does not arise as long as our main objective is not to gather information but to call up an imaginative picture. The point is that feminine fiction calls up visions, instead of conveying a decodeable Significant message.

Like Charlotte Brontë herself, the eponymous heroine of *Shirley* is wont to construct vividly realized scenarios, whose interest is quite divorced from the question of their reference to the way the world is. She imagines variously, on different occasions, Eve in the sunset, genius as a savage, and

---

[1]   Barthes, *Rustle*, pp.144, 146, 143, 147.

encountering a mermaid:

> I am to be walking by myself on deck ...something is to rise white on
> the surface of the sea, over which that moon mounts silent, and hangs
> glorious: the object glitters and sinks ... I think I hear it cry with an
> articulate voice: I call you from the cabin: I show you an image, fair as
> alabaster, emerging from the dim wave ... Are you not glad, Caroline,
> when at last, and with a wild shriek, she dives? (p.246)

The immediacy of the imaginary experience is emphasized by the use of the
present tense. Mrs Prior comments that the young ladies are 'fanciful' in
their conversation, and queries the very notion of fiction. 'We are aware that
mermaids do not exist: why speak of them as if they did?' *Shirley* is premised
upon the idea that communication about things, people, and events that we
know do not exist is worthwhile, because it (imaginatively) extends
experience, which is the stuff of life. And this, the novel suggests, is the case
whether the scenes imagined are fantastic, beautiful and extraordinary, or
plain and commonplace.

The replacement of the involuntary dreams and hallucinations of *Jane
Eyre* (their omens and symbolism suggestive of a universe that is the
manifestation of some universal intelligence) by the actively pursued
daydreams and imaginings in *Shirley* is indicative of the wider contrast
between the Christian framework of the former novel and the humanistic
materialism of the latter. In *Shirley* daydreams occur again and again – not
as abstract strings of ideas, but as sensuous constellations of *Vorstellungen*.

The daydreams in *Shirley* are not only about the impossible, but also about
the possible, and even the actual past or present. Caroline's

> imagination was full of pictures: images of Moore; scenes where he and
> she had been together; winter fireside sketches; a glowing landscape of
> a hot summer afternoon passed with him in the bosom of Nunnely
> wood; divine vignettes of mild spring or mellow autumn moments,
> when she had sat at his side in Hollow's copse, listening to the call of
> the May cuckoo, or sharing the September treasure of nuts and ripe
> black-berries, – a wild dessert which it was her morning's pleasure to
> collect in a little basket, and cover with green leaves and fresh blossoms
> ... Robert's features and form were with her; the sound of his voice was
> quite distinct in her ear; his few caresses seemed renewed ...the picture
> faded, the voices failed, the visionary clasp melted chill from her hand,
> and where the seal of lips had made impress on her forehead, it felt

now as if a sleety rain-drop had fallen. (p.173)

Recollections are one of the most common forms of daydream, and
Caroline's recollective experience demonstrates the difference between
imaginative and Significant reflection. There could be no alluring pleasure
in rehearsing the bare facts of a past love affair, and recalling the Significant
lessons it spelt out to us. Feminine fiction is frequently presented as a vivid
and emotional recollection, like Caroline's, shared with us by the narrator.
In the passage that begins *The Mill on the Floss*, the framing trope or
recollection is made the excuse for a paradigmatic and memorable piece of
sensuous and (relatively) inSignificant feminine description:

> As I look at the full stream, the vivid grass, the delicate bright-green
> powder softening the outline of the great trunks and branches that
> gleam from under the bare purple boughs, I am in love with moistness,
> and envy the white ducks that are dipping their heads far into the water
> here among the withes, unmindful of the awkward appearance they
> make in the drier world above. The rush of the water, and the booming
> of the mill, bring a dreamy deafness, which seems to heighten the
> peacefulness of the scene. They are like a great curtain of sound,
> shutting one out from the world beyond. And now there is the thunder
> of the huge covered wagon coming home with sacks of grain ... That
> ...waggoner is thinking of his dinner, getting sadly dry in the oven at
> this late hour ...his horses ... I fancy, are looking mild reproach at him
> from between their blinkers, that he should crack his whip at them in
> that awful manner as if they needed that hint! ... Look at their grand
> shaggy feet that seem to grasp the firm earth, at the patient strength of
> their necks, bowed under the heavy collar, at the mighty muscles of
> their struggling haunches! I should like well to hear them neigh over
> their hardly-earned feed of corn, and see them, with their moist necks
> freed from the harness, dipping their eager nostrils into the muddy
> pond ...the arch of the covered wagon disappears at the turning
> behind the trees. Now I can turn my eyes towards the mill again, and
> watch the unresting wheel sending out its diamond jets of water. That
> little girl is watching it too ... And that queer white cur with the brown
> ear seems to be leaping and barking in ineffectual remonstrance with
> the wheel; perhaps he is jealous, because his playfellow in the beaver
> bonnet is so rapt in its movement. It is time the little playfellow went in,
> I think; and there is a very bright fire to tempt her: the red light shines
> out under the deepening grey of the sky. It is time, too, for me to leave

off resting my arms on the cold stone of this bridge ...

Ah, my arms are really benumbed. I have been pressing my elbows on the arms of my chair, and dreaming that I was standing on the bridge in front of Dorlcote Mill.[2]

Shirley presents the imagination, and the concrete experience on which it feeds, as the greatest, most irreducible gift of humanity. Like Walton, Brontë considers fiction as a valuable extension of the range of experience, the medium of delight:

[Shirley's] book has perhaps been a good one; it has refreshed, refilled, rewarmed her heart; it has set her brain astir, furnished her mind with pictures ... A still, deep, inborn delight glows in her young veins ...the free dower of Nature to her child ...the swift glory spreads out, sweeping and kindling, and multiplies its splendours faster than Thought can effect his combinations ...that spring whose bright fresh bubbling in her heart keeps it green. (p.388)

The enjoyment of fiction, these recurring motifs powerfully suggest, is akin to that of daydream, though fiction allows for more sustained imaginings which, unlike those of the dozing narrator of *The Mill*, or Caroline's Helstone's reveries, can carry us far beyond the rehearsal of episodes from our own past experience.

Of course, like Caroline's dream, every imagined experience is liable at any moment to fade into chill abstraction. Moore imagines that walking the hedgerows at night, he will be haunted by Caroline: 'fancy the flutter of every little bird over its nest, the rustle of every leaf, a movement made by you; tree-shadows will take your shape; in the white sprays of hawthorn, I shall imagine glimpses of you' (p.255). He sees her clearly in what is, in fact, a white muslin curtain and a pot plant. To give Davis his due, one must acknowledge that the imaginings prompted by novels have less substance even than these visions; a literary description does not bear any direct relation to the thing it describes, either in resemblance or even in sense-modality. Whereas when we see a landscape picture, it may be, as Walton argues, that we imagine what we see is a real landscape, when we read a description, we do not imagine that the words we see are a real mountain. The words on the page suggest images and experiences, but only through strings of conventional symbols, which are themselves abstracted from the

---

[2]   Eliot, *The Mill on the Floss* (1860), ed. GS Haight (Oxford: Clarendon, 1980) (hereafter *MF*), p.3.

material states of affairs they would have us imagine. There can be no doubt that inSignificant fictions struggle perpetually against the abstraction of language.

Feminine fiction creatively explores the question of the modality of description and imagination. Brontë describes both Shirley and Caroline's day-dreams through the metaphor of representational fictions; 'pictures', 'sketches', 'landscape', 'vignettes'. And George Eliot similarly equates her task with that of the visual artist. She can, of course, never escape the shallow semantic quality of language; the fact that she works with conventional symbols, and that her art cannot reproduce the action of looking, as a painting can. However, in certain passages she limits her description to a single sense-modality, and a single perspective, so that as clear a picture of the scene as possible can be constructed in the mind's eye. In this passage Eliot attempts to allow the reader to picture a real scene, which the author knew well:

> ...a charming picture Cheverel Manor would have made that evening, if some English Watteau had been there to paint it: the castellated house of grey-tinted stone, with the flickering sunbeams sending dashes of golden light across the many-shaped panes in the mullioned windows, and a great beech leaning athwart one of the flanking towers, and breaking, with its dark flattened boughs, the too formal symmetry of the front; the broad gravel walk winding on the right, by a row of tall pines, alongside the pool on the left branching out among swelling grassy mounds, surmounted by clumps of trees, where the red trunk of the Scotch fir glows in the descending sunlight against the bright green of limes and acacias; the great pool, where a pair of swans are swimming lazily with one leg tucked under a wing, and where the open water-lilies lie calmly accepting the kisses of the fluttering light-sparkles; the lawn, with its smooth emerald greenness, sloping down to the rougher and browner herbage of the park ...on this lawn our two ladies, whose part in the landscape the painter, standing at a favourable point of view in the park, would represent with a few little dabs of red and white and blue. (*SCL*, pp.92–3).

Notice that the fact that here Eliot describes a real scene familiar from her childhood does not, crucially, reduce this passage to a factual, 'referential' statement. We do not read to get information about Arbury Hall, fictionalized as Cheverel Manor, but rather to imagine the scene. The passage relays Eliot's own pleasure in imaginatively calling it to mind.

Straining as they do to reach from the abstractions of conventional symbols to the concreteness of imagined sense-experience, verbal descriptions have, however, an advantage over painting in that they are not necessarily restricted to invoking one sense at a time. Eliot's sensual descriptions are like Mr Jerome's garden in 'Janet's Repentance', 'no monotony of enjoyment for one sense to the exclusion of another; but a charming paradisiacal mingling ...you gathered a moss-rose one moment and a bunch of currants the next ...in a delicious fluctuation between the scent of jasmine and the juice of gooseberries' (p.248).

It is impossible, in reading such texts, to feel that detail, while it 'is crucial for the creation of certain reality-effects ...finally ...is only a means to an end' as Crosby asserts.[3] The intellectual longing for abstraction and Significance is replaced in the narrative and its reader by a virtual presence of sensual particularities:

> Mrs Bellamy would perhaps be going out to gather the rose-leaves and lavender, and Tina was ...allowed to carry a handful in her pinafore ...they were spread out on sheets to dry, so that she could sit down like a frog among them, and have them poured over her in fragrant showers. Another frequent pleasure was to take a journey with Mr Bates through the kitchen-gardens and hot-houses, where the rich bunches of green and purple grapes hung from the roof, far out of reach of the tiny yellow hand that couldn't help stretching itself out towards them. (*SCL*, p.114)

The reader is tempted to turn up her face in passive welcome of the shower of phantom sense experiences, which carry, like fragrance, a freight of untheorized pleasure. The imagined scenes, like the grapes, remain ultimately out of reach, but they awaken in the receptive reader a ready eagerness to participate in their phantom world of the senses in all its delicacy and sweetness. Admittedly, such an urge is trusting and sensuous, and involves a submission to rules of sense that let us enjoy such a subtle game of the imagination.

vi. Realism and the reader's freedom

What I have been describing is not, however, a passive model of the reader's relation to the realist text. In the neglected difference in function between, on the one hand, statements that refer to real states of affairs and carry

---

[3] Crosby, p.16.

information (true or false) about them, and on the other, statements that create fictional states of affairs and demand that we imagine them, lies a whole new realm of freedom.

For Barthes the paradigm classic realist text leaves little for the reader to do but understand the words. A limited task of construction may be opened up for the reader through connotation, 'a secondary meaning, whose signifier is itself constituted by a sign or system of primary signification which is denotation'.[4] A limited plurality is found in the text as Significant structures are deciphered through the use of codes: the hermeneutic, the semantic, the symbolic, the proairetic, the cultural. The same word may take its place in more than one of these; the 'mansion', besides signifying a place, may also signify wealth, etc.: 'Everything signifies ceaselessly and several times, but without being delegated to a great final ensemble, to an ultimate structure'.[5]

Deconstruction has insisted that *all* texts are open in this way, rejecting, even more emphatically than Barthes, the idea that 'every text [is] univocal, possessing a true, canonical meaning', and contesting the 'hierarchy of denotated and connotated', the arrangement of 'all the meanings of a text in a circle around the hearth of denotation'.[6] Following and outstripping Barthes' lead, it insists that *no* verbal statement is immune to an infinite regress of signification; all allow the reader infinite play, 'to read is to find meanings, and to find meanings is to name them; but these named meanings are swept towards other names; names call to each other, reassemble, and their grouping calls for further naming', a game which can go on for ever.[7] Fiction, in this view, allows no special freedoms – there is nothing particularly 'imaginative' about it.

But fiction offers a radically alternative evasion of 'the pitiless divorce …between the producer of the text and its user, between its owner and its customer, between its author and the reader', by which the reader is 'plunged into a kind of idleness'.[8] Fiction alone is (partly) divorced from the question of reference, the practical business of conveying information, and given up to the unlimited sensuous production of imagined scenes as an end in itself without regard to reference. Even a provisional framing of the question of *Vorstellung* alters fundamentally the appearance of the role of authority in representational fiction.

---

[4] Barthes, *S/Z*, p.7.
[5] Barthes, *S/Z*, p.12.
[6] Barthes, *S/Z*, p.7.
[7] Barthes, *S/Z*, p.11.
[8] Barthes, *S/Z*, p.4.

This is the way Shirley reads Milton:

> Milton tried to see the first woman ...it was his cook that he saw; or it
> was Mrs Gill, as I have seen her, making custards, in the heat of
> summer, in the cool dairy, with rose-trees and nasturtiums about the
> latticed window, preparing a cold collation for the Rectors, – preserves,
> and 'dulcet creams' – puzzled 'what choice to choose for delicacy best;
> what order so contrived as not to mix tastes, not well-joined, inelegant;
> but bring taste after taste, upheld with kindliest change'. (p.320)

Milton does not intend to refer to Mrs Gill. He does intend to refer to Eve,
whom he believed was a real person – the bare bones of *Paradise Lost* are, in
this sense, non-fiction. Insofar as Milton believes that Eve existed, he asserts
that she bore such and such a character – in much the same way as he
might have asserted that the republic was a good thing. This assertion is not
fictional, and indeed it gives Shirley, as Barthes says, 'no more than the poor
freedom to accept or reject' it, as she would accept or reject news of the end
of the war.[9] As it happens, she rejects it. However, she does not reject the
text, whose fictionality offers her far more freedom. Insofar as it is fictional,
unlike news that the war has ended, it absolutely demands that she imagine
it, *create* referents for it in her mind's eye, as she does. The reader of *Paradise
Lost* has freedom to imagine an innumerable range of different Eves. There
are constraints on her imagination certainly – insofar as she imagines that
Eve never prepared meals, she is no longer engaging with *Paradise Lost.*
However, readers are perfectly free to imagine Eve just like Mrs Gill,
surrounded with nasturtiums, with a checked apron and floury fingernails.

Instead of 'gaining access to the magic of the signifier, to the pleasures of
writing' the reader of representational fiction, unlike the recipient of
information or commands, has available the possibility of interpretative
freedom outside the realm of language. Escape from passivity need not be a
matter of following up connotations, elaborating connections between one
sign and another. Davis's contention that 'the ideology of the novel *has* to
make readers forget about the fullness and sensuousness of lived experience'

---

9   There is not much interpretative freedom available to the reader of factual
    statements, but there is, of course, the at least as important extra-linguistic freedom
    to act upon information. Naturally, this freedom is not open to the recipient of
    'information' about Dorothea Brooke (though such 'information' might indirectly
    contribute to factual statements, or induce emotional reactions, that *could* prompt
    action).

could not be further from the truth.[10] In fact we enter a realm of sensual and experiential pleasure, a 'phantom', as Brontë calls it, of real experience, created in and by the reader. You are invited imaginatively, phantom-sensuously, to join Tina in playing with the medicine bottle, 'putting the cork in and drawing it out again, to hear how it would pop', and in strolling in the garden 'making little cawing noises to imitate the rooks, clapping her hands at the green frogs leaping in the moist grass, and fixing grave eyes on the gardener's fowls cluck-clucking under their pens'. Frogs recur in Eliot's story, but I defy anyone to find a secondary meaning, a deeper Significance for them – Eliot simply invites us to participate in her sensuous affair with the idea of the slippery, springy amphibians, to fall, like her, 'in love with moistness'. The only thing to which we are constrained in such instances is sensual participation; we can choose the easiness of chair, the peculiar flavour of tobacco, the very physical attitude of the vicar, relaxing 'by the side of his own sitting-room fire, smoking his pipe, and maintaining the pleasing antithesis of dryness and moisture by an occasional sip of gin-and-water' (SCL, pp.108, 136, 87). Such freedom of choice is beneath notice only in a scheme of things in which the particular has already been subsumed to the general, and the sensuous to the abstract.

vii.   Showing and telling: The elusive unity of the novel

I am suggesting that feminine fiction places exceptional and distinctive emphasis on this sensuous-imaginative function, which, though it is a function of all fiction to a greater or lesser extent, has been acutely under-theorized. It seems that an exceptionally large part of the 'point' of feminine fiction is that it deals not only with the meaning, or the aim, but also with the experience of life. In encountering the descriptive details of these novels the reader is expected, in other words, not to see what they *mean*, but to *see* what they mean.

However, the point must not be pushed too far. This imaginative function is less central to other fictional narratives, and even in feminine fiction there are passages, structures of oblique implication, formal and thematic choices, that are unmistakably Significant, implying abstract meanings and ultimately even statements with truth-content. To put it in the terms of Figure 1: while I argue that, in the course of any reading of feminine fiction, the bottom path is well trodden, this is not to say that other representational texts do not frequently send us off along one of the upper tracks first, and

---

10   Davis, p.154.

even in feminine fiction the upper ways are by no means abandoned. Frege's account of what is involved in the reception of an epic poem is not applicable to all fictional discourse – and we may suspect, indeed, that there is Significance behind the described scenes of classical epics that has become inaccessible with the passage of time. If literary criticism is to take seriously the ideas articulated by Walton about the imaginative function of representational art, it must start by applying them with discrimination.

Different novels rely more or less on this special appeal to sensuous imagination. Some fictions *are* best read, necessarily read, as self-contained formal structures of meaning, or as indirect statements about the real world, statements which we can legitimately judge true or false. The sensuous-imaginative function is important in all realist fiction (definitively?), and it may be combined with the most complex networks of abstract Significance – *Ulysses*, for example, is both luminous with hidden meaning and gritty with the stuff of Dublin life. However, the distinctive centrality of the sensuous function of feminine description is most obvious if we contrast it with the more deeply Significant role that description may be called upon to bear. Henry James, for example, is a relatively (though by no means absolutely) 'un-feminine' or 'masculine' realist. Scenes in James undoubtedly do often call for interpretation. The reader seems epistemologically and morally challenged to decipher the intricacy of the argument from the details of events. The scene in *Portrait of a Lady* in which Madam Merle is found standing in the sole presence of the seated Gilbert Osmond is briefly sketched, just as it fleetingly impresses itself upon Isabel, but we are not so much required to visualize the scene or to experience it imaginatively, as to comprehend the enormous Significance of the clues it communicates to Isabel, and, what is most important, to judge the part this Significance plays in determining the (non-fictional) 'meaning' of the narrative, and that meaning's wider aesthetic and moral implications. It is not just that the actions and descriptions of this novel are deeply Significant, but that we experience them almost entirely as such; we speculate, rather than imagine. James's novels seem the ultimate detective story; not only must we find out what is going on, but we must find out what the action is intended by the author to mean, metaphysically and morally speaking. When Percy Lubbock and other champions of James called for a replacement of 'telling' by 'showing', they tracked an inclination in him which, far from conquering the impulse to 'tell' (in the sense of assert and Signify, give your text a deeper 'message'), simply re-directs its energy, saturating the 'showing' with an indirect, indeterminate but all pervasive Significant 'telling', thus approximating the formal organic whole which is James's ideal of fiction.

RP Blackmur's observation that overt explanations were never necessary, 'hints and notes and observed appearances [being] always enough' to carry the full freight of James's meaning, nicely sums up the latter's investment in deep Significance, although it overstates the consistency with which he ever followed out his own principles.[11]

One primary question for a criticism that would take *Vorstellung* seriously would be to account for why it is that we do sometimes choose to imagine rather than to pursue Significance in our reading. For the fact is, that though in some novels, like James's, Significance may be obscure, and inextricably embodied in the detail which conveys it, this does not seem to obviate what Frege calls the 'striving for truth that drives us always to advance from the sense to the *Bedeutung*'. Neither are we prevented from thirsting for some stable meaning by the conviction that there is no referential destination, no statement about any state of affairs, behind the superficial meaning, but only an infinite chain of Signification. Perhaps it is because we are so used to language uses that have referents, that say something about the world, that this striving is difficult to overcome. The extent to which it is aroused is, if anything, directly proportional to the felt difficulty or even impossibility of ever satisfying it. Even modernist and postmodernist texts that deny their fictions an ultimate 'Significance' are often driven, nevertheless, by stimulation and frustration of the urge to find it.

In the feminine fiction dealt with here, however, the imaginative-fictional path, on the one hand, and the directly or indirectly referential or truth-bearing path on the other, have grown very far apart, and often have little relation to one another. Our impulse to 'find the meaning', extract the Significance, is discreetly accommodated and sated by the narratorial commentary and apostrophes to the reader that are so characteristic of the sub-genre. These non-fictional or transparently and directly Significant intrusions (which carry us either straight to (**D**) or by a very short way to (**B**) or (**C**)) meet and assuage our need to advance beyond sense and its associated sensuous ideas to grasp the 'message' or truth-content of the novel, so that when we come to the descriptive passages we amble off along the bottom path to (**E**), without interpretative anxiety. James's emphasis on the notion of over-determined unity was perhaps a reaction to this bifurcation within feminine fiction, where showing and telling were relatively separable activities. He defines himself precisely in opposition to my feminine writers in his fictional practice and ideology, limiting the

---

[11]   RP Blackmur, Introduction to Henry James, *The Art of the Novel*, p.xxvii.

sympathetic engagement, omniscience and reflective scope of his third person narrators in the cause of 'objectivity'. He emphasizes how far his own work differs from that of other realist novelists through its subordination to a rigorously unifying discipline, which demands, on the one hand, 'the imposed absence of that "going behind" to compass explanations and amplifications', and, on the other, resistance to the impulse to 'drag odds and ends from the "mere" story teller's great property-shop of aids to illusion'. His vigorous words on 'kinds' apply equally to the unifying, purist impulse behind his aesthetic practice, and to a particular – and, in Hutton's sense, 'masculine' – idea that the novelist's duty is to present the material world as a theatre of Significant essences, rather than of material specifics. With a critical glance towards the English novel tradition, he insists that '"Kinds" are the very life of literature, and truth and strength come from the complete recognition of them, from abounding to the utmost in their respective senses and sinking deep into their consistency ...the confusion of kinds is the inelegance of letters and the stultification of values'.[12] The typical, feminine, mid-century novel that James characterised as 'baggy', one of the more formally unified examples of which (*Middlemarch*) he could call 'a treasure-house of detail but ...an indifferent whole', indeed reflects in its fractures, its miscellaneousness, its rambling structure and its typically incomplete form, the irreducible, meaningless mess of sensuous and material experience that it takes as its subject-matter.[13]

Perhaps because we are still under James's modernising influence, in writing of the novel it is difficult to avoid assuming that there is some strategy at work to unite the distinct functions of presenting pictures and of creating referential or deeply Significant meanings, even when the two are manifestly pulled apart for us. There is extra temptation in this regard for the literary critic, who has traditionally 'interpreted' and deciphered fiction, distilled its Significance. Catherine Gallagher manifests both a persistence in looking for unity in the face of division, and the assumptions about the function of criticism which lie behind this persistence, when she comments of Eliot's *Felix Holt* that 'if appearances were as self-sufficient [i.e. deeply meaningful or Significant] as realists sometimes claim, there would probably be no need for novels, certainly no need for omniscient narrators with access to their characters' subjective inner lives, and surely no need for a body of critical explication'.[14]

---

[12]   James, *Art of the Novel*, p.111.

[13]   Henry James, unsigned review in *Galaxy*, 1873, in David Caroll (ed.) *George Eliot: The Critical Heritage* (London: Routledge and Kegan Paul, 1971), p.353.

[14]   Catherine Gallagher, 'The Failure of Realism: "Felix Holt"', *Nineteenth-Century Fiction*

Gallagher cites a 'claim' – that is, that appearances are self-sufficiently meaningful, and therefore moral – which is nowhere manifest in the fiction of the author of *Felix Holt* (which she discusses) or in the feminine narratives examined here. Gallagher herself enthrones as paradigmatic a comment in a letter from *Flaubert* to Maupassant: 'When you pass a grocer sitting in his doorway [or] a porter smoking his pipe, show me that grocer and that porter, their attitude and their whole physical aspect, including, as indicated by the skill of the portrait, their whole moral nature'.[15] She does not mark the crucial disaffinity between Flaubert's method, his 'objective' narration and his prefiguring of the Jamesian aestheticized and moralized stress on a subsuming of the telling in the showing, in the cause of an overall monolithic unity, and that of Eliot, who, both in the earlier *Scenes* and the later *Middlemarch*, is explicit that the narration serves precisely the role of introducing Significance and deeper meaning where there could be none otherwise, 'so much subtler is a human mind than the outside tissues which make a sort of blazonry or clock-face for it'.[16] Eliot justifies her narratorial intrusion precisely on the grounds of the insufficiency of appearances:

> At present I have to make the new settler Lydgate better known to any one interested in him than he could possibly be even to those who had seen the most of him since his arrival in Middlemarch. For surely all must admit that a man may be puffed and belauded, envied, ridiculed, counted upon as a tool and fallen in love with ...and yet remain virtually unknown – known merely as a cluster of signs for his neighbours' false suppositions.[17]

It is unfortunate, to say the least, for Gallagher's argument that she cannot

---

35 (1980), 372–84, 376. A related argument, framed in Fregean terms, is propounded by JP McGowan in 'The Turn of George Eliot's Realism', *Nineteenth-Century Fiction* 35 (1980), 171–92. My argument against Gallagher is equally in opposition to McGowan's contention that 'Eliot's realism involves the refusal to recognize that literary language has no referent' (p.173) and his conclusion that in her fiction 'seeing' 'has more to do with conceptual and linguistic processes than with perceptual seeing' (p.189). We should not infer from the vagueness and metaphorical character of Eliot's comments on the relation between fiction and 'reality' that she recognizes no distinction between fiction and discourses whose literal statements have a referent – such a basic assumption is taken for granted, rather than (with an implausible degree of stupidity) overlooked.

[15] Flaubert to Maupassant, in Gallagher, 'Failure of Realism', 375–6.
[16] Eliot, *Middlemarch*, I, I, p.10.
[17] Eliot, *Middlemarch*, I, XV, p.139.

find any statement of the kind of naïve 'realist' beliefs that she wants to critique, either in Eliot's own substantial writings on realism, or in those of any of Eliot's British contemporaries, or even from a writer of a vaguely comparable temperament. It seems even more unfortunate when we consider that her own argument is an indirect descendent of Barthes', given that, as I have suggested, his arguments about the general function of fiction are also rather inadequately supported by no more than a brief analysis of a passage from Flaubert. Gallagher seeks to demonstrate the applicability of an argument drawn from Flaubert to Eliot with reference to another passage from Flaubert, which is not the best argumentative strategy. But does her argument really rely upon this kind of support from an explicit statement of authorial intention?

The answer is both yes and no. The post-structuralist elaboration of Barthes' preoccupation with connotation offers her an easy way of making her point without recourse to such statements. Barthes argues that 'there is no other *proof* of a reading than the quality and endurance of its systematics; in other words: than its functioning', but the poststructuralist denial that any reading can in the end function at all, leaves us with a situation in which, in effect, any reading of connotation goes.[18] Gallagher's argument rests, ultimately, not only on the supposed 'claims' or 'aims' of the realist writers, but also on what she proclaims, with an un-falsifiable certainty, to be the *Significance* of their practice, the connotations of their primary representational strategies. But by her very assumption that feminine representational strategies do have any Significance, any connotations, at all, she begs the question against any inSignificant reading. Furthermore, from a historical perspective (as Gallagher's purports to be), there is scope for considerable scepticism about the extent to which formal and rhetorical strategies are intended by authors, or taken by readers, to imply a statement about the structure of reality. And a statement neither intended nor received could have no historical interest, even if we could imagine such a thing.

Gallagher is led astray by her inability to conceive of fiction outside a model of reading focused on Signification. She marks the influence on fiction I discussed in **ii,** of the transition from the belief of Martineau and her religious contemporaries that 'all facts emanate from values inherent in a God's benign purpose ... Reality itself thus furnish[ing] an illustration of principles', to a more sceptical attitude.[19] She makes the obvious point that Eliot explicitly links morality with the realist method. However, she also

---

[18]   Barthes, *S/Z*, p.11.
[19]   Gallagher, 'Failure of Realism', p.374.

makes the unwarranted assumption that that link must be of a peculiar kind, 'meaning is encrusted in the details of everyday reality; the universe is orderly and determined; facts and values are inseparable'.[20] This idea that the link between facts (the details of fiction?) and values must be objective, the notion that the moral 'value' of realist fiction is primarily a matter of the 'meaning' or Significance of its described scenes, emerges, it is clear, not from Eliot's own novelistic practice but from Gallagher herself. The equation between value and Significance or meaning is one which feminine fiction rejects, and as I shall argue in **viii–x**, the realistic narrative is not moral in its meaning, but rather has morally desirable effects and affects.

Gallagher, of course, does not have the discovery of coherence in Eliot's work as her ultimate goal – what she wants to find is an attempt at unity and Significance that achieves only contradiction: she wants to show that 'realistic fiction …invariably undermines, in practice, the ideology it purports to exemplify'.[21] But we are given no evidence whatsoever that realism 'purports' to exemplify the ideology she attributes to it. The contradiction she finds is constituted as such only by her own projection of an intended unity, that would fuse empirical detail with didactic lesson-teaching.

Gallagher cites an observation made by Felix Holt as illustrative of the way that Eliot's Significant realist project inevitably begins to contradict itself:

'Let a man once throttle himself with a satin stock, and he'll get new wants and new motives. Metamorphosis will have begun at his neck-joint, and it will go on till it has changed his likings first and then his reasoning, which will follow his likings as the feet of a hungry dog follow his nose'.

Gallagher comments that Felix 'actually believes …appearances to be absolutely related to inner states. He reverses the normal causality of metonymy: instead of believing that meanings find expression in signs, he believes that signs cause their meanings. In Felix's image, the sign literally becomes the meaning'.[22] Here is another clear instance of a conclusion following inevitably and trivially from the starting theoretical assumptions, with gross distortion of the text examined. For surely the point, as Gallagher herself has just said, is that 'these so-called signs are not signs at all', not that

---

[20] Gallagher, 'Failure of Realism', p.375.
[21] Gallagher, 'Failure of Realism', p.376.
[22] Gallagher, 'Failure of Realism', p.381.

the relation between sign and meaning (if we can comprehensibly apply such a distinction here) has been bizarrely reversed or condensed. Felix is commenting on the close relation between external material and internal subjective being, but he is not suggesting that external appearances reliably Signify deeper essences. There is no reason even to assume that anyone but the wearer knows that the stock is satin, it is not a 'sign' for anyone but Gallagher. Felix's insight parallels that which Althusser takes from Pascal (a great influence on Eliot), who 'says more or less: "Kneel down, move your lips in prayer, and you will believe"'.[23] Felix's point is that the 'essence' is not separable from the material embodiment; the latter is constitutive of the former. It is not Eliot, but Gallagher, who reduces the material to the Significant. Furthermore, Felix gives us a hint of an idea we will return to later – that reasoning follows liking, and not the other way around – that good or bad morality depends not upon a rational or irrational interpretation of the Significance of the world, but of the nature of our passionate relation to it.

As we may extrapolate from this manifest confusion on the part of an eminent critic, the claims to appreciation of 'feminine' narratives are ill-served by an exclusive critical focus on the deeper meaning/Significance of their representational passages. For a large proportion of the interest and appeal of feminine fiction lies outside the 'telling' parts of the narrative, the abstract authorial comments and portentous and patterned narrative events. The only distinctive 'message' they really persuasively or consistently establish is a direction not to over-value the Significant dimension of narrative, not to slight the 'merely' fictional, the insignificant production of *Vorstellungen* for their own sake. Unless we can establish some way of speaking about that which is left out by accounts of deep and structured Significance, the appeal of these novels must remain a mystery, and their functional role cannot be accurately analysed. Perhaps what we need for this purpose is not so much a hermeneutics, nor a poetics of meaning, nor a deconstruction of either of these projects, but rather a rhetoric capable of appreciating *realistic hypotyposis*, of analysing the fictional production of *Vorstellung*. Even if it turns out that this is in principle or in practice hard or impossible to construct, no critic with a historical conscience can advance from this epistemological difficulty to claims about the political function or ontology of the novel.

---

[23] Louis Althusser, 'Ideology and the Ideological State Apparatus', in *Lenin and Philosophy and Other Essays*, trans. Ben Brewster (London: New Left Books, 1971), pp.121–80, 158.

viii. Tea and sympathy: Sharing experience

The rapid social change of the nineteenth century made the discontinuity and fragmentariness of human experience visible as never before. Such an awareness is flagged up at the start of *Mary Barton*, as one of the premises of the narrative. Gaskell points out

> the effect of contrast in these commonplace but thoroughly rural fields, with the busy, bustling, manufacturing town ...left but half-an-hour ago. Here and there an old black and white farm-house, with its rambling out-buildings, speaks of other times and other occupations ... Here in their seasons may be seen the country business of haymaking, ploughing, &c., which are such pleasant mysteries for townspeople to watch.[24]

We might be tempted to surmise that these narratives sought to close up the breaches in nineteenth-century experience. Eliot insisted that 'Art is the nearest thing to life; it is a mode of amplifying and extending our contact with our fellow men beyond the bounds of our personal lot'.[25] Certainly our own enjoyment of the Victorian novel seems inextricably related to the thrill of an intimate engagement with the nitty-gritty of other kinds of lives, distanced from our own by historical change.

Yet the scenes conjured in these narratives are often enclosed spaces – the walled garden, the hollow, the small houses of Gaskell's and Eliot's Bartons, Tina and Janet's bedrooms. Such restricted spaces, as I have suggested, intimate the inherent privacy of the experience that the novelist strives to make available to a reading community for imaginative construction. Caroline imagines she would have need of magic to escape the bounds of her woman's experience – 'if a magician or a genius ...offered me Prince Ali's tube ...and if ...I had been enabled to take a view of Robert – to see where he was, how occupied – I should have learned, in a startling manner, the width of the chasm which gaped between such as he and such as I' (*Shirley*, p.229). Frege suggests that the *Vorstellung* conjured by sense 'is an internal image, arising from memories of sense impressions which I have had' in connection with that sense. But if the experiences recorded here are fundamentally unique, new, private, how can they be conjured in the mind

---

[24]   Elizabeth Gaskell, *Mary Barton* (1848) ed. Macdonald Daly (London and New York: Penguin, 1996), p.5. Hereafter, *MB*.

[25]   George Eliot, in *Essays of George Eliot*, ed. Thomas Pinney (London: Routledge and Kegan Paul, 1963), p.271.

of the reader?

It is the aim of these novels to transcend as far as possible the limits of individual experience; to allow readers to recall basic elements of their own experience, and to construct, mosaic-like, a new imagined experience from these memories. The imaginative conception of the unknown is always an extension from the known, just as Shirley imagines Caroline's 'herds' of whales 'pasturing about the bases of the "everlasting hills", devouring strange provender in the vast valleys' (*Shirley*, p.245).

Of course, the conundrum of the opacity of language, its conventionality, can be put off but never denied. But the conjuring of sensuous imaginative experience is a far more modest task than the establishment of a consensus about transcendent Significance, as Amos Barton discovers, when called upon to preach to a half-crazy audience of workhouse paupers. The 'Eleusinian   Mysteries'   of   university   education   alongside   'able mathematicians' at Cambridge have not prepared him for such a task:

> ...he must bring his geographical, chronological, exegetical mind pretty nearly to the pauper point of view ...he must have some approximate conception of the mode in which the doctrines that have so much vitality in the plenum of his own brain will comport themselves *in vacuo* – that is to say, in a brain that is neither geographical, chronological, nor exegetical ...he talked of Israel and its sins, of chosen vessels, of the Paschal lamb, of blood as a medium of reconciliation ...Barton's exposition turned on unleavened bread. Nothing in the world more suited to the simple understanding than instruction through familiar types and symbols! But there is always this danger attending it, that the interest or comprehension of your hearers may stop short precisely at the point where your spiritual interpretation begins ...Barton ...succeeded in carrying the pauper imagination to the dough-tub, but unfortunately was not able to carry it upwards from that well-known object to unknown truths which it was intended to shadow forth. (*SCL*, pp.24, 27)

Since, unlike Amos, the descriptive passages of feminine fiction do not wish to move the reader on from the dough tub, their task seems comparatively encompassable.   The   continuing   comprehensibility   of   materialistic descriptions, orientated towards some kind of imaginative picture, is less vulnerable to historical difference than that of more abstract or complex communications. The descriptions in the *Odyssey* are the most accessible part of it; we may have difficulty fathoming their Significance, but we have little difficulty 'seeing' when they would have us see (if not exactly what they would have us see). The more basic the terms, the less narrowly their range of availability as imaginative props will be circumscribed.

In 'Mr Gilfil's Love-Story', Eliot attempts to unpack the abstraction of time itself into sensuous details that also overflow the abstract categories of 'season', and are related in the historical present tense, as a succession not of cause and effect but of contingent impressions:

> Daises and buttercups give way to the brown waving grasses, tinged with the warm red sorrel; the waving grasses are swept away, and the meadows lie like emeralds set in the bushy hedgerows; the tawny-tipped corn begins to bow with the weight of the full ear; the reapers are bending amongst it, and it soon stands in sheaves; then, presently, the patches of yellow stubble lie side by side with streaks of dark red earth, which the plough is turning up in preparation for the new-thrashed seed. (*SCL*, pp.121–122)

The imaginative passages of feminine fiction work hard to achieve a relative breadth of sensually suggestive power by anatomizing experience in detail. But the ease of conjuring images to the mind across cultural divisions is never taken for granted. In *Shirley*, Caroline cannot understand how it is that no one has recognized the mature Mrs Pryor as the young wife they once knew. Mrs Pryor reminds her that 'I was very different ...you cannot fancy me a slim young person, attired in scanty drapery of white muslin, with bare arms, bracelets and necklace of beads, and hair disposed in round Grecian curls above my forehead?' (p.438). Given details such as these, Caroline and the reader can indeed now fancy the steady matron as a girl.

Shirley, as a historical novel, dwells on the differences of hairstyle, dress, and other minutiae that mark the whole story as something foreign even to its contemporary readers. For all the novelists dealt with here, these details are essential to the reality of times past, as of times present, and thus to their idea of an alternative 'history'. Their practice has links to an evolving tradition of female historiography in the mid–Victorian period that focused on aspects of daily life excluded by mainstream historiography. Eliot pays attention, for example, to matters such as the changes of fashion in female handiwork indicated by Miss Linnet's array of fancywork, 'japanned boxes, the alum and sealing-wax baskets, the fan-dolls, the "transferred" landscapes on the fire-screens, and the recent bouquets of wax-flowers, showed a disparity in freshness which made them referable to widely different periods', and the method of flower-painting according to 'the ingenious method then fashionable, of applying the shape of leaves and flowers cut out in cardboard, and scrubbing a brush over the surface thus conveniently marked out' (*SCL*, pp.214, 215–6). Her researches for *Romola* indicate how seriously she took the material details of lives in the remoter past also: 'We have in Varchi a ...clear description of the ordinary male costume of dignified Florentines in my time; but for the corresponding feminine costume the best authority I have seen is the very incomplete one of a certain Genevra's *trousseau* in the Ricordi of the Rinuccini family of rather an earlier period'.[26]

In the same spirit, Charlotte Brontë makes sure we can apprehend the material specifics of what is involved, for the niece of a country clergyman, in that commonest occurrence of the nineteenth-century novel, the tea party:

> 'I put off the baking to-day because I thought there would be bread plenty fit while morning: we shall never have enow'.
>
> 'Are there any tea-cakes?' ...
>
> 'Only three and a loaf. I wish these fine folks would stay at home till they're asked: and I want to finish trimming my hat' ...
>
> 'Then', suggested Caroline, to whom the importance of the emergency gave a certain energy, 'Fanny must run down to Briarfield and buy some muffins and crumpets, and some biscuits: and don't be cross, Eliza, we can't help it now'.
>
> 'And which tea-things are we to have?'
>
> 'Oh, the best I suppose: I'll get out the silver service', and she ran upstairs to the plate-closet, and presently brought down tea-pot, cream-ewer, and sugar-basin. (*Shirley*, p.113)

And just as Brontë here breaks down and particularizes the complex idea, 'tea party', so too does Gaskell is an equally meticulous description of the similar preparations of a Manchester factory-worker's family:

> 'Run, Mary, dear, just round the corner, and get some fresh eggs at Tipping's (you may get one apiece, that will be fivepence), and see if he has any nice ham cut, that he would let us have a pound of'.
>
> 'Say two pounds, missus, and don't be stingy', chimed in the husband.
>
> 'Well, a pound and a half ...get Cumberland ham, for Wilson comes

---

26   Eliot, *Letters*, IV, p.43.

from there-away, and it will have a sort of relish of home with it he'll like, and Mary ...you must get a pennyworth of milk and a loaf of bread ...thou must get sixpennyworth of rum, to warm the tea; thou'll get it at the "Grapes". And thou just go to Alice Wilson; he says she lives just round the corner, under 14 Barber Street ...and tell her to come and take her tea with us; she'll like to see her brother ...'

'If she comes she must bring a tea-cup and saucer, for we have but half a-dozen, and here's six of us', said Mrs Barton.

'Pooh, pooh, Jem and Mary can drink out of one, surely'. (*MB*, p.16)

Gaskell's and Brontë's two scenes are different; we may think *Significantly* different. The Barton's poverty is 'Signified' by their concern for prices, etc. But, in their respective contexts, we do not read these scenes in just this way. They both also, perhaps primarily, conjure a complete picture, reveal an overall experience, which is more than the sum of the 'statements' of 'information' extractable from their details.

These novelists show a persistent awareness of how words can conceal potential chasms of understanding caused by discontinuities of experience. 'Tea' on its own, let alone 'tea party', allows for a wide range of experiential inference, as Eliot observes:

...the flickering of Mrs Patten's bright fire is reflected in her bright copper tea-kettle, the home-made muffins glisten with an inviting succulence, and Mrs Patten's niece ...is pouring the rich cream into the fragrant tea with discreet liberality.

Reader! *did* you ever taste such a cup of tea as Miss Gibbs is at this moment handing to Mr Pilgrim? Do you know the dulcet strength, the animating blandness of tea sufficiently blended with real farmhouse cream? No – most like you are a miserable town-bred reader, who thinks of cream as a thinnish white fluid, delivered in infinitesimal pennyworths down area steps ... You have a vague idea of a milch cow as probably a white-plaster animal standing in a butterman's window, and you know nothing of the sweet history of genuine cream ...how it was this morning in the udders of the large sleek beast ...how it fell with pleasant rhythm into Betty's pail, sending a delicious incense into the cool air, how it was carried into that temple of moist cleanliness, the dairy, where it quietly separated itself from the meaner elements of milk, and lay in mellowed whiteness, ready for the skimming-dish which transferred it to Miss Gibb's glass cream-jug. If I am right ...Mr Pilgrim, who is holding that cup in his hand, has an idea beyond you.

(*SCL*, p.11)

Or he had, before Eliot helped us construct an apį ɔximation of the complex 'idea', and a phantom experience to go with it, for ourselves.

The variety of human experience, and the way in which fiction and language can stand in the way of the perception of one part of humanity by another, is countered in the descriptions of *Mary Barton* even more rigorously than it is thematized or Signified in that novel. The novel begins with a string of highly developed scenes, in which Gaskell moves away from the sordid clichés, so dulled in their affective strength, that are customarily employed to describe urban poverty. The holiday halting-place in 'Green Heys Fields' is described in great detail, the stile

> leading from the large pasture field into a smaller one, divided by a hedge of hawthorn and blackthorn; and near this stile, on the further side, there runs a tale that primroses may often be found, and occasionally the blue sweet violet on the grassy hedge bank ...factory girls ...wore the usual out-of-door dress of that particular class of maidens; namely, a shawl, which at midday or in fine weather was allowed to be merely a shawl, but towards evening, or if the day were chilly, became a sort of Spanish mantilla ...broug ɩ over the head and hung loosely down, or was pinned under the chin. (*MB*, p.6)

Gaskell captures a scene so alien to the bulk of her reading audience that she conveys one of its details through comparison with the literally foreign, the Spanish mantilla. However, she seeks to establish a balance between the perception of the urban working-class experience as radically different and as imaginatively accessible; these people, like their leisured rural contemporaries, take pleasure in primroses and sweet violets.

I think Davis is once again rather mistaken in thinking that 'novels, by using landscapes and the objects in them not for their usefulness but as part of a system of meaning, regard these things for their symbolic exchange value as part of a symbol-system alone'.[27] *Mary Barton*, like an imagist poem, presents the most banal of objects in all their vivid specificity:

> ...there was a gay-coloured piece of oil-cloth laid. The place seemed almost crammed with furniture ...Beneath the window was a dresser ... Opposite the fire-place was a table, which I should call a Pembroke, only that it was made of deal ... On it, resting against the wall, was a

---

27   Davis, p.86.

bright green japanned tea-tray, having a couple of scarlet lovers embracing in the middle. The fire-light danced merrily on this, and really (setting all tastes but a child's aside) it gave a richness of colouring to that side of the room. It was in some measure propped up by a crimson tea-caddy, also of japan ware ...if you can picture all this, with a washy, but clean stencilled pattern on the walls, you can form some idea of John Barton's home. (*MB*, p.15)

Once again let me stress that I am not making the absurd suggestion that these pictures are 'objective' 'reflections' of an external reality, even when they break down the package of meaning contained within a single word. They are always constructions from a particular perspective. For a start, the Barton's house would 'seem' pretty different from a dog's point of view – the concentration on the visual as opposed to the olfactory, the accurate discriminations of colour, and so on, are all distinctive of the human point of view, which, as the feminine novelists are always aware, is 'well wadded with stupidity'. Almost as importantly, the distribution of attention, the particular discriminations, are relative to a particular social moment, and, of course the description, even more decisively than most human acts of perception, is couched in language – an inherently social structure. Eliot's description of tea invokes a network of 'ideological' attitudes that could be interestingly analysed, and have their influence on the reader. But it in no way follows that all or even most of what goes on when we imagine is an abstract and ideological reverberation within the halls of Significance. We only ever perceive through a consciousness radically shaped by language, but we do perceive, and in the same way, while a fictional scene is certainly embodied in language, our imagination of it is, nevertheless, partly sensuous and extra-linguistic. And for these novelists, it is just such sensuous imaginings that must overcome the gulfs between the experience of different sections of humanity, which if they were to become absolute would seem forever unalterable and necessary.

ix. Simulation, fiction and morality: The extension of our sympathies after all?

The greatest benefit we owe to the artist, whether painter, poet, or novelist, is the extension of our sympathies.   ELIOT, *Essays*

If art does not enlarge men's sympathies, it does nothing morally ...opinions are a poor cement between human souls; and the only effect I ardently long to produce by my writings is that those who read them should be better able to imagine and to feel the pains and joys of those who differ from themselves in everything but the broad fact of being struggling, erring, human creatures.

ELIOT, *Letters*

...sympathy – the one poor word which includes all our best insight and our best love.

ELIOT, *Adam Bede*

Davis claims that 'Novels rely on the fact that realism acts as a technique by conceptualizing the world as delineated objects that are autonomous and separate from ourselves. The sensuous and immediate relationship with nature that Marx posits as a quality of unalienated life is dramatically cut off in the novel twice over'.[28] This statement has no application to the feminine narratives here dealt with.

Objecting to the reduction of Mr Tryan to a 'text for a wise discourse on the characteristics of the Evangelical school in his day', by the 'critic from his bird's eye station', who dismisses him as 'Not a remarkable specimen; the anatomy and habits of his species have been determined long ago', the narrator of the *Scenes* insists that he conjures these experiences from Mr Tryan's subjective angle:

I am not poised at that lofty height. I am on the level and in the press with him, as he struggles his way along the stony road, through the crowd of unloving fellow-men. He is stumbling ...his heart beats fast with dread ...his eyes are sometimes dim with tears ...a sensitive failing body ...surely the only true knowledge of our fellow-men is that which enables us to feel with him ... Our subtlest analysis of schools and sects must miss the essential truth, unless it be lit up by the love that sees in all forms of human thought and work, the life and death struggles of separate human beings. (*SCL*, pp.266–7)

As the physicality of this passage suggests, such a sense of another's experience is inextricably linked with materiality. Without these details, the reader will comprehend nothing new, but only the contours of a familiar generality, deadened by abstraction. The narrator, aware that the story of Tryan is inseparable from the material details of his life, tells us that if 'at the mention of a clergyman's study' we imagine 'a perfect snuggery' with 'strong ecclesiastical suggestions ...an easy-chair with a Gothic back ...velvety

---

[28]   Davis, p.133.

simulation of church windows ...the portrait of an eminent bishop ...a refined Anglican taste ...indicated by a German print from Overbeck ...the light ...softened by screen of boughs with a grey church in the background', we will have come up with an already familiar picture of the general (and literary) idea 'clergyman', which does not embody the experience of this particular clergyman, who has 'an ugly view of cottage-roofs and cabbage-gardens ...the sole provision for comfort ...a clumsy straight-backed arm-chair covered with faded chintz' (SCL, p.269).

Mr Jerome decides, like Felix Holt, that no divorce can be made between the subjective attitudes of men and their material surroundings, the particulars of their embodied experience. The vision of experience determined by physical surroundings, and of understanding therefore reliant on experience of a particular material habitat, is doubled – Mr Jerome understands Tryan by entering his habitat, and what he understands is that Tryan has chosen such a habitat because it alone allows for an intensity of sympathetic engagement with the poor in his parish:

> It seemed to him, as his eyes rested on this scene of Mr Tryan's labours, that he could understand the clergyman's self-privation without resorting to Mr Stickley's theory of defective spiritual enlightenment. Do not philosophic doctors tell us that we are unable to discern so much as a tree, except by an unconscious cunning which combines many past and separate sensations; that no sense is independent of another, so that in the dark we can hardly taste a fricassee, or tell whether our pipe is light or not, and the most intelligent boy, if accommodated with claws and hoofs instead of fingers, would be likely to remain of the lowest form? If so, it is easy to understand that our discernment of men's motives must depend on the completeness of the elements we can bring from our own susceptibility and our own experience ...the keenest eye will not serve, unless you have the delicate nerve filaments, which elude scientific lenses, and lose themselves in the invisible world of human sensation. (SCL, p.268)

In the fiction dealt with here, character is dependent on the material reality that surrounds it, and we can only imagine the objects that constitute it subjectively. We are offered not the 'spiritual enlightenment' of Significance, but a foreign, sensuous and embodied experience. It is simply not true of these narratives that 'characters ...are formed from a series of discrete and isolated moments designed by the author for their impact' while 'the isolation of the character from any deep involvement in the quotidian renders character the ultimate in alienated consciousness'.[29] These narratives seek to give us the phantoms of alien material experiences that can widen our sympathies, by drawing, as Eliot says, on our 'unconscious cunning which combines many past and separate sensations', and orchestrating these sensations into the imagination of novel situations.

In order to pursue this last idea, it will be useful to consider Eliot's suggestion that 'our discernment of men's motives must depend on the completeness of the elements we can bring from our own susceptibility and our own experience' more carefully. She gestures towards a model of social cognition and emotion that has recently been put forward in the philosophy of mind and in developmental psychology.[30] The consolidation of theories of mental simulation, of which I will here provide the briefest of summaries, promises to solve long-standing conundrums about the human capacity for sociability on the one hand, and about the nature of fiction and our engagement with it on the other, and, indeed, suggests that these two questions may be closely linked.

What is the basis of the highly developed human capacity to understand and predict the behaviour of others? One theory is that it is theoretical. We are either born with, or inductively put together, a range of axioms about human behaviour, desire and reasoning, upon which we base calculations about how individuals are likely to respond in any given situation. According to this so-called 'theory theory', our predictions of the thoughts and behaviour of other humans is founded upon the same processes as our prediction of the weather, or any other part of nature. The competing explanation is that understanding others is a matter of simulation.[31] We run a 'mental simulation', an imaginative mock-up of the experience and situation of others *from their point of view*, and extrapolate their likely behaviour from the emotional and cognitive 'output' of the simulated situation that we register within ourselves. We capitalise on the fact that other people are humans like us; we do not need to calculate how they would feel on being left out in the cold, we imagine their experience, and see how we feel *as them*. This is a re-description of what we talk about as imaginatively 'putting ourselves in other people's shoes' – although it implies that we do this much more of the time than we realize.

---

[29] Davis, p.155.

[30] See Martin Davies and Tony Stone (eds.), *Mental Simulation* (Oxford: Blackwell, 1995) and Peter Carruthers and Peter K. Smith (eds.), *Theories of Theories of Mind* (Cambridge: Cambridge University Press, 1996) pp.1–8.

[31] Peter Carruthers and Peter K. Smith (eds), *Theories of Theories of Mind* (Cambridge: Cambridge University Press, 1996), pp.1–8.

This simulative capacity may account not only for our understanding of others but also for our feeling for them. Running a simulation of their experience gives us access not only to a good guess at the content of their thoughts, but also a *felt* approximation of their emotional state. The output of the simulation is not just insight into how they feel, it is an imagined, phantom version of their emotion itself.

Gregory Currie and Kendall Walton argue that it is simulation that is going on when we feel interest in and emotional involvement with the experience of fictional characters.[32] This supposition solves long-standing philosophical conundrums posed by the fact that we seem to feel for characters we know to be fictional. It also has an overwhelming, though as yet unrealized, appeal for the literary critic.

Especially for the critic of Eliot. For this imaginative, simulative capacity is what George Eliot called 'sympathy'. For her, sympathy was not just another virtue like pity, not one moral attitude among others; it was rather the necessary condition of all morality, a fundamental mode of understanding. In *Daniel Deronda* she observes that 'there is no escaping the fact that want of sympathy condemns us to a corresponding stupidity. Mephistopheles thrown upon real life, and obliged to manage his own plots, would inevitably make blunders'.[33] Simulation theory suggests that Eliot is right in supposing that the possibility of human society may depend on the 'completeness of the elements we can bring from our own susceptibility and our own experience' of mental simulation.

The accuracy and vividness of our simulations may, in turn, depend upon the recollection of our own first-hand experiences, and on the clarity, vividness, detail and facility with which we can string these into a complete simulation. GH Lewes was clear that 'states of consciousness, whatever their origin, are feelings capable of being *re*-felt in the form of images and memories', and Eliot builds this assumption into her conception of sympathy as 'a living again through our own past in a new form'.[34] It is not towards objective structures of moral meaning or Significance, but towards this

---

[32]   Gregory Currie, 'The Paradox of Caring: Fiction and the Philosophy of Mind', and Kendall Walton, 'Spelunking, Simulation, and Slime: On Being Moved by Fiction'; both in Mette Hjort and Sue Laver (eds.), *Emotion and the Arts* (Oxford: Oxford University Press, 1997), pp.63–77, 37–49.

[33]   George Eliot, *Daniel Deronda* (1876), ed. Graham Handley (Oxford: Clarendon Press, 1984), VI, xlviii, p.555.

[34]   GH Lewes, *Problems of Life and Mind* (London 1879), III, p.88; Eliot, *SCL*, p.300. cf. Li's differently supported argument that 'Eliot had a clear understanding of how feelings can be associated with thought by way of memory' in Hao Li, *Memory and History in George Eliot* (London: Macmillan, 2000), p.17.

subjective, emotional understanding that Eliot's realism is oriented. Sympathy, Eliot suggests, is a power and a skill, 'we can no more wish to return to a narrower sympathy, than a painter or a musician can wish to return to his cruder manner, or a philosopher to his less complete formula'.[35] Many animals indulge in forms of play that develop the capacities most essential to their existence. Fiction perhaps functions as play in which humans learn the skills of sociability, co-operation and social insight.[36]

The details of feminine fiction are inextricably related to its sympathetic function. Hume, whose theory of sympathy is echoed both in the novel tradition and in simulation theory, remarked that 'the imagination is more affected by what is particular than by what is general ...the sentiments are always mov'd with difficulty, when the objects are in any degree, loose and undetermined', and Eliot agrees: 'emotion links itself with particulars, and only in a faint and secondary manner with abstractions'.[37] 'Feminine' passages that rarely entice us to look for a factual statement beyond Frege's 'internal image, arising from memories of sense impressions which [we] have had and acts, both internal and external, which [we] have performed' conjured by language, are particularly adapted to this emotive purpose.

Such imagining is essentially perspectival and subjective. Indeed, it is impossible to conceive of imagining something, making it sensuously almost present, without doing so from a subjective perspective; as Christopher Peacocke points out 'to imagine something is always at least to imagine, *from the inside*, being in some conscious state'.[38] The passage from *The Mill on the Floss*, quoted on page 88 above, illustrates this principle particularly

---

[35] George Eliot, *Adam Bede* (1859) ed. Carol A. Martin (Oxford: Clarendon Press, 2001), VI, liv, p.530.

[36] Here, perhaps, is a scientific grounding for Hartman's call for the revival of the doctrine 'which links genius to the sympathetic imagination, sees the progress of humanity in terms of an ability to feel for others, a progress facilitated by a faculty that can acknowledge – represent from the inside – situations different from one's own' (Geoffrey Hartman, *The Sympathy Paradox: Poetry, Feeling, and Modern Cultural Morality* (Texas: University of Austin, 1996), p.5). It seems to me that this is unlikely to be the clue to musical genius, or even to the genius behind most, let alone all, literature or even fiction. Simulation theory will be most useful to the literary critic as one tool amongst others in the discussion of genre, not as a comprehensive theory of fiction, literature or art.

[37] David Hume, *Treatise of Human Nature*, p.371, Eliot, *Essays*, p.371.

[38] Christopher Peacocke, 'Imagination, Experience, and Possibility', in John Foster and Howard Robinson (eds.) *Essays on Berkeley* (Oxford: Clarendon, 1985), p.21, my itals. See also his *Sense and Content* (Oxford: Oxford University Press, 1983), Ch. 5.

emphatically: here the subjective perspectives are nested and multiple – we imagine things from the point of view of the narrator, the ducks, the waggoner, the horses, the dog, and the little girl.

In *Shirley*, Caroline Helstone's excitement at the thought of visiting the Hebrides is tuned to the notion that it will offer some limited access to the reality of the Norsemen. The lived experience that these materialities help to determine seems to her inextricably twined around them. Similarly, her dejection is not reducible to her disappointed love for Moore. It is bound up with the Jew basket, the cold cellars of her uncle's house, her remembrance of the beautiful hollow. Even common feelings, such as disappointed love, are defamiliarized by being reduced to their material descriptions, so that we engage with their basic constituents and come to feel them all the more. 'Strange', thinks Caroline, 'that grief should now almost choke me, because another human being's eye has failed to greet mine' (*Shirley*, p.172).

Mrs Gaskell's descriptions of Manchester life have much in common, stylistically, with Eliot's account of Mrs Gilfil's locked room, where each material detail does not so much signify as imaginatively contain the daily actions and feelings in which it is involved:

> they turned into a little paved court, having the backs of houses at the end opposite to the opening, and a gutter running through the middle to carry off household slops, washing suds, &c. The women who lived in the court were busy taking in strings of caps, frocks, and various articles of linen, which hung from side to side, dangling so low, that if our friends had been a few minutes earlier they would have had to stoop very much, or else the half-wet clothes would have flapped in their faces. (*MB*, p.14)

The scene is not still but full of activity and the traces of activity, and it is described without the kind of scientific air of assessment manifest in the Blue Books and some of the novels constructed with their help. As Wright observes, 'the very manner in which the scene is handled suggests that these horrors are to be seen in terms of human rather than statistical or objective truth'.[39]

The interiors of the houses are described in a similar way – Gaskell dwelling on details that would be of remark chiefly to a 'foreigner', but blending the acknowledgement of the strangeness of these details with hints of the habits and feelings that they produce, and that have produced them:

---

[39]	Terence Wright, *'We are not Angels'* p.21.

On the right of the door ...was a longish window, with a broad ledge. On each side of this, hung blue-and-white check curtains, which were now drawn, to shut in the friends met to enjoy themselves. Two geraniums, unpruned and leafy, which stood on the sill, formed a further defence from out-door pryers. In the corner between the window and the fireside was a cupboard, apparently full of plates and dishes, cups and saucers, and some more nondescript articles, for which one would have fancied their possessors could find no use – such as triangular pieces of glass to save carving knives and forks from dirtying table-cloths. However, it was evident Mrs Barton was proud of her crockery and glass, for she left her cupboard door open, with a glance of satisfaction and pleasure. On the opposite side to the door and window was the staircase, and two doors, one of which ...led into a sort of little back kitchen, where dirty work, such as washing up dishes, might be done, and whose shelves served as larder, and pantry, and store room, and all. (*MB*, p.15)

In *Mary Barton*, the univocal objectivity of History is democratically dispersed into subjective perspectives. Gaskell wrote that she 'wanted to represent the subject in the light in which some of the workmen certainly consider to be *true*, not that I dare to say it is the abstract absolute truth'.[40]

Feminine fiction, then, rejects the 'objectivist' account of what is, which, if extended to human experience, turns so easily into a determinism that transforms *is* into *ought*. It suggests that truly social being, comprising both understanding and the desire for social good, cannot be arrived at through the abstractions of political economists – the 'ingenious philosophers' who by assessing the 'arithmetical proportion' of social hardship see it only as part of a 'balance of happiness' as unchangeable as the laws of nature, and who find 'ground for complacency in statistics' – nor through the religious abstraction which validates and ignores injustice through recourse to the 'doctrine of compensation', nor through any 'other short and easy method of obtaining thorough complacency in the presence of pain' (*SCL*, p.314).

Gaskell's fictional endeavours were shaped by opposition to the popular embrace of a callous Malthusian social theory and Ricardian laissez-faire economics that is illustrated in Martineau's diagrammatically didactic *Illustrations of Political Economy*, (which, as Brantlinger tellingly points out, are 'fiction almost by accident').[41] Eliot wrote in opposition to the emergence of

---

40   Gaskell, letter to Mary Ewart, 1848, in Caroll, *Critical Heritage*, p.83.
41   Patrick Brantlinger, *The Spirit of Reform* (Oxford: Oxford University Press, 1978), p.23.

Social Darwinism. Feminine fiction sets its face against theories of social determinism and the indifference that can result from its 'convenient doctrines'; it attempts to intervene in the mental habits of readers, to cultivate a sympathetic habit of mind, to alter not their beliefs but their very natures in a manner that will prohibit their embracing with comfort the proclaimed necessities of science and History as moral law. Gallagher's assertion that 'Harriet Martineau and George Eliot ...held similar metaphysical assumptions', overlooks the fact that Eliot's method, like that of Brontë and Gaskell, is constructed with the object of countering precisely Martineau's brand of realism, and the exclusively theoretic and systematic habits of mind with which it is associated, which reject the data of sympathy.[42] It seemed to Eliot and her fellow feminine novelists that trusting morality to objectivized abstract knowledge was a sure route to misunderstanding, laissez-faire irresponsibility, and social indifference.

If pain is presented merely in theory, it *can* be considered with complacency; if, on the other hand, it is the subject of sensuous imagination, the phantom-emotional product of simulation, complacency becomes impossible. Eliot was eager to distinguish her brand of fiction from that which is, like Martineau's, 'understood to have a scientific and expository character'.[43] Feminine fiction insists on making an emotional and sensual as well as theoretical appeal, dealing in detail rather than abstraction; 'the emotions ...are but slightly influenced by arithmetical considerations':

> Doubtless a complacency resting on that basis is highly rational; but emotion, I fear, is obstinately irrational ...it absolutely refuses to adopt the quantitative view of human anguish [leaving] a clear balance on the side of satisfaction. This is the inherent imbecility of feeling, and one must be a great philosopher to have got quite clear of all that, and to have emerged into the serene air of pure intellect, in which it is evident that individuals really exist for no other purpose than that abstractions may be drawn from them – abstractions that may rise from heaps of ruined lives like the sweet savour of a sacrifice in the nostrils of philosophers, and of a philosophic Deity. (*SCL*, pp.314–315)

It is by cultivating the virtue of sympathy, not by teaching moral precepts, nor by presenting any kind of general system or theory, that these narratives fulfil the promise that seems so outrageous to Davis, that 'novelists, particularly, are capable of opposing certain destructive forces in society by

---

[42] Gallagher, 'Failure of Realism', pp.374, 375.

[43] George Eliot, letter to Frederic Harrison, 15 August 1866, in *Letters*, IV, pp.300–1.

simply representing them in fiction'.[44] For Eliot,

> ...the highest aim in education is ...to obtain not results but *powers*, not particular solutions, but the means by which endless solutions may be wrought. He is the most effective educator ...who does not seek to make his pupils moral by enjoining particular courses of action, but by bringing into activity the feelings and sympathies that must issue in noble action. On the same ground it may be said that the most effective writer is not he who announces a particular discovery, who convinces men of a particular conclusion, who demonstrates that this measure is right and that measure wrong; but he who rouses in others the activities that must issue in discovery, who awakes men from their indifference ... He does not, perhaps, enrich your stock of data, but he clears away the film from your eyes that you may search for data to some purpose. He does not, perhaps, convince you, but he strikes you, undeceives you, animates you.[45]

Hutton may have been on to something when he observed that feminine fiction treats 'even ...art as a craft, as a manipulation of *effects*, thinking little of that dull, laborious understanding of abstract studies'. It is, I think, true that its practitioners approached their art with 'little of the *spirit* of science', but that is their strength and not, as he thought, their weakness.[46]

We can see, in this light, that Gallagher's contention that Eliot 'insists on equalizing by raising all to the level of significance; and ...hopes that inclusion and acceptance will of themselves lead to the production of meaning, order, and universal understanding' imposes a completely foreign preoccupation with Significance, 'meaning', and 'order' onto Eliot's pragmatic cultivation and extension of the skill of sympathetic mental simulation in her readers.[47] This sympathetic function, and the tendency it fosters, precisely obviate the necessity for the meaning, system and order of theory. 'Realistic metonymy' in fiction, if it is indeed founded on a belief that 'a detailed recording of everyday life might ineluctably lead to moral

---

[44] Davis, p.132. My argument here follows TR Wright's suggestion that, in accordance with the Comtean Postitivist emphasis on the role of emotion in morality, 'George Eliot's novels can be understood ...as an attempt to improve her readers by exercising their altruistic instincts.' TR Wright, *The Religion of Humanity* (Cambridge: Cambridge University Press, 1986), p.199.

[45] Eliot, *Essays*, p.213.

[46] Hutton, *Relative Value*, p.22.

[47] Gallagher, 'Failure of Realism', p.377.

progress' does not hinge that belief on the idea that meaning, codes of morality, are Signified, written out by the world. Feminine fiction's aspiration to moral amelioration *cannot* be founded as Gallagher thinks on 'the assumption that observable appearances bespeak deeper moral essences', so that 'we arrive at moral essences by accumulating the specific details of appearance that surround these essences'.[48] For such a process could only produce something like a mathematical diagram of morality, appealing for recognition to the intellect, but not in any way altering our relation to it in the process. As Eliot puts it, 'Appeals founded on generalizations and statistics require a sympathy ready-made, a moral sentiment already in activity; but a picture of human life such as a great artist can give, surprises even the trivial and the selfish into that attention to what is apart from themselves, which may be called the raw material of moral sentiment'.[49]

The *Scenes* begins with a passage about the march of History, which alludes to a specific political ideology connected with the 'ingenious philosophers' mentioned above. 'Immense improvement! says the well-regulated mind, which unintermittingly rejoices in ...guarantees of human advancement, and has no moments when conservative-reforming intellect takes a nap', while 'imagination' questions the 'new-varnished efficiency, which will yield endless diagrams, plans, elevations, and sections, but alas! no picture' (*SCL*, p.7). The wish for a picture is not, in the context of Eliot's theory of sympathetic understanding, an aestheticisation of political life, but rather an appreciation of the need to understand and plan as a human for humans. She insists that feeling, thinking, experiencing beings, with social and creative capacities, are too complex and too dynamic to be predicted or guided by the cold, rationalistic and deterministic equations of political economy.[50]

The incidental subjective descriptions of feminine fiction function as vehicles of sympathy precisely because they distinguish themselves from narratives which 'do not pretend to work on the emotions, or ...couldn't do it if they did pretend'.[51] From our own perspective, we can only surmise how much these narratives, and the imaginative sympathy they encouraged, did to prevent the experience and suffering of the Others of History from being

---

[48] Gallagher, 'Failure of Realism', p.375.

[49] Eliot, *Essays*, p.270.

[50] The conviction, which Eliot shares with simulation theorists, that humans can be understood quite differently from non-human phenomena, is probably also part of her intellectual inheritance from Vico and Herder.

[51] Eliot to Harrison, *Letters*, IV, p.300

utterly submerged from sight and so exposed to violence. The possibility that it may be partly due to such imaginative appeals 'that things are not so ill with you and me as they might have been' seems a very real one.

x. The growing good of the world

Mary Barton begins with a passage that strongly recalls Eliot's picture of Mr Jerome's Garden. Gaskell describes the citizens' gatherings near a

> rambling farmyard, belonging to one of those ...gabled, black and white houses ...overlooking the field through which the public footpath leads. The porch of this farmhouse is covered by a rose-tree; and the little garden surrounding it is crowded with a medley of old-fashioned herbs and flowers, planted ...when the garden was the only druggist's shop, and allowed to grow into scrambling and wild luxuriance − roses, lavender, sage, balm (for tea), rosemary, pinks and wallflowers, onions and jessamine, in most republican and indiscriminate order. (*MB*, p.6)

Whether or not Eliot remembered Gaskell's description, the echo suggests a peculiar magnetism in the image. If James's fiction is like his 'golden bowl', feminine fiction is as much like this rambling farmhouse and its garden overlooking the public path, in which the aesthetic and the functional, the striking and the familiar are altogether blended; it serves diverse pleasures and purposes. If it was planted with an element of design, that design was clearly not one of any unifying or autotelic aesthetic, nor of single-minded utilitarianism. The various elements have grown through and over and around one another into a scented yet thorny tangle, that poses a formidable challenge to any one who would identify the species and the plan that shaped the planting. I hope, however, that my assemblage of sensuous passages from feminine fiction has highlighted some distinctive blooms justifying this investigation.

In my passing engagement with this task, I have come across some well-known folk remedies whose recent passage through suspicion and disrepute as mere superstitions is perhaps just a necessary stage in their progress towards recognition in the light of modern theory. I have argued that, as Eliot and generations of other critics since her time have maintained, fiction does good work through the extension and cultivation of our capacity for sympathy. I hope I have done something to provide theoretical justification for this common gut response. What Belsey calls 'the order of a universe whose sole inhabitant is "Eternal Man" ...a subjectivity ...whose silent presence both determines and transcends history, a "human essence" float[ing] free of the destructive forces of a mass society', is precisely what we will *not* find in feminine fiction.[52] In imaginative engagement with such fiction, the subjectivity of the reader is not 'interpellated', as they say, as rational, 'transcendent and non-contradictory', the 'unified and unifying subject' of its ideology.[53] It is rather shaped and moulded through its interaction with imagined materiality outside itself, as it flows from subject position to subject position – imaginatively occupying a certain house, spending a certain budget, wearing a certain costume – all by the reading of a novel. Eliot captures the spirit of feminine fiction in her remark, made in ironic allusion to Kant's *Critique of Pure Reason,* that for the men of Shepperton 25 years ago, '"something to drink" was as necessary a "condition of thought" as Time and Space' (*SCL,* p.15). Materiality, its contingent details as well as its constants, saturates mind through and through. The diverse subjective perspectives of feminine fiction are each moulded by a particular material experience. Davis's criticism, that 'in effect, reading novels is a solitary activity in which readers define themselves by what they are not, put themselves into locations they have never been'[54] is not the crime but the moral justification of fiction.

The detailed descriptions of feminine fiction may be constructed by the reader into a simulated subjective experience. These experiences both overlap with and extend the reader's own experience, so as to produce pleasure and interest on the one hand, and on the other a sense of history with a small 'h', the lived experience behind, before and around us. The very mode of the creation of this historical sense guarantees that it will be an emotional, sympathetic one that outstrips the ego, creating identification between individuals and a wider social body, motivating action and instigating change. This fiction creates a sympathetic and imaginative habit of mind; it cultivates a virtue that may alter the reader's relation to the real world.

Terence Wright remarks of one of Gaskell's short stories that 'the story itself [acts] out far more than can be contained in a moral'.[55] Brontë ends *Shirley* with a mocking challenge to the reader to reduce her narrative to a Significant structure: 'The story is told. I think I now see the judicious reader putting on his spectacles to look for the moral' (*Shirley,* p.646). Eliot wrote of her fear of 'the habit of pedagogic moralizing' and of any form of

---

52 Belsey, 'ReReading', p.127.
53 Belsey, *Critical Practice,* p.78; Steven Heath, 'Narrative Space', *Screen* 17:3 (1976), 68–112, 85. See also Crosby, Barthes, and Davis.
54 Davis, pp.135–6.
55 Terence Wright, *'We are not Angels',* p.15.

encroaching abstraction in narrative, 'If it lapses anywhere from the picture to the diagram – it becomes the most offensive of all teaching'. She seeks instead to fit her fictions to 'lay hold on the emotions as human experience' and '"flash" conviction on the world by means of aroused sympathy' by means of the power of words to 'produce in the mind analogous emotions to those produced by the object itself' to which they usually refer.[56] Feminine realist histories seek to replace the ineluctability of Significance and abstraction with the solidity of the texture of life, just as Tina seeks refuge from the suspense and desire of her solipsistic fantasies by sitting 'with her forehead pressed against the cold pane', her teeth set 'tight against the window-frame' (*SCL*, pp.131–2), foreshadowing Dorothea Brooke, who similarly 'besought hardness and coldness and aching weariness to bring her relief from the mysterious incorporeal might of her anguish: she lay on the bare floor and let the night grow cold around her'.[57] There is a utopianism about this aspiration certainly, but also a subversive conviction of the irreducibility of human experience in the face of science and History, and of its transcendence of, rather than by, abstraction.

---

[56] Eliot, *Essays*, p.379, and *Letters*, IV, pp.300–01, and 'Ruskin's Lectures', in *George Eliot: A Writer's Notebook (1854–79) and Uncollected Writings*, ed. J. Warren (Charlottesville: Virginia University Press, 1981), p.240.

[57] Eliot, *Middlemarch* VIII, lxxx, pp.774–5

CHAPTER 3

The Personal, the Political and the Human, Part I: Sympathy – A Family Affair?

[The historian confronting] fundamentally divergent thought-systems and
...widely differing modes of experience and interpretation [needs] the
courage to subject not just the adversary's point of view but all points of
view, including his own, to ideological analysis.

KARL MANNHEIM

i. The family and political theory: Rehearsing old dilemmas

Let any ...inclined to be hard ...inquire into the comprehensiveness of
her own beautiful views.   GEORGE ELIOT, *Middlemarch*.

In this chapter and the two that follow, I move away from questions to do
with the representational modes of Victorian fiction, and the metaphysical
stance implicit in or propagated by those modes. For alongside the imposing
battery of arguments against the novel on these fronts, politicized criticism
has marshalled forceful objections against its subject matter.

Foremost among these is the objection to the 'personal' focus of Victorian
fiction. Various allegations have been made against this focus. It is said to
divert readers' attention away from political problems and political solutions
towards a preoccupation with 'human nature' – a trans-historical notion
that, far from reflecting anything outside the structures of language and
power, serves to curtail political critique. It is also said to perpetuate the
arch-ideological illusion that it is people, rather than political structures, that
make history; in other words, that human subjects are ontologically prior to,
rather than mere effects of discourse. And, finally, it is said to reinforce the
deep division in Victorian ideology and practice between the private and the

social, and by doing so to facilitate the strategic displacement of criticism away from the latter.

Closely related to these objections, there are two further complaints about the Victorian novel. There is the argument – or, perhaps we should rather call it a assumption – that it is an individualist genre representing the self-fulfilment of the individual hero as opposed to society, and that it celebrates the individual's unconfined freedom to assert, develop and discover himself. Then there is also the argument of opposite tendency: that the role that the Victorian fictional imagination apportions to women is usually one of self-abnegation and confinement within the closed domestic and private sphere; that female self-fulfilment and economic independence are too often sacrificed.

I could spend some time illustrating the absurdity of the coexistence of these two opposite arguments, for there is some absurdity about it. But the two of them are tenuously reconciled by the conception (outlined in the extensive literature on the subject of 'separate spheres') of bourgeois ideology as being bifurcated along gendered lines. It is certainly true that the political/personal, public/domestic, masculine – individualism/feminine – altruism binaries were primary structuring devices of the Victorian imagination. Nevertheless, something can yet be said on behalf of Victorian fiction's political function and insight. For it is precisely in the light of a full consideration of just how real and deep is this public-private split in both the culture and the material life of capitalist society that the novel's uniquely incisive engagement with and contestation of this divide can be appreciated. 'Separate spheres' ideology, as I shall show, was not a settled and serviceable discourse; behind its fragile appearances of equilibrium there raged a heated and complex struggle between two radically divergent conceptions of the nature of human beings and their relations to each other.

These binaries have structured thought about ethics and politics – have indeed been the very condition of thought about either ethics or politics – since the Victorian era, up to and including our own time. As I hope to show, modern reasoning and feeling are torn between two irreconcilable systems. It is disingenuous simply to scapegoat the novel as an expression of the division and ignore our own profound investment in it.

The problem of the human subject and its relation to social structures is a persistent one, not as easily dismissed, emptied out, or reduced to non-human, mechanical terms as theorists from the seventeenth century through to Althusser and his literary-critical legatees have imagined. As Victorian domestic fiction illustrates, all political discourse assumes some sort of model of human nature and subjectivity. It is only the nature and the explicitness of that model that are at issue. In its engagement with this question, as I hope to demonstrate, Victorian domestic fiction makes a unique and multivalent contribution to the fundamental struggle over the claims of individualism.

This chapter sketches the genesis of the modern conception of the separate realm of family, and the contest over the nature and importance of the human subject with which it is so closely connected. It shows a historical struggle with dilemmas that we have not so much conquered as forgotten.

I argued in Chapter 2 that sympathy, as a fundamentally social dimension of human subjectivity, may be an important, perhaps even a necessary factor in the impulse towards social critique and the commitment to social change. If so, we should not expect to find sympathy blandly embraced by the mainstream thinking of an unequal Victorian society. In the eighteenth century, the very notion of sympathy – along with that of subjectivity and the role of the passions more generally – had been hotly debated. Was sympathy the stuff of society itself, or was it a dangerously subversive and enthusiastic passion? For the Victorians, on the other hand, the contest was, for the most part, no longer over the nature and desirability of emotional subjectivity and sympathy, or about the spontaneous altruistic action and communal conception of goals that they produce. Rather, there was a struggle over the proper scope of sympathy. It was not its suppression, but its containment that was at issue. The narrow space in which it was attempted to contain sympathy was feminine and domestic, and the rhetoric justifying its confinement within this space was the doctrine of separate spheres. However, if the family arena became thus the site of the enslavement of emotional subjectivity and sympathy, it also became the base for their revolt.

So extensive and successful was the Victorian effort thus to contain affectivity and sympathy, that we ourselves have come to associate emotion, and the feminine and domestic discourse with which it became identified, with containment. We have come to connect sentiment, instinct and altruism with the oppression of women, and with narrow, individual or family interests *as opposed* to public, political ones. In doing so we have come to regard sympathy and feeling exactly as separate sphere ideologues would have wanted. Victorian domestic novelists, on the other hand, were not so quiescent.

ii. **Human creatures**

Mary Poovey's *Uneven Developments* is one of the most impressive of the many recent studies that have set out to contest the 'Victorian' 'notion that "instincts" and "natural" differences between the sexes delineate social roles'. She sees the demonstration of 'the historical specificity of this conception of nature' as part of the wider task of challenging the idea that 'certain instincts, however they are defined, "lie ...unanimously in the hearts of humanity ...in all times and amid all people"', an idea that she also associates with the Victorians.[1] She opposes to this idea the standard politico-critical vision of human subjectivity as a product of discourse.

It is worth noting that these two allegedly Victorian ideas – the idea of gender difference, and the idea of universal human propensities – are both logically and rhetorically divergent. A consideration of gender difference is not a consideration of what makes us all human. This is one reason why Poovey's narrower and wider projects are not as consonant as she thinks. But the more profound problem with her account lies in the fact that the Victorians themselves used the notion of gender difference to shelve precisely the kind of serious reflection on biologically determined needs, dispositions, and modes of subjectivity that evolutionary theory makes possible. It was not the idea of a biologically determinate human nature but rather the rejection of such that was the characteristic nineteenth-century bourgeois metaphysical myth, designed to disguise the prescription of individualism as objective neutrality. The biological essentialism that was characteristic of the Victorian discussion of the condition of women was actually symptomatic of the extent to which all acknowledgment of *man* as an animal was repressed and displaced in favour of a picture of man as the locus of an atomic, self-asserting rationality that was taken to transcend or supplant nature. Through the establishment of 'separate spheres', liberal individualist ideology suppressed a political acknowledgment of the reality of feeling and the necessity of reproductive labour and human interdependence. By focusing on gender difference, it contained the political implications of human biology and emotional subjectivity.[2]

Of course, the argument that there are *no* qualities shared *ceteris paribus* by all human subjects is not a logical space open either to the Victorian liberal or to Poovey. Nothing, and no type of thing, has no qualities, and we are

---

[1]   Mary Poovey, *Uneven Developments* (London: Virago, 1989), p.2.

[2]   I use the word 'liberalism' throughout these chapters to mean classical liberalism, with its central emphasis on the principle of self-ownership. The word 'libertarianism' is now often used instead, sometimes, as by Jerry Cohen in *Self-Ownership, Freedom and Equality* (Cambridge: Cambridge University Press, 1995), in opposition to contemporary liberalism as propounded by John Rawls, Ronald Dworkin et al., who have renounced the stronger interpretations of this principle (although Rawls still makes use of some of the attitudes towards human nature with which it is so closely associated). However, to use the word 'libertarian' in a nineteenth-century context seems anachronistic.

only able to say that something changes with time and with history if there is some constant that indicates that it is one type of thing that is changing. The anti-biological position (in theoretical practice, if not in meta-theory) is to maintain that the only things that all human subjects share are a set of abstract, immaterial and non-biological characteristics: the Victorian liberal would have said these included reason and self-ownership; Poovey would probably say something like embeddedness within a system of significance and a dynamic of power and desire. There is a strong family resemblance between the two views.

It is surprising that the theoretical untenability of conducting any analysis of human society that is independent of assumptions or hypotheses about a more or less determinate human nature has not been acknowledged by politicized criticism. But even setting such fundamental, though abstract, considerations aside (arguments founded on matters of mere logic do not always cut much ice), it seems extraordinary that the focus is always on the politically conservative stances associated with biological essentialism, and never on the equally notable ideological evasions that spring from the attempt to marginalize or deny the biologically given characteristics of human subjects. I turn now to a brief examination of the places of, and connections between, the ideology of separate spheres and liberal theory's 'thin' conception of human nature and human subjectivity.

iii. Separate spheres

In the middle of the nineteenth century, the production and exchange of commodities, and the profit incentive according to which they are organized, finally separated from and took priority over both state and family.[3] By its removal from the home, production was finally divorced from non-productive work, with which it had once been seamlessly integrated. With this separation, this subordination of other forms of labour to those that realized profit through manufacture and exchange of commodities, came the ideology of separate spheres. Women who remained in the home were now deprived of some of their work and of the prestige of the rest. They were offered – as a sop, it might seem – the recompense of a doctrine

---

[3] Karl Polanyi in *The Great Transformation* (Boston: Beacon Press, 1957), p.60, defines the market economy as a distinctive formation in which the production of commodities takes structural precedence over other modes of work, so that the movements of goods, labour, land and money is governed by the action of the market. In his account, it is only with the repeal of the Speenhamland Law in 1834 that the last of these elements, labour, becomes a commodity in England.

of 'influence' in exchange for the power whose locus had now shifted to the economic sphere; that is, though they might not now have the means to assert their will, their good wishes could find fulfilment through the willing and gratuitous deference of their husband to their purifying influence. Non-competitive relations and activities within the home no longer counted as possible spheres of action and power.

This period also saw the enthronement of instrumental reason as the proper basis for political discourse and decision-making. The domestic sphere became the radically separated domain of activities and subjective attitudes that, though now economically and logistically subordinated to the dynamic of the production of commodities, remained absolutely necessary to civilized society: for the purposes of sexual reproduction; the raising of children as socialized individuals; the care of the sick and elderly; the regulation of intimate relationships; the accommodation of the basic daily physical and emotional needs of working individuals; and as the crucible for the fundamental emotions which motivated all these activities. The establishment of separate spheres is sometimes spoken of as though it were primarily a strategy for establishing ideological coherence and hegemony, rather than first and foremost a material development. The wide currency of this misconception is evidence of the ideological relegation of domesticity, emotion and biology themselves to secondary and merely super-structural status that attended this material development, and that lives on in our own time.

Although the establishment of a separate domestic realm was primarily a material, rather than an ideological necessity, its maintenance did demand particular ideological negotiations. The public realm of economics was made possible only by the fact that within the household went on various forms of work, and various modes of subjectivity and relation that could not be sustained by the individualist ideology that governed the political and economic realms, and which by their very ineradicability undermined the most basic premises of that ideology. Thus the separation of and discontinuity between the attitudes towards human subjectivity that characterized the domestic realm on the one hand, and the public arena on the other, were of crucial importance for the perpetuation of both. It is worth sketching the context within which this separation arose and was maintained, and it is to that context, rather than to novels, which this brief chapter is devoted. I hope this diversion will be justified by the purchase it gives me on domestic fiction in the two following chapters.

iv. Self-ownership and the social contract

The progressive separation of family from the rest of social life correlated with the rise of contractarian political theory in the seventeenth and eighteenth centuries. Hobbes, Locke and Rousseau all hypothesized states of nature in which each man was radically separate from the next. As Hobbes put it, 'Let us …consider men …as if but even now sprung out of the earth, and suddenly, like mushrooms, come to full maturity, without all kind of entanglements to each other'.[4] Mary Midgley remarks that

> this model shows human society as a spread of standard social atoms, originally distinct and independent, each of which combines with others only at its own choice and in its own private interests. This model is drawn from physics, and from seventeenth-century physics, at that, where the ultimate particles of matter were conceived as hard, impenetrable, homogenous little billiard balls, with no hooks or internal structure. To see how such atoms could combine at all was very hard.[5]

Human beings are treated as individual bodies whose blind forward-motion is the positive principle of their existence. Interaction between human beings is a matter of collision, producing reaction and no more. The state embodies the transference of some of this energy, and so it moves in the same direction. What we should notice about this view of human nature is that it is not really a view of *human* nature at all, but rather a theoretical subjugation of the latter to a wider conception of nature in general. Men are considered as mushrooms or atoms, but not as men. Instead of working from this metaphorical analogy towards relevant distinctions, liberal theory represses such distinctions by further extending the analogy, and so convinces itself that it has evaded any contentious assumptions about human nature. The forces of physical bodies become the instrumental-reason-governed self-assertion of the individual man, or, for Poovey (after Althusser), vectors in the ineluctable though uneven development of the cultural structures of power. The extended metaphor comes to look like a neutral and parsimonious description of human existence in the most basic of terms.

In Locke's state of nature, men are in 'a *State of perfect Freedom* to order

---

4   Thomas Hobbes, 'Philosophical Rudiments Concerning Government and Society', in *The English Works of Thomas Hobbes,* ed. W Molesworth, 12 vols (London: Routledge/Thoemmes Press, 1992), II:108–9.

5   Mary Midgley, 'Duties concerning Islands', *Encounter* 60/2 (1983) 36–44, 37.

their Actions, and dispose of their Possessions, and Persons as they think fit, within the bounds of the Law of Nature, without asking leave, or depending upon the Will of any other Man'.[6] Locke's Law of Nature, which is something very like common-sense self-interest, decrees only that man should not needlessly interfere with the business of another, insofar as it would be irrational to do so given that such interference would set a precedent according to which he himself might be interfered with. However, finding that, as the population increases, his interests clash with increasing frequency and complexity with those of his fellow men, the natural man may choose to trade in his natural capacity (and *hence* right) to self-defence and free self-assertion in exchange for membership of a civil society under a government, where his own rights will be protected for him. The basis of these rights is every citizen's '*Property* in his own *Person*', which he does not resign, but merely entrusts to the care of others under a government.[7]

As an extension of the principle of self-ownership, Locke defends the appropriation and accumulation of private property: 'Whatsoever then he removes out of the State that Nature has provided …he hath mixed his Labour with, and joyned to it something that is his own, and thereby makes it his *Property*'.[8] In classic liberal theory, for which Locke helps lay the foundations, the function of the state is to protect the self-ownership and property of each man, his right to pursue his own conception of the good life; liberalism 'has only one overriding aim: to secure the political conditions that are necessary for the exercise of personal freedom'.[9] The ethical theory associated with this political attitude regards the central tenet of morality to be respect for the rights of others, embodied in the principle of non-interference in their exercise of self-ownership. Any search for a more elaborated conception of the good is an unwarranted convolution of the fundamentality of the Newtonian conception of man as just another body.

The political state is constituted so as to do justice to the power distribution in the state of nature, which is a '*State* also of *Equality*, wherein all the Power and Jurisdiction is reciprocal, no one having more than another'.[10] Men only consent to the social contract whereby they forswear interference with others because it is rational for them to do so, on the

6   John Locke, *Two Treatises of Government*, ed. Peter Laslett (Cambridge: Cambridge University Press, 1960), *Second Treatise*, II.4.3–7 p.309.
7   Locke, *Second Treatise*, V.27.2–3 p.328.
8   Locke, *Second Treatise*, V.27.5–8 p.329.
9   Judith Shklar, 'The Liberalism of Fear', in Nancy Rosenblum (ed.), *Liberalism and the Moral Life* (Cambridge, Mass.: Harvard University Press, 1991) pp.21–38, p.21.
10 Locke, *Second Treatise*, II.4.3–5 p.309.

grounds that other men have the power to punish their abuses. The notion that all human beings are equal is not a normative principle but a factual premise within liberalism. *Given* that all men are equally able to assert themselves, it follows that if only all legal fetters on the freedoms of each individual are removed society will be an even playing field in which individual excellence will emerge, and each individual will rejoice in the fulfilment of his or her true self.

In elaboration of the contractarian view, Hume comments that

> Were there a species of creature intermingled with men, which, though rational, were possessed of such inferior strength …that they were incapable of all resistance, and could never …make us feel the strength of their resentment …we …should not …lie under any restraint of justice with regard to them, nor could they possess any right or property …as no inconvenience ever results from the exercise of power, so firmly established in nature, the restraints of justice and property, being totally *useless*, would never have place in so unequal a confederacy.

Hume was the first, and almost the last, to notice that whatever we make of justice, so conceived, as a strategy for social life, it is an imperfect principle, a 'cautious, jealous virtue' that would give way to spontaneous and impassioned generosity if man could either reach a state of sufficient abundance, or cultivate his natural benevolence to a sufficient extent. In which case 'the whole human race *would form only one family*'.[11] The abstract categories that characterize modern accounts of society and of the political subject (or, equally, the inverse reflection of liberal political subject – that is, the subject-as-vector that populates contemporary theory), as well as the norms such as rights and justice that are extrapolated from these descriptions, are final and universal descriptions and principles only given certain assumptions about human nature and the limits of emotion and

---

[11]   David Hume, 'An Enquiry concerning the Principles of Morals', in *David Hume: Enquiries*, ed. LA Selby-Bigge and PH Nidditch (Oxford: Clarendon, 3rd edition, 1975). III:I:152 p.190, and 'Principles of Morals', III:I:145–46 pp.184–5, italics mine. There is a debate about whether Hume is here offering an explanation (and a critique) of the origins and foundations of what we call justice (for one version of this approach see JL Jenkins and Robert Shaver, '"Mr Hobbes Could Have Said No More"', in Anne J Jacobson (ed.), *Feminist Interpretations of David Hume* (Philadelphia: Pennsylvania State University Press, 2000)), or actually condoning this principle as Thomas Reid assumed at the time (and as is argued by David Gauthier, 'David Hume, Contractarian', *Philosophical Review* 88 (1979)).

emotional mutuality. These assumptions are in turn reliant on the axiom that we behave differently inside and outside the family.

v. Liberalism and the family

Locke, in the course of his argument against patriarchal justifications of government, assiduously denies that there is any continuity or similarity between the family and the state. The family is not part of the public arena but rather an extension of each man's private realm, tailored to his own will, which he has contracted with the state to protect as private.

With a contrary emphasis, however, Locke also argues that even family, through marriage, its central relation, is a contractual arrangement. 'Conjugal society is made by a voluntary compact between man and woman'. Insofar as both parties respect the contract, the power of the husband over his wife is limited, but 'the Husband and the Wife, though they have but one common concern ...will unavoidably sometimes have different wills ...it therefore being necessary, that the last Determination, i.e. the Rule, should be placed somewhere, it naturally falls to the Man's share, as the abler and stronger'.[12] As Locke's conception of the rights of the individual is inextricably linked with his tracing of the roots of society to a natural law characterized by rational self-assertion, individual strength provides a crucial and inalienable claim to power.

Surely, according to this second emphasis, the family is continuous with the other contractual relationships that constitute the public realm? Locke simply cannot rest comfortably with the opposition between family and society, even though that opposition is integral to his arguments against the patriarchal political theory of the past. He is aware that the family poses a challenge to (what looks like) the elegance and parsimony of his account.

The spirit of Locke's *Treatise* is most fully realised in the middle of the nineteenth century, when liberal apologists, after Locke, theorize the family as necessarily radically apart and in opposition to society at large. However, despite immediate appearances, these apologists in the last instance, like Locke, deconstruct the division. Their stance on the family follows naturally from the minimal and distinctive consideration they give to human nature. In illustration of their argument, I will look briefly at two examples taken from quite distinct discursive realms.

Sarah Ellis, in her many conduct manuals, was the most famous proponent of the notion of a separate domestic sphere of peculiar virtues.

---

[12]   Locke, *Second Treatise*, VII.78:1–2 p.362, VII.82.1–6 p.364.

Though at moments a stern critic of the standards of civil society, her mode of handling the division between the civil and the domestic realm was extremely characteristic of her time. Like other liberals, she finds the domestic virtues she preaches continually encroached upon by the values of the overarching system, and vice versa.

Ellis uses her domestic perspective to diagnose the deficiencies of the civil arena. In using familial language in her description of the marketplace, she draws upon the intuitive notion that there ought to be one principle governing all areas of life. She places the need for a regeneration of domestic virtue in the critical condition of the civil arena, which constitutes 'a strife, no less than deadly to the highest impulses of the soul'.

> Alas! there is no union in the great field of action in which [man] is engaged; but envy, and hatred, and opposition, to the close of the day – every man's hand against his brother, and each struggling to exalt himself, not merely by trampling upon his fallen foe, but by usurping the place of his weaker brother, who faints by his side, from not having brought an equal portion of strength into the conflict.[13]

Her critique of the alienating effect of work in the bourgeois world is acute. 'Every morning brings the same hurried and indifferent parting, every evening the same jaded, speechless, welcomeless return – until we almost fail to recognize the man, in the machine'.[14] Ellis is aware that there is some part of what we recognize as full 'humanity' which is not accommodated by the civil arena. However, she is convinced that there is no scope for these extra 'human' values to have any impact on the situation she criticizes. 'The man of enlightened understanding, who neglects his [business] for the sake of hours of leisure, must be content to spend them in the debtor's department of a jail. Thus, it is not with single individuals that the blame can be made to rest. The fault is in the system'.[15] Ellis's sense of the resistance of the 'system' to any accommodation of 'human' values foreign to it, displays on the one hand an incisive perception, and on the other, in its lack of qualification, an unreasoned fatalism that is characteristic of contractarian thought.

Having thus resigned the possibility of extending domestic values to encompass the public sphere, Ellis soon finds public competition swamping the distinctiveness of domesticity. In asserting the inevitability of the

---

[13]   Ellis, *The Women of England* (London: Fisher, Son and Co., 1839), p.52.
[14]   Elllis, *Women of England,* p.56,
[15]   Elllis, *Women of England,* p.56.

individualistic dynamic of the public realm, she falls back upon a conception of human nature that casts great doubt on the family's status as at once 'natural' and emotional and sympathetic. 'The little child ...is a perfect bundle of selfishness ...implanted in the nature of the child ...a portion of the elementary nature of the human being'.[16] Such selfishness, she thinks, should not be stamped out altogether, being essential to survival in the civil arena. While 'Selfishness' is the 'first principle of our common nature', pity, on the other hand, 'cannot ...be classed amongst our spontaneous emotions ...pity has to be taught ...children are not naturally compassionate'. Ellis argues that it is a law of nature that 'men in general are ...apt ...to act and think as if they were created to exist of, and by, themselves'.[17] Furthermore, 'Love of property is one part, and a very useful one, of that original selfishness ...one of the most active tendencies of our nature. It is the stimulus to industry ...it gives stability to national and individual prosperity'.[18]

Against this background is projected a picture of the family which looks strangely like a microcosm of the bourgeois economic arena and its mores. On the topic of pocket money, Ellis comments that 'it is better that a child should possess a little, and that that little should be as truly its own as the father's property is his own. Indiscriminate taking, using and appropriating in a family may wear an agreeable outside appearance of unselfishness and liberality, but ...out of such confusion of property there will arise confusion of claims, and there will follow disputes and quarrels. Neither is there any true generosity in the giver when all is held in common'.[19] Ellis uses exactly the same justification for private property *within* the private sphere that Locke uses in describing the evolution of society at large.

With what I will argue is a characteristically liberal emphasis, Ellis is in fact extremely anxious to limit the scope of feeling in general, and family affection in particular. She urges the good wife to 'avoid ...any very close contact with [your husband's] nearest relatives ...you may not yourself be sufficiently amiable to bear it'. The extended family is envisaged as a zone of tension, to be kept at arm's length; 'a warm-hearted, dependent, and affectionate young woman ...will be predisposed to lean upon the kindness of [her husband's] relatives, and even to enter rashly into the most intimate and familiar intercourse with them. But ...this amiable impulse must be

[16] Ellis, *Education of the Heart* (London: Hodder and Stoughton, 1869), pp.19–20.
[17] Ellis, *Education of the Heart*, pp.155, 124; *Wives of England* (London: Fisher, Son and Co, 1843), p.69.
[18] Ellis, *Education of the Heart*, p.121.
[19] Ellis, *Education of the Heart*, p.158

checked', because 'unless the husband's relatives are somewhat more than human ...amongst themselves there will not be perfect unanimity ...They will probably be divided into little parties'. The good mistress must make sure her relations are 'made to understand that you do not wish them, in your own house, entirely to share all things in common'.[20] Economic factors must be considered when it comes to family politics, 'such is the weakness of human nature ...that the good and the happiness of all parties seem to require as little mixing up as possible ...of rich and poor relations. When the poor have to be provided for ...it is better ...to do this at a distance, or at least not associated as one family'. The family suddenly shows itself as a realm quite as full of conflict and individual interest as civil society. Even the closest family relationships are not exempt from this principle of division. 'The love of a parent for a child ...can never bind that child beyond a certain period ...the love of a child for a parent must necessarily be interrupted ...The love of a brother of a sister must ever be ready to give place to dearer claims'. With the definitive gesture of the liberal family ideologist, Ellis declares that, far from being an agent for unlimited social regeneration, 'it is only in the married state that the boundless capabilities of woman's love can ever be fully known or appreciated'.

This restriction of the essence of family to chosen, contracted sexual partners is an attempt to get past the radical challenge suggested by a more comprehensive consideration of family relationships to the model of the autonomous and atomic human subject. Ellis' moral scheme has no real place for the physical and emotional interdependence that the domestic arena accommodates. She comments that 'illness is to men a sufficient trial and humiliation ...as it deprives them of their free agency'.[21] Even the affectivity of sympathetic family relations is rejected in the last analysis; 'the mere generosity of impulse ...deserves no better a name than self-gratification. Indeed, all acting from mere impulse, may be classed under the head of selfishness'.[22]

In the end, the family is not set up in opposition to, but rather as a training ground for the public realm of economic competition, as Ellis's overwhelming emphasis on the mother's duty to train her children in the protocol of property relations makes clear. 'Incalculable in amount is the weight which a strict regard to the claims of property would throw into the right scale of that balance which a wise mother has to hold in her hands.

[20] Ellis, *Wives of England*, pp.23, 39, 42.
[21] Ellis, *Wives of England*, pp.323, 137–8, 141, 79.
[22] Ellis, *Daughters of England* (London: Fisher, Son and Co, 1845), p.411

Loose, vague notions about mine and thine, about property in general, are always dangerous'.[23] Because of her inheritance of a particular model of the human subject, the preacher of family values and love shared much ground, even in her vision of family, with the nineteenth-century advocates of social and economic individualism.

The warmest of such advocates was Herbert Spencer, the most rigorous proponent of the atomic and egoistic conception of man, for whom the highest aim of humanity was to become conscious of the inevitability of deterministic process and the egoistic struggle for survival that is its universal principle. His Social Darwinism completely neglected both the appreciation of the innate interdependence and sociability of human nature on the one hand, and the rejection of nature as ultimate moral arbiter on the other, that an evolutionary perspective so obviously prompted.[24] He coined that notorious tautology 'the survival of the fittest', which captures so neatly the circularity, the emptiness and the surreptitiously objectified moralism of the politics of self-ownership. The universality and transcendence of his conception of the impulse to survive and evolve, on which he founded a whole metaphysics, prohibits any reflection on what makes us human.

Spencer's central principle was that 'Every man has freedom to do all that he will, provided he infringes not the equal freedom of every other man'. He opposed 'any arrangement which [might] prevent superiority from profiting by the rewards of superiority, or shield inferiority from the evils it entails'.[25] Inferiority meant inferiority in survival-strength, in whatever form. He proclaimed that 'inconvenience, suffering and death, are the penalties attached by nature to ignorance ...whoso thinks he can mend matters by dissociating ignorance and its penalties, lays claim to more than Divine wisdom, and more than Divine benevolence'.[26] Illnesses 'insofar as they do exist ...are among the penalties Nature has attached to ignorance and imbecility, and should not therefore be tampered with'.[27] With staggering confidence, and a characteristic disregard of the manifest fact of the matter,

---

[23] Ellis, *Education of the Heart*, pp.157–8

[24] The popular idea that there is something inherently individualist about Darwin has, of course, no foundation – if it had, it is not likely that Marx would have said that his theory 'in the field of natural history, provides the basis for our views' (Marx to Engels, 19 December 1860, in *Marx and Engels: The Collected Works*, 49 vols (London: Lawrence and Wishart, 1975–6), vol.41:232.

[25] Herbert Spencer, *Social Statics* (London, 1868), p.121, and *The Principles of Ethics* (London, 1881), v.i:189.

[26] Spencer, *Social Statics*, p.412

[27] Spencer, *Social Statics*, p.418.

he declares that 'Nature demands that every being shall be self-sufficing'.[28]

It is hard to see how a newborn baby could get through its first hours according to this ideology. However, Spencer attempted to make allowance for this powerful objection. Nature swerves from her lawful promotion of 'those shoulderings aside of the weak by the strong' only within the family, where her laws are reversed.

> Nature's modes of treatment inside the family group and outside the family group, are diametrically opposed to one another …the intrusion of either mode into the sphere of the other, would be fatal to the species.
> The radical distinction between family-ethics and State-ethics must be maintained …while generosity must be the essential principle of the one, justice must be the essential principle of the other …a rigorous maintenance of those normal relations among citizens under which each gets in return for his labour …as much as is proved to be its value by the demand for it: such return …as will enable him to thrive and rear his offspring in proportion to the superiorities which make him valuable to himself and others.[29]

This undefended distinction would seem extraordinary did it not reflect the actual practice of his time. However, the distinction is difficult to apply with consistency, and Spencer continually betrays it. In some places he allows the spirit of competition to invade the family. In 'What Knowledge is of Most Worth', for example, as Nancy Paxton observes, 'Spencer locates the "struggle for survival" …in the bosom of the family itself. Children, he explains, develop according to the same natural laws that operate in both the animal kingdom and in the laissez-faire world of human commerce'.[30] So, in terms of discipline, responsible parents should 'see that their children habitually experience the true consequences of their conduct – the natural reactions: neither warding them off, nor intensifying them, nor putting artificial consequences in place of them'.[31] One might have thought that the natural consequences of infant behaviour would be pretty disastrous. But the

---

[28] Spencer, *Social Statics*, p.414.
[29] Spencer, *Social Statics*, p.354, and *The Man Versus the State* (London, 1950), pp.80, 81.
[30] Herbert Spencer, 'What Knowledge is of Most Worth' in *Education, Intellectual, Moral and Physical* (London: G Mainwaring, 1861), Ch. 1; Nancy L Paxton, *George Eliot and Herbert Spencer* (Princeton and Oxford: Princeton University Press, 1991), p.73.
[31] Spencer, 'The Moral Discipline of Children', *British Quarterly Review* (1858–59) 364–90, 392.

family, insofar as it must function as a training ground for successful individualists, had, as Ellis had realized, to reflect as far as possible the spirit of the world outside.

In other places, Spencer anticipated the contrary danger that family-ethics might infect state-ethics. He was a paranoid opponent of anything tending towards paternalism. Early in his career he acknowledged that, according to his 'law of equal freedom' the 'rights of women must stand or fall with those of men'. Later, however, he became afraid that votes for women would be unlikely to foster 'the unhindered exercise of the faculties by each' which was the aim of the state. Their biological propensity for nurture and generosity, the natural sympathy for the weak which alone fits them to bring up children, might not after all slip from them as they left their home. In their voting, they would be likely to display 'a more general fostering of the worse at the expense of the better' which would retard the onward force of evolution.[32] His ideas on this point are closely in line with those of that hero of contemporary theory, Nietzsche, who wondered,

> are women able to be just at all, since they are so accustomed to loving, to at once taking sides for or against? ...they are less interested in causes, more interested in persons: if they are interested in a cause ...they at once become its vehement advocates and thereby spoil the purity of its influence. There is thus no little danger in entrusting politics or certain kinds of science (for example history) to them.[33]

Both these radical individualists share common ground with Sarah Ellis, who expressed her strong belief that women were unfitted for government by their innate familial virtues; 'the discord of Babel, or the heated elements of a volcano, could scarcely equal the confusion, the ebullition, and the universal tumult, that would follow the partial attention given to every separate complaint, the ready credence accorded to every separate story, and the prompt and unhesitating application of means, to affect at all times the most incompatible of ends' which would follow from the participation of women in government.[34] Women, these theorists fear, have not been told that nature has set up a bar between the family and civil society. The

32 Spencer, *Social Statics*, p.190, and *Principles of Ethics*, quoted in David Wiltshire, *The Social and Political Though of Herbert Spencer* (Oxford: Oxford University Press, 1978), p.115.
33 Friedrich Nietzsche, *Human, All too Human*, trans. RJ Hollingdale (Cambridge: Cambridge University Press, 1986), 7:416 p.154–5.
34 Ellis, *Wives of England*, p.72.

emotional and altruistic subjectivity of one half of the human race – on which the continuance and justification of the family depends – must be denied institutional expression for the sake of fostering the transcendent self-assertive essence of the other.

Liberal theory's supposedly objective picture of political society and the human subject is not in reality therefore a parsimonious depiction of basic human nature, but a reflection rather of the institutionalization and cultural prioritization of one particular principle, rational self-ownership, over others that are more congruent with a biological perspective on human subjectivity. Writers as diverse as Ellis and Spencer collude not only in confining non-self-assertive impulses within a very narrowly conceived domestic arena, taking it as read that not only are such impulses absent and, in any case, undesirable in the civil arena, but also in arguing that even within the family interdependence and emotion are secondary or marginal. Just as Victorian political discourse is characterized by the assertion of the absolute difference between the standards and impulses that govern family and those that govern the rest of society – an assertion that maintains a real material division – it is characterized also by a continual lapse into the recognition of a theoretical continuum between the two spheres. This recognition on the one hand challenges the necessity of that material division, and on the other hand prompts an effort to reassert the unity of experience through the degradation and concealment of domestic standards of behaviour and models of subjectivity at the expense of those assumed by public political discourse and the civil society it legitimates.

We are blinder to this last strategy than we are to the ideology of separate spheres, because it is the strategy that continues to shape our own consciousness. The notion of separate spheres is but one phase in the grand sweep of the marginalization, depreciation, and concealment of affective and interpersonal subjectivity and dependencies that has led to the establishment of our current ideologies of more or less unqualified individualism, and the complete theoretical abandonment of any fleshed-out picture of human nature.

vi. Human nature and the critique of liberalism

In *On the Jewish Question*, Marx provided what remains the most telling critique of the thin conception of human subjectivity upon which liberal political justice is founded. First, he pointed out, the very structures of liberal justice betray the elusiveness of the freedom, independence and equality of the individual. To declare, for instance, that each man is equal in the eyes of the State regardless of his economic status, is not to secure equality but rather to presume inequality. There will still be material inequalities that limit the options of individuals, but the State, by refusing to recognize them politically, washes its hands of them. But secondly, and even more profoundly, Marx observed that liberal rights are primarily rights of separation:

> None of the so-called rights of man ...go beyond egoistic man ...an individual withdrawn into himself, into the confines of his private interests and private caprice, and separated from the community ...he is far from being conceived as a species being; on the contrary, species-life itself, society, appears as a framework external to the individuals, as a restriction of their original independence ...the sphere in which man acts as a communal being is degraded to a level below the sphere in which he acts as a partial being ...it is not man as a *citoyen*, but man as *bourgeois* who is considered to be the *essential* and *true* man.[35]

In taking individual rights and impartial justice as ends in themselves, liberal theory begs the question, assuming that self-assertion and consequent conflicts of interest form both the basis and the highest potential of human society. The 'society of free competition' protected by liberal justice and universalized by political economy, is an ideal 'appropriate to their notion of human nature', and to no other.[36]

Marx's objection was not to the fact that liberal political discourse, and political economy likewise, make assumptions about human subjectivity, but that they pretend not to, and that the assumptions they make are politically strategic, demonstrably false, and morally repugnant. We can trace in Marx, as Elster, Creaven and numerous others have demonstrated, a conception of humanity as a species set apart by a particular combination of characteristics – sociability, self-consciousness, intentionality, language, tool making and co-operation.[37] To trace the dynamic of human mastery of material resources, of cultural coherence, disruption and control – or to hypothesize, as we like to do, such complex cultural phenomena as the circulation of power and its covert operations through systems of signs – simply demands that on some level we are conscious that human subjects are not sticks or stones, and that we assume something about what they are like. As Marx

---

35   Karl Marx, *On the Jewish Question* (1843), in *Collected Works*, V:3:164.

36   Marx, *Grundrisse* (1857) (Harmondsworth: Penguin, 1973), p.83

37   Sean Creaven, *Marxism and Realism* (London: Routledge, 2000), John Elster, *Making Sense of Marx* (Cambridge: Cambridge University Press, 1985).

puts it, 'the first premise of all human history is, of course, the existence of living human individuals. Thus the first fact to be established is the physical organization of these individuals and their consequent relation to the rest of nature ...all historical writing must set out from these natural bases'.[38]

Geras points out that for Marx 'essential human needs fulfil not just a theoretical function' but also, 'as befits Marx's revolutionary standpoint ...possess an overtly practical implication ...serving as a norm of judgment and of action' in that 'the necessity of social revolution is justified in the light of basic human needs'.[39] The search for 'a really human morality' depends upon assumptions about what humans need for a good life. As Marx commented in his critique of the incomplete foundations of Benthamite utilitarianism, 'to know what is useful for a dog, one must study dog-nature'.[40] Without a filled-out vision of human nature and subjectivity, there can be, as for Hobbes, 'no other goal, nor other garland, but being foremost'.[41] The liberal conception of the subject and the scheme of self-owning rights founded upon it, are alienated abstractions, mere contractarian schemes, disguising their normative judgements as objective descriptions of the way human subjects and society are and must be. Human progress demands that they be replaced by a more substantive consideration of our distinctively human needs, capacities and perspectives, not least of which are the sociability and self-consciousness that allow us to build upon and modify our present nature through culture. Marx's conceives socialism precisely as a 'fully developed humanism', which 'equals naturalism'.[42]

Geras has demonstrated conclusively that Althusser's famous contention, now the foundation stone of theory, that Marx turned his back on the idea of human nature in 1845 is simply unsupportable.[43] However, taking themselves to be building upon a basic and incontrovertible materialist premise, critics such as Steven Greenblatt and Catherine Gallagher have

---

[38] Marx, *The German Ideology* (1845), *Works* vol.5, I:2:31.

[39] N. Geras, *Marx and Human Nature* (London: Verso/New Left Books, c1983), p.70.

[40] Marx, *Capital*, V.35:605.

[41] Thomas Hobbes, *Element of Law Natural & Politic* (Cambridge: Cambridge University Press, 1928), I.9.21.

[42] Marx, *Works*, 3:296

[43] Geras's is the most concerted of the several attempts to explode the myth of Marx's anti-essentialism, which is supported only, as he demonstrates, by a highly contentious reading of one sentence in the *Thesis on Feuerbach*, and is refuted by innumerable other passages from Marx's later works. See also Michael Evans, *Karl Marx* (London 1975), p.53, Helmut Fleischer, *Marxism and History* (London 1973), pp.25–6, 46, John McMurty, *The Structure of Marx's World View* (Princeton 1978), pp.19–37.

pronounced as the primary axiom of new-historicism the principle that humanity is 'a species that is inherently – that is, abstracted from any particular historical manifestation of its being – without qualities'.[44] Taken literally, such a statement is, as Collier points out, 'meaningless outside the context of idealism'.[45] It relies for its plausibility on the same bracketing off of basic material human needs and impulses and their stubborn constancy that is so characteristic of liberal individualist ideology. Gallagher and Greenblatt's stance blinds them and their tradition to the fact that the refusal to recognise human needs, constraints and capacities can play a political part every bit as invidious as the most extremely formulated biologism or essentialism. It was precisely through a materialist consideration of man as a distinctive kind of subject with given needs and potentials that Marx rejected the premises that unite Victorian liberals and political economists and our own contemporary theorists in dismissing a thick concept of the subject in favour of abstractions like 'reason' and 'self-ownership' or 'language' and 'power'.

In rejecting this aspect of Marx, literary critics have clung to precisely the strands of timidity and concession that mark him as constrained by his historical moment. It is true that at some moments Marx, and still more often Marxism, seem, like political economy, to come close to the abandonment of all other evaluative/descriptive frameworks but that of mechanical forward motion. The only major theoretical difference between Marxism of this school and Spencer, is one of forecast. As Cohen argues, if Marxists have not consciously accepted the principle of self-ownership, they have often at least 'failed frontally to oppose it', in the way that might have been suggested by the second stage of Marx's early critique.[46] The very

---

[44]   Gallagher and Greenblatt, *New Historicism*, p.5. To save them from the most manifest absurdities of this view, we might charitably assume that they mean to advance some version of the argument that human nature, though it does exist, is not 'ontologically distinct', cannot be found or studied in its pure form, and therefore may as well be ignored. However, as Geras argues (p.115), this argument is hardly less untenable. Half the objects of our intellectual attention are not 'ontologically distinct' in that strong sense (e.g. gravity, relations of production, light), and yet to exclude them from consideration on that account would be impossible. The argument might work as an objection to a metaphysical, Hegelian-style consideration of the Essence of Man, but is no argument against building a materialist notion of human nature into political philosophy.

[45]   Andrew Collier, 'Truth and Practice', *Radical Philosophy* 5 (Summer 1973), 16.

[46]   GA Cohen, *Self-ownership, Freedom and Equality* (Cambridge: Cambridge University Press, 1995), p.119. For instance, the classical Marxist critique of capitalist exploitation relies on taking self-ownership as a given, revealing as it does an

standards, partly inherited from Marx, by which we distinguish 'idealist' from 'materialist' perspectives on human affairs, are themselves coloured by loaded classical liberal assumptions about human nature. Suspicion of the role of sympathy and impassioned social consciousness (as opposed to, or in addition to class struggle) as solutions to social and interpersonal conflicts, and the dismissal of such attitudes as mere social constructions incapable of transcending their historical moment and set up to block or occlude 'genuine' change, participate in precisely the naturalization of self-owning, self-asserting individualism as 'before' nature that was underway in the mid-nineteenth century, and that was under debate in the domestic novel. What we may call post-Marxist criticism has been particularly consistent in its exorcising of any faith in any form of human self-determination. It leaves us exactly where social Darwinism and political economy left us – in cynical/reverential prostration before the mechanical laws of nature, before which subjects must abandon all pretence of the capacity to be motivated by distinctively human feelings and value judgements.

vii. Double binds

...if she swims she's a witch, and if she's drowned ...a poor silly old woman.   GEORGE ELIOT, *The Mill on the Floss*

The family continues to exist within a capitalist system run according to principles inimical to it because of the fact that men do not, in fact, sprout like mushrooms from the ground. Rather men are produced, to be exact, by female labour, continue helpless and beholden to others for life for many years, and finally become adults who rely on others for the preservation of their lives in sickness, the preservation of their comfort and sanity in health, and for the value of their lives always. Considering the huge amounts of (predominantly female) labour 'mixed' in the thriving individual, it seems possible that his very soul is not his own. Independent self-ownership, instead of being the paradigmatic human state that allows of anomalies only to further itself, seems in this light reduced to a narrow band of economic competition propped up on either side by the family and the state. The intimate relations of family, the hidden web of vegetative mycelia beneath

---

appropriation of a proportion of the fruits of the worker's labour, theirs by right *according to the principle of self-ownership*. The deduction of tax for the maintenance of those who cannot work would be just as much a matter of exploitation. Thus the theory of exploitation works as a critique of the contradictions of bourgeois ideology, but does nothing to move us beyond that ideology.

the economically fruiting body, suggest that the individual independence that liberal politics defends as a basic right is a chimera.

Because of their failure to follow up the critique of self-ownership and the investigation of human nature, Marxists have been less attentive to the particular determinate material conditions of human reproduction than they might have been. Thus, in the course of an intelligent passage on the nineteenth-century family, Eric Hobsbawm encounters a conundrum to which he can find no answer:

> [The] connections ...between nineteenth-century family structure and bourgeois society remain obscure ...Why should a society dedicated to an economy of profit-making competitive enterprise, to the efforts of the isolated individual, to equality of rights and opportunities and freedom, rest on an institution which so totally denied all of these?[47]

The most obvious answer to this question is the observation that it would be impossible to have sufficient numbers of children painfully born, to have those children successfully reared, and to preserve the mental and physical health of their parents, if there were no arena ungoverned by the principles of independence, competition and equal rights, to accommodate 'personal dependence'. As Susan Moller Okin points out, 'the fact that human beings are born helpless infants, not the supposed autonomous actors who populate political theories, is obscured by the implicit assumption of gendered families, operating outside the scope of political theories'.[48] Every society must find some place for the interdependencies accommodated by family, and every society depends for its very existence upon the sympathetic and altruistic subjective attitudes that these interdependencies embody. These human characteristics are not merely a convenient and optional ideological device but rather a precondition for human existence.

One might have thought that feminism criticism would be alert to such considerations. But feminism has inherited an ambiguous relation to the principle of self-ownership. Because of this rather intimate ambiguity, the likes of George Eliot, Mrs Gaskell, and many other Victorian writers who set themselves resolutely against this principle pose something of a difficulty for feminist criticism.

For instance, any survey of the critical assessment of Eliot's treatment of gender, from Zelda Austen in 1976, through Elaine Showalter in 1980, to

---

[47] Eric Hobsbawm, *The Age of Capital* (1975) (reprinted London: Abacus, 2000), p.278

[48] Susan Moller Okin, 'Gender, the Public, and the Private', in Anne Phillips (ed.) *Feminism and Politics*, (Oxford: Oxford University Press, 1998), pp.116–41, p.121.

Kate Flint in 2001, starts by registering the insistent awareness amongst feminist critics of Eliot's failure to portray, celebrate or point the way for 'strong, successful women striking out on their own'.[49] By contrast, all Charlotte Brontë's novels, to take an example of a novelist of contrasting temper, are seen to exhibit notable examples of strong, successful women striking out (at least temporarily) on their own. For this reason Brontë's novels, and *Jane Eyre* in particular, are to some extent off the feminist hook, but are charged by Marxist critics with being mouth-pieces of bourgeois individualism, with its moral emphasis on strength and independence.[50] Here we see the double bind that nineteenth-century ideology presents for both the female Victorian novelist and the feminist critic. The choice seems between sympathy and altruism conservatively contained, on the one hand, or callous individualism, on the other.

In a social context in which it was more or less assumed that women were owned by others, it was in a way, of course, progressive for women to assert principles of self-ownership and independence. In the next chapter, I will examine in the work of Dinah Craik the attitudes towards political, public and family relations that correlate with the assertion of a 'standard of abstract right, including manhood and womanhood' 'the first of [the] common laws, or common duties' of which is 'self dependence'. Craik asserts that '"Heaven helps those who help themselves"', the independent type of woman who 'never was and never will be indebted to any one, except for love while she lives, and for a grave when she dies'.[51] But in this paradigmatic bracketing off of love and mortality, and thus of the *needs* of emotionally and physically vulnerable social human animals, she re-asserts the gendered bifurcation and prioritizing of competitive, productive, and self-asserting work over the personal, private, altruistic reproductive labour that enables it, so ensuring that demand for self-assertion is not disrupted or qualified.

Both the social subjection of women and their physical difference, manifested in comparative physical weakness, physical interrelation with

---

[49] Zelda Austen, 'Why Feminist Critics are Angry with George Eliot', *College English* 37 (1976), 549–61; Elaine Showalter, 'The Greening of Sister George', *Nineteenth-Century Fiction* 35 (1980), 292–311; Kate Flint, 'George Eliot and Gender' in *The Cambridge Companion to George Eliot* (Cambridge: Cambridge University Press, 2001), pp.159–80, p.160.

[50] Terry Eagleton, *Myths of Power: A Marxist Study of the Brontës* (London and New York: Macmillan, 1975).

[51] Dinah Mulock Craik, *A Woman's Thoughts about Woman* (1858), ed. Elaine Showalter (New York: New York University Press, 1995), pp.73, 75.

their offspring, and their consignment to the devalued sphere of non-productive, interpersonal 'reproductive' labour, makes the embrace of the ideology of self-ownership problematic on their part. In this light we should treat with caution the idea, voiced by Flint, that Eliot's ideas on gender simply lack 'boldness', in order to do justice to the resistance of women who are unwilling to heroise or idealize 'strong, successful' women *or* men 'striking out on their own'.[52] We should not leap to Shuttleworth's conclusion that the texts of Eliot and others like her do no more than 'reproduce, without challenge, some of the most deeply engrained ideological notions of gender of the age'.[53] From the right perspective, we will see that the domestic focus in Victorian fiction is the arena for a profound and desperate struggle over the nature of humans and their society, and over the proper scope of interdependence, sympathy and affective relations.

It is not easy to establish such a perspective. The feminism we have inherited was born with capitalism, and with the Protestant, more especially Puritan, ethic that nourished it. The profile of the bourgeois individual and the conception of human subjectivity and society that ground it are hallmarks of its original period of currency, and have ever marked one side of the revolutionary feminist coin. JS Mill, as the defender of women's rights on the one hand, and individual liberty on the other, embodied the link.

Despite its extraordinary mastery, Mill's radical and forward-looking defence of women's rights in *The Subjection of Women* is open to some of the criticisms that Marx levels at similar arguments for the legal emancipation of the Jews. Mill argues that women's position is an anomaly in a modern world, the 'peculiar character' of which is captured by the fact 'that human beings are no longer born to their place in life …but are free to employ their faculties …to achieve the lot which may appear to them most desirable'.[54] As the *Anthropological Review* remarked with outrage, Mill and his liberal contemporaries 'cannot help claiming the suffrage for the Negro – and the woman. Such conclusions are the inevitable results of the premises whence he started'. For the *Anthropological Review*, and many of Mill's contemporaries, rights for women were the 'reductio ad absurdum' of liberalism.[55] Mill

---

[52] Flint, 'Eliot and Gender', p.160.

[53] Sally Shuttleworth, Critical Commentary in *The Mill on the Floss* (London: Routledge, 1991), p.507.

[54] JS Mill, *The Subjection of Women* (1869), in *Collected Works of John Stuart Mill*, ed. John M. Robson, 33 vols (Toronto: University of Toronto Press, 1963–91), XXI:261–340, 272–3.

[55] *Anthropological Review* IV (1866), 115.

argues that, in the case of women as in all other cases, a choice of lifestyle
should be left 'to the unfettered choice of the individual'.

However, in seeking to talk down the potential consequences of such a
change for the sake of his conservative interlocutors, Mill comes close to
turning Marx's arguments against himself. The case of women may be like
that of apprentices – 'even the laws which required that workmen should
serve an apprenticeship, have in this country been repealed: there being
ample assurance that in all cases in which an apprenticeship is necessary, its
necessity will suffice to enforce it'.[56] Might it not be that being a man
remains a practical 'necessity' for pre-eminence in the economic or political
realm, despite equal legal access? Mill concedes that while all 'dignities and
social advantages are [*legally*] open to the whole male sex', 'many indeed are
only attainable by wealth …the difficulties, to the majority, are indeed
insuperable'.[57] As Marx argues, legal equality is in fact acquiescence in
actual inequality. Bearing in mind 'the great vitality and durability of
institutions which place right on the side of might', of which Mill is so well
aware, and 'how the good as well as the bad propensities and sentiments of
those who have power in their hands, become identified with retaining it',
the assertion that 'nothing more is needed for the complete removal' of
men's power over women than that 'wives should have the same rights, and
should receive the protection of the law in the same manner, as all other
persons', seems rather unreasonably optimistic.[58]

Mill denies that 'any one knows, or can know, the nature of the two sexes'
in the context of unequal social conditions, averring the lack of present
evidence that 'there is any difference, much more what the difference is,
between the two sexes considered as moral and rational beings'. His stress
on the idea that 'the true virtue of human beings is fitness to live together *as
equals*' is characteristic, and implies not only an equality of condition but also
an identity of natural power.[59] If women are to benefit from individual
rights, it must, according to the liberal contractarian model, be on the
grounds of their equal strength of self-assertion.

But, as Mill himself acknowledges, the social inequality of the sexes came
about only because there is no such identity in natural independent powers.
Through the limits of independence placed on her by her reproductive role,
as well as the comparative disadvantage of having a smaller body, woman

---

56 Mill, *Subjection of Women*, p.273.
57 Mill, *Subjection of Women*, p.274–5.
58 Mill, *Subjection of Women*, p.265, and *On Liberty*, in *Collected Works*, XVIII:213–310,
    p.301.
59 Mill, 'Subjection of Women', pp.276, 277, 294, my italics.

herself seems to slide within the liberal scheme towards the position of the right-less animal described by Hume.[60] Mill does not discuss political accommodation for physical differences between the sexes, confining himself to the consideration of more abstract 'moral and intellectual' equality.

While the feminist movement, which was given a shove by Mill in his essay, and which has come down little changed to our own time, is a tribute to the benefits of a struggle for rights, it is also a testimony to the limits of what such a struggle, on such terms, can achieve. As Christine DiStefano observes, 'in Mill's hands, women are dealt with in the terms of exceptional and masculine individualism …The "price" of liberal feminist liberation is transsexualism. Women must be disembodied, desexed, degendered, and made over into the image of the middle class and upper class men if they are to benefit from the promise of rational liberalism'.[61] The point is, of course, that women are disembodied and desexed only rhetorically, while a material and subjective reality of difference persists unrecognized.

Human biology inevitably challenges the scope of liberal rights, and the liberal picture of human subjectivity, and it is women who feel the tension most acutely. As Germaine Greer writes

> In order to compete with men Western woman has joined the masculine hierarchy and cultivated a masculine sense of self. The acknowledgement of her pregnancy means that she must step down from all that …what happens to her …can have convulsive effects upon what she has come to think of as unalterable, her personality. In exchange for her settled self-image she has a body which inexorably goes about its own business, including biochemical changes in the brain. The period following the birth of a child has been called the fourth trimester; mother and child remain attached as it were by an invisible unbiblical cord. A mother is no longer self-sufficient but at the mercy of the child's indomitable love and egotism.[62]

Families, and the mother-child relationship that is at their core, threaten to

---

[60] It is for something like this reason, I suppose, that in some feminist (and other) utopias, babies are all produced by test tube. There is something self-contradictory about this dream – if such a situation could really be brought about, there is nothing in the principle of self-ownership, to which such fantasies cater, that could motivate the perpetuation of human life anyway.

[61] Christine DiStefano, *Configurations of Masculinity* (Ithaca: Cornell University Press, 1991), pp.175–6.

[62] Germaine Greer, *Sex and Destiny* (Reading: Picador, 1985), p.12.

deconstruct the very notion of the individuated, independent, egoistic persons that populate political theory.

The family also accommodates other unequal alignments of power. It is the support not only of the infant but also of the sick man. In his weakness, do his rights, and therefore his humanity, fall from him? The family behind every bourgeois individual is a realm in which, though there is no equality of strength for self-assertion, there is duty, society, humanity and value. Whereas contract-based theories of rights privilege 'the duties which people owe each other *merely as thinkers*', and as self-interested thinkers at that, working from a metaphysical conception of the rational self-identical Man, the family asserts 'the laws of humanity', the partial feelings characteristic of human social animals – sympathy, sentiment and affection.[63]

Nineteenth-century women and their champions in fiction were faced with a difficult choice. While liberalism seemed to offer immediate advantages, female domesticity and biology provided a perspective from which the contradictions at the heart and the obstacles at the frontier of liberal rights were acutely visible. But any acknowledgement of this alternative perspective could be used to argue for women's 'natural' subordination as disenfranchized and unpaid domestic labourers, and to reinforce the dualistic divide between the standards of home and those of civil and political society.

viii. Feminism and nature?

There is still a widespread suspicion that any consideration of human subjectivity and biology that undermines the ideal of female independence implies a repressive or defeatist biological determinism. George Eliot was at pains to contest this conclusion. Like Marx, she consciously grappled with the relation of man to the rest of the world, recognizing that this relation is characterized by both continuity and difference. Rejecting both idealism and mechanistic materialism, she attempted to maintain a consciousness of material givens, on the one hand, and the potential for historical change, on the other. Her famous letter to John Morley (more often cited and ridiculed than analysed or carefully considered) was written to emphasize her complete rejection of the 'pitiable fallacy' of the 'intention of Nature' argument, which made biological difference between the sexes justification for the oppression of women. She acknowledged, like Mill, that the question of the extent of the biological difference between the sexes is an open

---

[63] Midgley, p.38.

question. Unlike him, she regarded the biological differences *not* in doubt as fit objects of political consciousness.

Where Marx draws attention to the economic, Eliot draws attention to the biological reality concealed behind the ideal of a political society of independent and rational equals. She clarifies her position as follows: 'as a fact of mere zoological evolution, woman seems to me to have the worse share in existence. But *for that very reason* I would the more contend that in the moral evolution we have "an art which does mend nature"'.[64] She is aware that according to natural laws, some disadvantages *are* laid at women's doors as social competitors. Their 'zoological' bond to their children, through pregnancy and until weaning, and perhaps beyond through instinct, undermines their independence; they are unaccommodated by a system designed for atoms.

But crucially, while she sees the need to take account of the givens of human nature, Eliot rejects these as in themselves arbiters of morality. To accept a clear-eyed and rounded consideration of human nature as a factor in establishing norms of human behaviour does not mean abandoning oneself to every natural distinction and impulse.[65] A feeling, human self-consciousness, embodied in 'moral evolution', requires an acknowledgement of biology but ensures that such an acknowledgement will have only rationally and sympathetically – that is, *humanly* – mediated implications.

A naturalization of ethics with reference to biology comes with a built-in self-reflexiveness, because social self-consciousness and emotion are also natural. Eliot's most explicit statement of this idea comes in her alterations to Lewes's volume on psychology in *Problems of Life and Mind*, in which she traces the modification of the basic animal 'sense of dependence on individual being or other-selves which lies implicit in the sexual and parental relation' through the 'enlargement of the mental range in the human being, and under the influence of the social medium which raises emotions into sentiments'.[66] The particular characteristics of our common nature, given due consideration, and viewed through the prism of our sympathetic, socialized self-conscious intelligence, will rule out the impoverished morality

---

[64]   Eliot to John Morley, 14 May 1867, *Letters* IV:364–5, my itals.

[65]   It is only with the assumption of a laissez faire attitude towards the drives of desire (of which, indeed, we do sometimes see a bizarre trace in post-Freud-and-Nietzschean theorizing), that a view of social possibility that takes into account the distinctiveness of the human seems dangerous.

[66]   Lewes, *Problems of Life and Mind* III.xi.158, pp.386–7, with Eliot's editorial additions (for detail of which, see KK Collins, 'GH Lewes Revised: George Eliot and the Moral Sense', *Victorian Studies* 21 (1978), pp.463–92).

of liberal individualism, and provide ground for a truer and better moral and social order.

Eliot insists that whatever might be discovered about the difference of the sexes should have no normative bearing, except – and the exception is significant – in one respect: insofar as it directs our efforts towards a negation of what we judge to be biological and social evils (such as selfishness) and towards a perpetuation of biological and social virtues, such as sympathy and altruism.[67] Such judgements, for Eliot, can only be founded upon a feeling consciousness of what we *are*, biologically and socially. She withheld her enthusiasm from systems that had at their core an implicit belief in the autonomy of the individual and/or the beneficent normativity of the mechanical workings of the material world of which humanity is just another part. Instead, like Marx, she constructed her morality from an acknowledgement of the human situation as a struggle between determinate circumstances, human needs, and a range of human capacities, particularly sympathy and self-consciousness, that endow us with unique power to transform those circumstances to meet those needs.

Eliot alludes to the natural lottery as a recalcitrant source of inequality. For her, the highest aim of society should be not only to reward individual merit, but also to aid weakness; not just to recognize innate equality but to give natural inequality social remedy, not just to reward talent and strength, but also to compensate weakness, not only to respect natural rights and avoid interference, but to cultivate 'regenerating tenderness' and sympathy. She argues for a society which is not only just but sympathetic and loving: 'It is the function of love in the largest sense, to mitigate the harshness of all fatalities' in striving for 'as near an approach to equivalence of good for women and for man as can be secured by the effort of growing moral force to lighten the pressure of hard non-moral outward conditions'.[68]

---

[67] As I suggested in the previous chapter, here Eliot is closely in line with the thinking of Auguste Comte, who, as TR Wright shows, argued that 'morality ...was a matter of "compressing egoism" and "developing altruism", developing the personal instincts and channelling them in useful directions' *Religion of Humanity*, p.31. I deal further with this connection below. The picture I give of Eliot's morality and social theory bears a very close resemblance, in many respects, to Comtean Positivism: how much this is a matter of direct influence, and how much of influences in common, it is hard to say. I regard my own placement of Eliot's thought in the wider context of a struggle over the consolidation of contractarian political theory and liberal individualism as consonant, rather than in any sense in tension, with Wright's convincing and wide-ranging demonstration of Comte's influence on Eliot.

[68] Eliot to Morley, *Letters*, IV:364.

ix. Family resemblances

We see here how far Eliot differs from her friend Herbert Spencer in maintaining the conception of the human as both continuous with the natural world and its immutable laws, and capable of conscious reflection and reaction upon those laws. She was aware of her friend's danger of falling into an 'enervating fatalism', which, as Wiltshire puts it 'could rob human betterment of its motive force'.[69]

The conundrum of human freedom, which plays its part in Eliot's conception of the family (which I explore in the final chapter), is central not only to Eliot's own fiction but also to her age. Mill recalls in his autobiography how he struggled with it, feeling 'as if I was scientifically proved to be the helpless slave of antecedent circumstances'.[70] It is a conundrum we have inherited, and which is currently being debated in a number of areas, not least in cultural studies, with its problematic theories of subversion and containment. In allowing ourselves to be sucked once more into this difficulty, we seem to forget that mechanistic social determinism is itself a bourgeois dogma. The notion of social determinism is theoretically or politically productive only when it is qualified; we noted such a sophisticated qualification in Dickens, and will come across it again. Both Mill and Eliot found alternatives to stultifying notions of determinism through their acquaintance with the French socialism that also influenced Marx. Eliot was exposed to these ideas particularly via August Comte, who placed discrimination between phenomena that are inevitable and those that are historically determined, and consciousness of their interaction, at the centre of his philosophy.

The richness of his theory in this regard allowed Comte to argue forcefully against the atomic and mechanical conception of human nature and of society. Like Eliot, he saw rational reflection on our own species-nature as a necessary shaper of our natural virtues, 'scientific study of the relation which each individual bears to the whole race is a continual stimulus to social sympathy'.[71] There is also a family resemblance between his ideas and those of Marx. Cooperation, for Comte as for Marx, was not only desirable but absolutely unavoidable; 'The man who dares to think himself independent of others, either in feelings, thoughts, or actions, cannot even put the blasphemous conception into words without immediate self-

---

[69] Eliot, quoted in Wiltshire, p.40.
[70] Mill, *An Autobiography* (London: 1879), p.168–9.
[71] Auguste Comte, *System of Positive Polity*, trans. JH Bridges and others, 4 vols, (London: 1875–7), I:177.

contradiction, since the very language he uses in not his own. The profoundest thinker cannot by himself form the simplest language', said Comte; 'Production by an isolated individual outside society …is as much of an absurdity as is the development of human language without human beings living together and talking to each other', echoed Marx, three years later.[72]

It may have been from Comte also that Eliot derived her insistence on the natural, sentimental foundations of morality. His Positive Religion, as Wright demonstrates, 'founds it hopes on benevolent human instinct'. In a passage (quoted by Wright) from *The Catechism of Positive Religion*, Comte thus opposes positivist virtue to Christian morality 'which proclaims that the benevolent sentiments are foreign to our natures'.[73] This emphasis also placed positivism in diametric opposition to the liberal individualist conception of human nature as we have seen it exemplified in Ellis and Spencer.

Free of liberal baggage, Comte was able to dispense with the radical distinction between family and society. As Wright argues, for Comte 'Domestic life is …a preparation for social life …The distinction between private and public is abolished: work and wealth become social responsibilities, open to the moral supervision of public opinion'. The family was the natural school of the most advanced social behaviour, and Comte's ideal society would be founded on the extension to the whole of society of the principles cultivated within it. As 'the first and smallest community to which everyone belonged', the family 'played a crucial role in the Positivist development of the sympathies'.[74]

However, Comte's prescriptions for the activity of women, like so much of the rest of the details of his scheme, were by no means as free of conservative bias and as faithful to his positivist principles as he seemed to imagine. Nevertheless, although, as Wright demonstrates, George Eliot's support for his views was rather equivocal, she recognized the value of the kind of extended vision of sympathetic familial relationships of which his dogmatic insistence on a particular pattern of gender roles was a corruption.

---

[72] Comte, I:177–8, Marx, *Grundrisse* p.84.

[73] TR Wright, *Religion of Humanity*, p.27.

[74] TR Wright, *Religion of Humanity*, pp.29, 31. Wright also tells us, in demonstration of the connection between Comte's and Eliot's views on this subject, that the latter copied into two different notebooks a passage from the English translation of the *Système* about solidarity with Humanity as an extension of family feeling (p.180).

x. Feminism and domesticity

It is difficult, from a contemporary feminist perspective, to appreciate even the partial appeal of Comte in the face of the manifest conservatism of some of his views, for if essentialism is one of our current bêtes noires, domesticity, family life itself, is the other. Feminism has understandably tended to view domestic labour according to the standards of the period of its own birth. In the nineteenth century, the imperative of expanding capitalism dictated an ideology in which domestic labour and relations were considered at best secondary and at worst degrading. Only such an ideology could expand the productive labour force, control and delimit its bodily indulgences, private activities, and pleasures, and guarantee that it remain flexible and unconstrained by any logic save that of the market. Tilly and Scott argue against the idea that

> 'woman's proper place', with its connotations of complete economic dependency and idealised femininity is a traditional value. In fact it is a rather recently accepted middle class value not at all inconsistent with notions of 'the rights and responsibilities of the individual'. The hierarchical division of labour within the family which assigned the husband the role of breadwinner and the wife the role of domestic manager and moral guardian emerged only in the nineteenth century.[75]

They demonstrate that women held important authoritative and economic roles from within the home in earlier stages of society. It is only with the nineteenth century's radical contraction of the family, its radical separation of family from society at large, and its increasing tendency to measure achievement in economic and competitive terms, that a role centred within the family becomes oppressive for man or for woman.

This argument radically undermines the popular account of the progress of women outlined by Goode: 'the crucial crystallising variable – i.e., the necessary but not sufficient cause of the betterment of the Western woman's position – was *ideological*: the gradual, logical, philosophical extension to women of originally Protestant notions about the rights and responsibilities of the *individual* undermined the traditional idea of "woman's proper place"',

---

[75] Joan W Scott and Louise Tilly, 'Women's Work and the Family in Nineteenth Century Europe', in CE Rosenberg (ed.), *The Family in History* (Philadelphia: University of Pennsylvania Press, 1975), pp.145–78, p.151.

within the family, that is.[76] In fact, the demeaned and separatist conception of 'woman's proper place' was a stage in the process of marginalizing and making invisible domestic labour, intimate relations and feelings themselves. As Scott and Tilly point out, there was no correlation whatever between agitation and legislation for the extension of women's rights, and the actual number of women at work dictated by the market. Women went out to work because of changes brought about by a structural and economic marginalization of labour based around the cohesive family group, rather than because society learnt to respect their autonomy. Any linking of these two developments is pure rationalization.

The acceptance of the marginalization and devaluation of reproductive domestic labour is complicit in capitalism's self-serving vision of man as a rational independent spirit without bodily or emotional dependencies; a vision under construction, and contestation, in the mid-Victorian period. Margaret Homans speaks bitterly of the way George Eliot 'humiliatingly and sentimentally dwells upon Dinah [Morris]'s obsession with housework', revealing Dinah's degrading emotional investment in 'domestic servitude', and how she adds insult to injury by having Adam Bede join in, while scandalously depriving us, on the other hand, of any celebration of Maggie Tulliver's work as a seamstress.[77] In speaking so, Homans is guilty not only of an anachronism, but also of reproducing the fetishistic attribution of worth to alienated public productive work at the expense of reproductive domestic labour and the feelings which go with it (demoted to the status of humiliating drudgery and shallow illusion), that was contested in the mid-nineteenth-century novel.

We should not assume that nineteenth-century authors who value the domestic are opposed to or uninterested in 'the betterment of woman's position'. As we shall see, for Charlotte Yonge and for Eliot, as for other female novelists, the boldest path seemed not to reject the feminine feelings and values of the domestic sphere, but to combat the debasement of such feelings and values and their restriction to the home. They were aware of the danger that 'the proposal that we extend the norms of the public sphere into the private sphere will not ...extend the norms of justice and fairness to the domestic. It will actually extend the norms of instrumental power relations into a sphere that still manages to operate according to other, more

---

[76] William Goode, *World Revolution and Family Patterns* (London: Collier-Macmillan, 1963), p.56

[77] Margaret Homans, 'Dinah's Blush, Maggie's Arm: Class, Gender and Sexuality in George Eliot's Early Novels', *Victorian Studies* 36 (1993), 155–78, 164.

moral, norms'.[78] Domestic fiction serves, above all, as a medium for the exploration of non-instrumental norms and modes of subjectivity.

Novelists, above all, show that political argument is inevitably linked to some conception of what humans are – whether that conception be an idealist vision of a rational and transcendent intelligence, or a materialist one of a needy, working, feeling and intending body. And the domestic conventions of the fiction I will examine in the next chapters allow, as do the parameters of no other discourse, for an examination of this question. Only in domestic fiction do the gloves come off as the contest over human nature and subjectivity, which is at the back of all political debate, reveals itself for what it really is. Imaginative pictures of human beings in their most basic social groupings vie with one another in a struggle to determine the starting point of political existence.

The notion of the separate domestic sphere, and the focus on biological roles that went with it, was little more than a quibble, a token concession in the argument for individualism. But an examination of the kind of objections that this quibble sought to meet, the kind of activities it attempted to maintain through a period of transition, may remind us of problems attendant upon individualism that we might have forgotten. Poovey, and others who follow her line, are in danger of rejecting the Victorian quibble only to swallow the central argument, to whose fallaciousness the quibble might provide the key. The private realm of the individual, the touch-stone and motivation of liberal thought, derives both its material possibility and many of its concrete pleasures, its value, from family life conducted according to principles and attitudes inimical to its own. In dismissing domestic fiction as no more than an ideological manifestation of a double standard, we avoid precisely the confrontation with the choice of standards to which it was an inconclusive, though suggestive, response.

If the mother's relation to her baby sets the limits to an individualist rights-based social ethic, it embodies a different model: the unforced and yet unalienable duty of nurture by the stronger of the weaker, carrying with it no taint of humiliation to the nurtured or of burden to the nurturer. The ethics of sympathy and 'altruism', a word coined, as TR Wright points out, by GH Lewes in an essay on Comte's positivism,[79] cannot be considered without an estimation of their relation to the struggle over the establishment of an individualist ideological hegemony as it was articulated with reference to the family.

---

[78]   Judith Squires, on the feminist theory of Jean Bethke Elshtain, in *Gender in Political Theory* (Cambridge: Polity, 2000), p.49.
[79]   TR Wright, *Religion of Humanity*, p.56.

CHAPTER 4

The Personal, the Political and the Human, Part II: Which Family Values?

Nancy Armstrong, in *Desire and Domestic Fiction* (OUP, 1987), and Catherine Gallagher, in *The Industrial Reformation of Fiction* (University of Chicago Press, 1985), examine the modes in which the ideology of domesticity functions in the nineteenth century. Both assume that portrayals of domesticity have nothing to do with any persistent facts of human nature, but rather constitute an attempt to invent the very idea of such facts as a tool for the naturalization of attitudes that are really shaped by 'political history' and the class struggle. Their studies share one particular angle on the more general argument that, in nineteenth-century fiction, the focus on the domestic serves as a rhetorical evasion of social problems.

Significant though their project is, it requires no consideration of fiction's reflection of and influence on the shape of real families, or of the political impetus of the shape of family, considered not only as a discursive figure in relation to public and class politics but as a real determinant of the course of people's lives. Because, in other words, they assume that even to engage with the idea of 'domesticity' or 'human nature' already implies a displacement of the political, they overlook the political struggles that go on over *the very terms* of that engagement. As I have argued, however, given that that engagement is not one that any political discourse can evade, the negotiation of its terms is really the focus of the political action.

Susan Moller Okin expounds her famous slogan 'the personal is political' as implying that 'neither the realm of domestic personal life, nor that of non-domestic and political life, can be understood or interpreted in isolation from the other'.[1] It seems to me that Armstrong, Gallagher and Poovey

[1]   Susan Moller Okin, 'Gender, the Public, and the Private', in Anne Phillips (ed.) *Feminism and Politics* (Oxford: Oxford University Press, 1998), pp.116–141, p.124.

interpret the domestic in the light of (what has been conceived as) the political, but not vice versa. Their studies do little to challenge the classical liberal vision of the whole realm of intimate bonds and domestic activity as secondary supplements to public, political life. I will treat the politics of domesticity neither as a buttress to, nor as a reflection or reiteration of public politics, but as a primary sphere of conflict in itself, on the results of which the shape of public politics hangs.

It is not the invocation in domestic fiction of trans-historical human characteristics *as such* that is complicit in the strategies of bourgeois power; such invocations are a constitutive element in any discourse about humanity. On the contrary, the fact that the evaluation of human nature in domestic fiction is conscious and explicit, rather than unconscious and covert, makes the genre as a whole potentially subversive of a wider liberal discourse that imagines itself independent of any substantive presuppositions on this front. If we give our attention to this rare explicitness, we find that in the details of domestic fiction's particular and contrasting pictures of the human subject and the family we can trace an enduring struggle still structurally embedded at the heart of modern society: a struggle over the scope of sympathy.

i.   The family: Nuclear versus extended

In this chapter, I will compare the opposing versions of family fictionalized by Dinah Mulock Craik and Charlotte Yonge, two extremely popular nineteenth-century fiction writers who were on opposite sides of the main political debates of their time. In temperament, background, readership and ideals they were entirely dissimilar, but they both wrote fiction that was domestic in the strongest sense. Their novels focus not on inter-familial personal relationships, but primarily on intra-familial ones, and give accounts not only of courtship but also of family life. The contrast between their two very different accounts reveals the extent to which Victorian family ideology was not a coherent and settled body of opinion, conservative in virtue precisely of its 'domesticity', but was rather a site for thrashing out wider political ideals. What you made of family depended on what you made of the human subject and the rest of the social world. And it may be, as these novelists demonstrate, that what your society made of family determined what family made of you.

Craik's frame of reference is distinctively (classically) liberal, and that background determines many of her starting assumptions about family. However, because her fictional world is so vividly realised, her novels illustrate not only liberal family ideology, but also the inadequacy and contradiction of that ideology in confrontation with the nitty-gritty of life.

With Yonge, on the other hand, a contrastingly anti-liberal political perspective manifests itself in a totally different understanding of family. In rejecting liberalism, Yonge avoids many of the problems and tensions encountered by Craik. Her model of family, focused on domestic virtues, rejects radical gender divisions along with the possibility of separating public from private. Like the writers discussed by Monica Cohen, she uses 'home' as 'a trope for expressing hostility towards, and indeed a wish to repudiate, the psychological language of individualistic subjectivity Poovey and Armstrong identify as characteristic of domestic ideology'.[2]

The distinction I am pursuing is directly related to that marked by Greer, between the Family with a big F, a traditional and pre-capitalist social formation, which I associate with Yonge, and the nuclear family, which Greer defines in highly specific terms, and which I associate with Craik:

> I will only describe a family as nuclear when the relationship [between sexual partners] takes precedence over all others, and involves more time and more attention than are given to any blood relationship ... I will not exclude even that with the children of the nuclear unit, who are given less time in the nuclear family than the spouses give to each other ...for the ...housewife, the relationship with the children is secondary to her relationship with her husband (and with her husband's employer). The woman in a nuclear family who puts her children before her husband is 'asking for trouble' ... The family becomes nuclear when it is stripped down to this function, all other relations of blood and affinity having atrophied and fallen away.[3]

This picture of the family is a clearly recognizable feature of post-industrial society. From this incontrovertible diagnosis Greer moves to the rather more contentious attribution of this state of affairs to the 'irresistible force of industrialization pulling people away from the land ...the ideology of sexual love, [and] liberalism'.[4]

Other historians such as Goode agree that this model of family is historically specific: 'whenever the economic system expands through industrialisation ...Extended kinship ties weaken, lineage patterns dissolve,

---

2   Monica F Cohen, *Professional Domesticity in the Victorian Novel* (Cambridge: Cambridge University Press, 1998), p.8.

3   Germaine Greer, *Sex and Destiny* (Reading, Picador, 1985) pp.222–3.

4   Greer, p.225.

and a trend towards some form of the conjugal system begins to appear'.[5] On the other hand, Peter Laslett and others have denied that any such movement from the extended to the nuclear family ever took place, and have argued instead that the 'nuclear' family, comprising only mother, father, and children living under one roof, has always been the basic social unit in northern Europe and is not a marker, as has so long been thought, of the transition from traditional to industrial society.[6] Greer, with Rosemary O'Day and others, has been unsatisfied with Laslett's demonstrations.[7] My own attempt to discover 'the truth' about the evolution of the family through a survey of the history books has been completely in vain. Instead of consensus, I have found a debate raging with extraordinary rancour, in which the stance of historical objectivity is strained in a way I have never seen elsewhere in recent historiography. Many of the key players are either self-confessedly 'for' the nuclear family, presenting it as either universal and 'natural' (Laslett, Mount), or a symptom of social progress and improvement (Goode), or they are 'against' it, viewing it as an oppressive manifestation of capitalism. Fundamental political and ethical questions – and also, one might suspect, profound questions of personal identity – are clearly at stake here. It seems that the family as a locus of ideological conflict has endured, and I hope to show why this is not surprising.[8]

I am not particularly interested in denying the trans-historicity of the nuclear family as Laslett defines it, which is simply as a description of typical units sleeping under one roof. The post-industrial 'nuclear' family is not so much a living arrangement as a highly distinctive ideological configuration. As Greer remarks, Laslett's statistics do little towards 'quantifying the difference between the soulscape of a young man who says that he is Doug's boy and another who says he is a Piscean'.[9] Not only does Laslett not

---

[5]   William Goode, *World Revolution and Family Patterns* (London, Collier-Macmillan, 1963) p.7.

[6]   Peter Laslett, in his Introduction to *Household and Family in Past Time*, ed. P. Laslett (Cambridge: Cambridge University Press, 1972), and *The World We Have Lost* (London: Methuen, 1965).

[7]   Rosemary O'Day, *Family and Family Relationship 1500–1900* (Basingstoke: Macmillan, 1994).

[8]   These two models correspond to the opposed uses of 'the family' in recent British party politics. Thatcher drew on the tradition of the first when she said that 'there is no such thing as society, only individuals and their families.' New Labour has used the second as a way of rhetorically 'de-politicizing' the Party's socialist objectives. The second model is much harder to contain, much less amenable to the capitalist economy, where allegiances and duties are a shackle.

[9]   Greer, p.224.

attempt to trace such a distinction himself, but he also categorically rules out as unreliable one medium in which it might be traced – literature. As I will demonstrate however, nineteenth-century fiction provides illustrations so pointed and elaborate of the contest over the meaning and value of family as to provide evidence of a specific cultural tension over the breadth of the family, as well as a fleshing out of the wider political implications of that tension. Specifically, as we shall see, the nuclear family, as Greer defines it, is in the nineteenth century polemically connected with an ideal of an independent and completely self-determining human subject, that subject's right and responsibility over himself and over his property, and that subject's power of free choice: an ideal derived from the contract model.[10]

The nuclear family is the form into which inevitable human relation and emotional intersubjective bonds are compressed within an inherently un-relational view of man. It represents a minimal, contracted concession to man's dependence on others. Its fictional representation reveals the stresses it is under as such – as the concentrated focus of a powerful contradiction in the conception of what the individual is and needs.

Fictional portrayals of the wider Family, on the other hand, stress the individual subject's inescapable reliance on, attachment to, and responsibility towards the beings around it. The paradigmatic relation of the Family is the mother and child – not a relation of equal independence but of unchosen emotional bonds, gratuitous self-sacrificing affection, and non-demeaning dependence.

Domestic fiction shows us the nuclear family violated by competition, and the Family making a mockery and a misery of individual self-determination. The self-owning individual goes to work to find himself haunted by relations, and comes home to find his hearth-stone shattered by competition. Between these two visions of family, we find worked out on the pulses of everyday relation the fundamental tensions manifested in Victorian political practice and theory between rival visions of the human subject and human society. These are contradictions that we may recognize still at the heart of contemporary political controversy, and as shaping forces in our own personal and public lives.

---

[10]   It is probably no coincidence that Laslett is not only the champion of the 'naturalness' of the nuclear family, but also the respectful editor of Locke's *Two Treatises of Government.*

ii. Self help and the nuclear family

Dinah Mulock Craik's best-seller, *John Halifax, Gentleman* (which, published in 1856, sold 250,000 copies) is a fable of economic and social progress, and at the same time a narrative of the establishment of a nuclear family, in Greer's sense. It is a celebration of a vigorous and self-confident liberal individualist ideology, and also, essentially, an exploration of the place of the family within such a scheme.

The narrative is premised upon some distinctive metaphysical assumptions. God has created a world 'which, so far as we can see, He means like all other of His creations gradually to advance toward perfection'.[11] Part of this advancement is a natural tendency for all things to find their right place and proportions, a redistribution of rewards towards the deserving. 'John ...had strongly this presentiment of future power which may often be noticed in men who have carved out their own fortunes. They have in them the instinct to rise; and as surely as water regains its own level, so do they, from however low a source, ascend to theirs' (*JHG*, p.361). The natural laws of economic competition and self-assertion reveal a divinely ordained hierarchy, not passed on by authority but emerging through the natural process in which each individual human billiard ball is potted in just the right order, in what Craik calls 'the harsh, practical, yet not ill-meaning world, where all find their place soon or late'.[12] Craik decisively puts off the worry about the incommensurability of moral standards and the way of the material social world, which I described in Chapter 2 as characteristically problematic for Victorian fiction.

Because the progress of everything towards its right place is God-given, it is every man's duty to try to advance himself in the world. John can proclaim that 'I am what God made me, *and* what, with His blessing, I will make myself' (*JHG*, p.181, my italics). The metaphysical scheme is translated into didactic terms, into the Protestant, and capitalist, ethic of self-advancement. Although liberal individualism has tended to produce secularism, as Midgley points out, 'the intense individualism which has focused our attention exclusively on the social-contract model is itself thoroughly mystical. It has glorified the individual human soul as an object having infinite and transcendent value, has hailed it as the only real creator, and bestowed on it much of the panoply of God'. For Midgley, it is a short

---

[11]   Dinah Mulock Craik, *John Halifax, Gentleman* (1856) (London and Glasgow: Collins, c1930), p.336. Hereafter *JHG*.

[12]   Dinah Mulock Craik, *A Woman's Thoughts about Women* (1857–58), ed. Elaine Showalter (New York: New York University Press, 1995), p.70.

step from Protestant theology to liberal individualism, and Nietzsche's thought is not the deconstruction but rather the culmination of this 'new theology'.[13]

Becoming what you essentially are necessitates keeping yourself disentangled from and untainted by other people. John triumphs by limiting his ties to other human beings. His first claim to advancement is his refusal to beg, "'I never begged! I either worked or starved'". He sleeps out of doors; having once tried lodging "'at the decentest place I could find ...'" – here an expression of intolerable disgust came over the boy's face – "'I don't intend to try that again ...Better keep my own company and the open air'" (*JHG*, pp.197, 41). His difference from other poor people is evident to himself and to others, his inner gentlemanliness radiating through his external circumstances; 'though his clothes were threadbare, all but ragged, they were not unclean; and there was a rosy, healthy freshness in his tanned skin, which showed he loved and delighted in what poor folk generally abominate – water' (*JHG*, p.13).

John is that distinctive nineteenth-century phenomenon, the man-mushroom, appearing without parents or other associations, seemingly born self-sufficient. Dependency is worse than death to John, the individual must be free to exercise his property in his own person, and to extend this to other property; "'I'm a person of independent property, which consists of my head and my two hands, out of which I hope to realise a large capital some day'" (*JHG*, p.14).

But again like the paradigmatic Victorian hero, he moves smoothly from being an orphan without ties to being a married man, and, in the very process, asserts his independence through the conquest of a high-born wife. John's passionate desire for Ursula, like Pip's for Estella in *Great Expectations*, is inextricably connected with his sense of his place in society. It is also a desire to demonstrate "'the truth – which I may prove openly one day – that we *are* equals'" (*JHG*, p.198). She makes him, like Pip, ashamed of his working hands, and he dresses up in gentlemanly clothes when likely to see her. Craik treats the melding of social aspiration and love with none of the irony Dickens directed at it a few years later. In the terms of the novel, Ursula's acceptance of John proves that what he 'really' is, what his 'own, free natural self' is, is John Halifax, Gentleman, not 'the tanner's 'prenticeboy' (*JHG*, p.182). Choosing and winning Ursula is his first manifestation of, and thus proof of his entitlement to, individual power. 'He

---

[13] Mary Midgley, 'Duties Concerning Islands', *Encounter* 60/2 (1983) 36–44, p.43. See also her 'Creation and Originality', *Heart and Mind: The Varieties of Moral Experience* (Brighton: Harvester Press, 1981).

would use his own judgement, and follow his own will, in spite of anybody' (*JHG*, p.41). The core and essence of the nuclear family is embodied in a couple *who have freely chosen each other, and who are each the reward of the other's merit.* The love match is a confirmation of the individual's power of free choice. The emphasis upon *choosing* a spouse, even, or especially, in the face of parental and family opposition, is key in defining this model of family, and is an emphasis that is recurrent in Craik's fiction — most particularly in *The Woman's Kingdom* (to which I turn later) but also in many other novels — even the passive Eleanor in *The Ogilvies* asserts herself unbendingly in her choice of husband, and Dora in *A Life for a Life* insists on marrying Max despite her family's overwhelmingly reasonable grounds for opposition (he killed her brother). As Goode puts it, 'the ideology of the conjugal family is a radical one, destructive of the older traditions ...it grows from a set of more general radical principles which also arouse these groups politically ...It asserts the equality of individuals, as against class, caste, or sex barriers ...proclaims the right of the individual to choose his or her own spouse, place to live, and even which kin obligations to accept ...it asserts the worth of the *individual* as against the inherited elements''.[14]

The middle-class nuclear family lives 'wholesomely and decently' aloof from others, an elevated model for 'poor families' who have to be discouraged from 'herding together like pigs in a sty'. 'They visited nobody, and nobody visited them' (*JHG*, pp.321, 270). According to a political-economic reduction, individual self-assertion is the only form of social responsibility. 'Being their superior in many things, he is their master and they his servant', and as such John will do nothing to alleviate the distance between himself and his workers: 'there was not a gentleman in the country whose name so seldom headed a charity subscription as that of John Halifax' (*JHG*, pp.341, 488).

Faced with a starving mob, the embodiment of social inequality, John 'heroically' saves his master's property by propitiating them with a single meal. The scene gives tokens of his natural ascendancy and the basic principles on which it is based.

'I'm not one of you. I'd be ashamed to come in the night and burn my master's house down' ... They listened, as it were by compulsion, to the clear, manly voice ...

'What do you do it for?' John continued. 'All because he would not sell you, or give you, his wheat. Even so — it was *his* wheat, not yours.

---

[14]   Goode, p.19

May not a man do what he likes with his own?' The argument seemed to strike home. There is always a lurking sense of rude justice in a mob – at least a British mob. (*JHG*, p.111)

Indeed, this Lockean (and Nozickean) argument, on the self-evidence of which the plot is founded, is straightforward enough. However, the radical distinction between it and the 'evil' Squire Brithwood's contention that "Might's right, and possession's nine-tenths of the law' is less easy to discern (*JHG*, p.248).[15] The retrospective restriction of the attribution of a sense of justice to *British* mobs shows a distinctively anglo-bourgeois anxiety to repress the relation between the principle of self-ownership and the possibility of social revolution. The rightful power that John advocates is inherently a function of individual desert. But personal capital and social capital are continually confounded, and their relation to moral desert systematically blurred. John's 'youth, health, courage, honour, honesty' are described as his original 'capital'. His wealth is foreshadowed in his physical strength, which can hardly have much to do with his moral desert (*JHG*, p.181).

Where such a moral premium is put on personal strength and vigorous independence, it is hard to see how John can choose a physically weaker and economically dependent woman as his equal and the validator of his identity. His wife, however, is also 'rather tall, of a figure built ...for activity and energy ...at once warm and tender, strong and womanly' with as much 'independent dignity' as himself. 'Her manner in girlhood was not exactly either "meek" or "gentle" ...she comported herself ...with a dignity and decision – a certain stand-offishness' (*JHG*, pp.135, 141, 268). The union between Ursula and John is presented as one of equality and reciprocity; a bond so strong that it overshadows all others. The two are 'simply and equally friends', struggle and competition are submerged in reciprocation and affective bonds, and the transition in the tone of the narrative is a great relief.

Craik's depiction of the couple's mutual dependence and respect is really moving, and made all the more so by their isolation in a world in which help cannot be expected from anyone else. The couple's co-operation and love cast an irresistible aura of warm humanity over their efforts to rise in the world. John wishes to make money in order to buy his wife some grey long-tailed ponies she has longed for since a child, Ursula takes a keen interest in

---

15 As Nicholas Jolley points out in this regard, 'the *Second Treatise on Government* is haunted by the ghost of Thomas Hobbes', *Locke: His Philosophical Thought* (Oxford: Oxford University Press, 1999), p.196.

John's engineering schemes, and John is proud that his wife can make suggestions in that regard better than any man. Their labour, in the early stages of their marriage when their income is modest, is all transformed into the labour of love.

> Ursula ...would often sit chatting ...having on her lap a coarse brown pan, shelling peas, slicing beans, picking gooseberries ...Or else, in the summer evening she would be at the window sewing – always sewing – but so placed that with one glance she could see down the street to where John was coming. Far, far off she always saw him; and at the sight her whole face would change and brighten, like a meadow when the sun comes out. Then she ran to open the door, and I could hear his low 'my darling!' and then a long, long pause, in the hall (*JHG*, p.270).

The emotional intensity of the family, its sanctity, is created by its exclusion from the world's raw power relations, and the very starkness of the terms in which they have been outlined. The family exists in opposition to society; its essence depends on the strict maintenance of its boundaries, which always tend to exclude all but sexual partners.

For the egalitarianism of the conjugal pair cannot be comfortably extended to include the entire family. The fact that children are not strong and independent immediately from birth makes care for them too much like a burden and not enough like a freely engaged in contract. Family relations that are biological cannot be given equal prestige with the chosen bond between John and his wife. Parental and sibling relations are too liable to extend in time and space, blurring the division between family and wider world; siblings must not expect to retain their bonds once they are established within their own nuclear units. The novel manifests a tension between the idyllic vision of the family, the emotional intensity of which Craik captures so well, and the consciousness that, according to the individualist logic of the novel, it must be submitted to a dynamic of rivalries and torn apart. No amount of virtue and wisdom, the novel suggests, can preserve sympathy and interdependence anywhere outside the marriage bond.

It is made progressively apparent that John and Ursula's wider family is an arena of competition. Each parent has a favourite child, each brother a favourite sister, the disfavoured in each case being slighted at the favourite's expense. John and Ursula are the inner sanctum, and they alone, as Craik moralistically reminds us, ought to admit no rival in their affections. Barbara Thaden is, as far as I know, the only critic to have noted just how pointedly

Victorian liberal and conjugal ideology 'forced women to privilege the wifely role over the maternal role and forced them to break their primary libidinal bonds with their infants'.[16] This is the final, brutal step in the stripping down of the nuclear family. John's temporary absences show Ursula 'what in the passion of her mother-love she might have been tempted to forget – many mothers do – that beyond all maternal duty, is the duty that a woman owes to her husband; beyond all loves, is the love that was hers before any of them were born' (*JHG*, p.504).

It is this moralistic struggle against a wider and more equal sympathy that troubles the course of the novel. While the narrative on the one hand conveys a poignantly strong sense of exorbitant, unmeasured tenderness between siblings and their parents, on the other it also struggles against that sense, reminding us that some bonds trump others, and eventually demonstrating with pointed violence that this spreading love cannot last. The reading experience is an uncomfortable testament to Craik's skill in plumbing the depths of an emotional tension structural to the modern family, and her failure finally to reconcile such tension.

The middle section of the novel depicts an idyllic family group, the seeming organic wholeness of which is emphasized in the knowledge that it is illusory. 'It was such a picture – these five darlings, these children which God had given them – a group perfect and complete in itself, like a root of daisies, or a branch of ripening fruit, which not one could be added to, or taken from' (*JHG*, p.392). John is passionately fond of one of his children, the most dependent of all, little blind Muriel. As if as a discipline for his over-fondness, Muriel dies in childhood, and the narrator dramatically queries the justice of the divine scheme of things, only to reassert the faith which alone can calm discontent:

> 'Oh God! My only daughter – my dearest child!' Yes, she was the dearest ... Strange mystery, that He should so often take, by death or otherwise, the dearest – always the dearest. Strange, that he should hear us cry – us writhing in the dust, 'O Father, anything, anything but this!' But our Father answers not; and meanwhile the desire of our eyes – be it a life, a love, or a blessing – slowly, slowly goes – is gone. And yet we must believe in our Father ... Thanks be to God if he puts into our hearts such love towards Him that even while He slays us we can trust Him still. (*JHG*, p.387)

---

16 Barbara Z Thaden, *The Maternal Voice in Victorian Fiction* (New York and London: Garland, 1997), p.8.

As the novel enters its final stage, this emotionally daring form of argument becomes central. It is *because* the way of the world seems so impenetrably unjust, as the weaker fall by the wayside, seemingly unpitied, that we must be thankful for our continued faith, and humble before the edicts of fortune that are embodied in the triumph of the strong. The other side of the confidence of individualism is an abject prostration before mechanical process, a despairing abandonment (like Herbert Spencer's) of the human right to judge and react against the inhuman.

Childhood mortality, and its representation in fiction, is an important litmus test for Victorian conceptions of providence. Craik wrote to Margaret Oliphant with a reproof for striking the wrong note on this subject in *Agnes* – 'I think you will yet be sorry for having written "Agnes": – because it does *not* "justify the ways of God to men"'.[17] In Oliphant's novel, maternal passion breaks the bounds within which Craik so insistently confines it, and a discrimination is forcefully asserted between the brute, amoral fact of the mowing down of the weak and innocent on the one hand, and normative *human* judgement and love on the other.

Within Craik's scheme, the warmth of family relation, elegiacally captured on page after page, is a resistance to the God-warranted struggle of life. John is held back on his social climb by the memory of his dead favourite:

> 'Once, I hoped to do some wonderful things when I was forty-five. But somehow the desire faded' ...all the active energies and noble ambitions which especially belong to the prime of manhood, in him had been, not dead perhaps, but sleeping. Sleeping ...under the daisies of a child's grave at Enderley.
>
> I know not if this was right – but ...A certain something in him seemed different ever after, as if a portion of the father's own life had been taken away with Muriel, and lay buried in the little dead bosom of his first-born, his dearest child. (*JHG*, p.404)

It is the mother, we are told, who has borne the special weight of giving up to the earth 'a portion of her own being', 'her very flesh and blood, the fruit of her own womb' (*JHG*, p.399). But in this image of strange sympathy, John himself is feminized by a metaphoric extension of the physical interdependence, the rupturing of individual integrity embodied in the

---

[17]   Letter from Craik to Margaret Oliphant, 27 October 1865, in collection at the National Library of Scotland, Record MS.23210:36–75.

relation of mother and child.

However, like the hero that he is, John struggles against the tempting passion of mother-love, and conquers the damper put on his self-assertion by his fatherly affection. The strange, contradictory logic of the narrative, torn as it is between the appeal of relational existence and emotion as they are experienced within the family, and the ethic of individualist self-assertion that is germane to civil society, makes the acquisition of wealth a painful duty, and individualism a stance of social altruism. John wonders whether 'now that our children are growing up, and our income is doubling and trebling year by year, we ought to widen our circle of usefulness, or close it up permanently within the quiet bond of little Longfield', and decides '*not* the latter, because it *is* the happiest' (*JHG*, p.409).

With what seems like masochistic energy, Craik shatters the illusion of mutuality and harmony within the family, smashing it into contact with the spirit of competition, and beating it back to the discrete affection between husband and wife. She seems compelled, as the novel goes on, to address every painful contradiction that the early history of John seemed to gloss over so easily.

The family is after all the training ground of independent men like John: bonds of dependence must be broken; each individual, with his spouse, must go forth alone to find his deserved place. On the night of the death of their sister, in the silence can be heard only 'Guy and Edwin arguing vociferously in the dark, on the respective merits and future treatment of their two sisters, Muriel and Maud'. A markedly strange time for an argument, and a strange argument it is, over the 'ranking' and rewarding of sisters. The last part of the novel is taken up by the violent rivalry of two brothers, who 'excellent lads both, as they grew into manhood, did not exactly "pull together"' (*JHG*, pp.39, 416). The tension between the two boys seems to unpick the ideological work done by the first half of the novel. They pull apart the contradictions embodied by John. Edwin is good at business, reserved, fortunate and prudent; Guy is 'warm-hearted', pleasure-loving, generous, hasty and unlucky. It is constantly implied, though never admitted, that Edwin is, in fact, ignoble and selfish, while Guy is noble and generous, and that the latter qualities are of little use for self-advancement. The ageing John's defence of his business-like son in the face of criticisms from his warm-hearted brother, comes perilously close to the contradictions the book seeks to reconcile:

'This is very ill news. Ten bank failures in the *Gazette* to-day'.
'But it will not harm us, father'.

'Edwin is always thinking of "us", and "our business," remarked Guy, rather sharply ...

'Edwin is scarcely wrong in thinking of us, since upon us depend so many'.

(*JHG*, p.416)

In the relation between the sons, the tussle between self-regarding continence and generous openness is naked. Their rivalry finds a focus in their competition for the affection of the governess. 'A sorrow had entered' the family, 'not from without, but from within – a sorrow which we could not meet and bear, as a family'. Guy proposes to her, only to discover that his reserved brother has already won her love. The two brothers are found 'struggling together like Cain and Abel. And from the fury in their faces, the quarrel might have a similar ending'. The crisis is represented as unresolvable; none blame Guy's bitter resentment of his brother's good fortune, or hatred for the woman who has inadvertently disappointed him. And yet the household's 'solemn upholding of the pre-eminent right and law of love' prevents any idea of sacrifice on Edwin's part from entering into the equation. In love, both brothers are absolutely entitled to exorbitant self-interest. And so the dawn of sexual love, inevitably and even desirably, 'makes the family cease to be a family, in many things, from henceforward. The two strongest feelings of life clash; the bond of brotherly unity, in its perfectness, is broken forever'. The rivalry over the governess is merely the overflow of the inevitably growing struggle for self-assertion between the brothers, the desire to possess her is as much a sign as it is a cause of their antagonistic competition (*JHG*, pp.474, 472, 470, 470):

Edwin [was] standing by, proud and glad, with his arm clasped round Louise. He did not remove it. In his brother's very face – perhaps because of the expression of that face – the lover held fast his own. ... The girl's hand, which was sorrowfully and kindly extended, Guy snatched and held fast ....

'I shall claim my right – just for once – may I, sister Louise?' With a glance of defiance at Edwin, Guy caught his brother's betrothed round the waist and kissed her – once – twice – savagely. (*JHG*, p.482)

As this ethic of independent self-assertion is reduced to the basic level of sexual competition and physical violence, its possible cost for women, as the socially and physically weaker sex, becomes apparent. Craik brings into clear relief the contradiction between the two views of women upon which capitalist society is founded. A reconciliation of the notion of woman as free self-owner with the notion of woman as altruistic carer can only be achieved by the love match, so when Guy's choice in love is thwarted, the novel breaks down into emotional dissonance. The narrative seems to demand that at one and the same time we both respect and condemn the woman who has rejected him. Guy, 'had not only lost his love, but what is more precious than love – faith in womankind'. This 'faith' is founded upon the trust that women are available as reward for the growing individual; this prize denied him, Guy's violence is directed at women in general, in particular weaker or more dependent women (*JHG*, pp.466, 476):

> Guy, snatching up his little sister, lifted her roughly on his knee.
> 'Come along, Maud. You'll be my girl now. Nobody else wants you. Kiss me, child'. But the little lady drew back.
> 'So, you hate me, too? Edwin has been teaching you? Very well. Get away, you cheat!' He pushed her violently aside. (*JHG*, p.478)

Female dependence is in the end despicable like all other dependencies, whatever their cause, and female independence is tolerated only as long as it affirms the independence of men, rather than marking the limits of their power. The household once ruptured by the enemy within, 'neither joy nor affliction would ever find [it] a family again' (*JHG*, p.474). Its members turn against one another with a disturbing sexual violence.

The startling thing is that Craik treats all this as not only inevitable, but also desirable. It becomes slowly apparent that John and his wife are unmistakably and virtuously selfish, 'as all lovers are'. Rejoicing in their own limitless wealth, and looking back on the hardships of the past with sentimental tears, they offer their oldest son the chance, on his marriage, to 'start in poverty', in the same position as they, as orphans with no one to help them, originally began theirs. Like all else that John does, this selfishness is presented as a moral duty, '"I fear we have been too anxious to play *Deus ex machina* with our children,"' he says. The narrator concurs, in another equation of the expedient with the normative: 'they cannot help their children ...those children must learn to stand alone, each for himself, compelled to carry his own burden and work out, well or ill, his individual life'. The warfare over, and the extended family established as a set of voluntary relations between independent couples, John remarks, '"all our young birds will soon be flown ...We shall be very happy. We need only one another"' (*JHG*, pp.476, 461, 471. 474, 568).

John's death finally shows that other family bonds are as nothing to that one exhaustive piece of interrelation that is marriage. The self-possessed Ursula tells her children, 'I want to be left ...alone with my husband'. She herself then dies only a short space after her husband (*JHG*, p.574).

John dies on 1 August 1834, the day on which England emancipated its slaves. Herein lies a reminder of the abuses which John's brand of post-Lockean liberalism has been so instrumental in eradicating.[18] The confluence of events also highlights, however, the intimate relation between a political emphasis on freedom through self-ownership and a particular idea of family. On this day of emancipation John and Ursula are freed from mortal shackles – represented most immediately in the form of their own children. The wider family, as a metonym of all non-conjugal social relations, is no more than an unnatural burden at whose dissolution we are invited, tearfully, to rejoice.

There is one gap in the universal happiness that this independence is seen to create – a gap invisible because it is the originating locus of these narratives of self-sufficiency. The narrator, Phineas, the feeble cripple whose only fault is his physical weakness, is left without a future. Having served as the first rung in John's climb to eminence, his story has gradually become no more than the relating of others' stories. A book in which independence is the primary virtue is narrated by a voice with none. His relation to John, 'he of whose heart mine was the mere faint echo', has been such that it has no place in the binary models of relation which the book offers: independent, symmetrical and dispassionate regard on the one hand, passionate and mutual sexual union on the other. Phineas's feeling for John is so anomalous – he refers to him as 'my more than brother' – that it leaves no trace on John's conventional family life. The death of John leaves Phineas an empty shell. We can only believe that his existence is concluded with his narrative, and that he has now but to wait for death, as his last words to John – 'it is but a little while' – imply. The fate of Phineas is a peripheral revelation of the other side of this model of relation in which the one great marital tie is substituted for all others. When John meets Ursula, Phineas reflects: 'although I rejoiced in his joy, still I felt half-sadly for a moment, the vague, fine line of division which was thus for evermore drawn between him and me of no fault on either side, and of which he himself was unaware. It was but the right and natural law of things, the difference between the married and unmarried, which only the latter feel' (*JHG*, pp.220, .571, 259). This

---

[18] Locke himself, of course, did not oppose slavery, but legal equality between both races and sexes is the obvious conclusion of his premises, which have been the pivot of the struggle for the achievement of such equality.

strange breach in sympathy is not blameable, because it is natural. Love, like all else, has its hierarchies, and its competitions, as Phineas knows all along. 'Being in so many things his opposite' because of his crippled condition, Phineas cannot ever hope to have, like John, a 'character the key-stone of which was that whereon is built all liking and all love – *dependableness*'. Phineas can only depend, and he can never enter into that sole magical relation, marriage, in which dependence on another is justified: 'my character was too feeble and womanish to be likely to win any woman's reverence or love' (*JHG*, pp.133, 38, 63).

In *A Woman's Thoughts about Women*, Craik argues that women should be able, are indeed already able, to work:

> Fear not the world: it is often juster to us than we are to ourselves. If in its harsh jostlings the 'weaker goes to the wall' – as so many allege is sure to happen to a woman – you will almost always find that this is not merely because of her sex, but for some inherent qualities in herself …
> The world is hard enough, for two thirds of it are struggling for the dear life – 'each for himself, and de'il take the hindmost'; but it has a rough sense of moral justice after all. And whosoever denies that, spite of all hindrances from individual wickedness, *the right* shall not ultimately prevail, impugns not alone human justice, but the justice of God.[19]

Craik is haunted by the saying 'de'il take the hindmost' (which recurs in *John Halifax*); her fiction and prose add up to a sustained struggle to define her world-view, and her view of women in particular, in relation to it.

In allowing women to assert themselves as individual producers, she insists that they accept the value system of the economic arena, 'we must learn to rate ourselves at no ideal and picturesque value, but simply as *labourers* – fair and honest competitors in the field of the world; and our wares mere merchandise, where money's worth alone brings money, or has any right to expect it'.[20] Her value for individuals is inherently related to their ability to assert themselves in the world of commodities; to women, as well as men, she applies the adage 'The value of a thing/Is just as much as it will bring'. Conventional scales of value are not open to question, nor is the general principle of leaving the fate of men and women to the mercy of market forces. Woman's destiny, 'her home, her life, her lot, are all of her own making'. Because the valuable individual is by definition autonomous,

---

[19]   Craik, *A Woman's Thoughts*, p.78.
[20]   Craik, *A Woman's Thoughts*, p.83.

the notion of criticizing social as opposed to personal failings is outside Craik's conception. She disapproved of novels that left the reader 'inclined to arraign society, morality, [or], what is worse, Providence'.[21]

Nevertheless, when Craik, the righteous moralist and powerful delineator of passion, gratuitously chastens with an ironic and scornful 'womanish' both herself and her most sympathetic character, there is a significant schism within the narrating voice. RH Hutton remarked that such figures in her fiction are really women in disguise:

> ...it is difficult to suppress the fear that Phineas Fletcher will fall hopelessly in love with John Halifax, so hard is it to remember that Phineas is of the male sex ...when he professes to be an uncle, the reader is aware constantly that he is really an aunt ...it is scarcely possible to persuade one's self that the tender, devoted manner in which courage comes for the first time in thinking and acting for another, and the self-sacrificing resignation with which all monopolizing desires are resigned on the glimpse of that other's dawning passion, – are not taken from the experience of a mother, or at least a sister, very thinly disguised under the masculine pretensions of Phineas Fletcher.[22]

Perhaps in strategic allegiance to the cause of feminist individualism, Craik does not make her dependent character female. However, the treatment of Phineas reveals a residual and ambivalent allegiance to 'feminine', sympathetic values. Even in its moralistic and dutiful resignation to the triumph of the fittest, it raises a consciousness of injustice, a feeling of rebellion, and a deep movement of compassion; the sentiments of the weak and oppressed, and of the nurturer; the tempting passion of the mother.

iii. Getting rid of the relations.

> No one cares about distant relatives nowadays. They went out of fashion
> years ago.   OSCAR WILDE, *Lord Arthur Savile's Crime*

John Halifax's idealistic advocacy of liberal individualism is presented in the light of a particularized, emotional and broad-ranging exploration of its

---

[21]   Craik, *A Woman's Thoughts*, pp.79, 71, 194. The last remark is a glance at Gaskell's *Ruth*.
[22]   Hutton 'Authoress of "John Halifax"', p.475.

outcomes in both family and wider social life. Craik's later novel, *The Woman's Kingdom* (1869), is more single-minded in its didacticism, presenting the link between the individualist ethos and a clearly distinct model of the family even more explicitly.[23]

While John Halifax rose from nowhere to a position in which he could help emancipate the slaves and place his son in parliament, Will Steadman is a doctor who rises to be a rather better-off doctor. The ambition of the earlier novel is contracted in scale; here we have individualism as a policy of battening down the hatches and looking after the nuclear family, as opposed to anything more ambitious.

The novel begins with two strong siblings nursing two weaker ones; the former end happily, the latter unhappily. The novel shows how this comes about, with a pointed insistence that the involuntary bonds of fraternity, which bind weak to strong, be sundered in favour of voluntary and symmetrical marital relations that allow the strong to fulfil themselves. In the universe of the novel, there is an inexorable judgement hanging over the heads of the weak. If they cannot help themselves, no one else has a duty or even the right to help them. Only the love match is excluded from the rule of absolute independence; only within its bounds do individuals feel the sympathy inclining them to do more for one another than what a very minimally conceived notion of duty demands.

In such a context, the reader's desire for romance is heightened to an incredible pitch; one expects of it a redress of all the deficiencies and hardnessess exhibited elsewhere. Craik encourages such an attitude:

> This will be a thorough 'love' story. I do not pretend to make it anything else. There are other things in life besides love: but everybody who has lived at all, knows that love is the very heart of life, the pivot upon which its whole machinery turns: without which no human existence can be complete, and with which, however broken and worn, in part, it can still go on working somehow, and working to a comparatively useful and cheerful end ... A life without love in it must of necessity be an imperfect, an unnatural life. (*WK*, p.15)

Marriage is the gift with which the Saved are marked out, the union in which individuals find legitimation. 'Heaven guides all true lovers that are to be husband and wife – leads them from the farthest corners of the world ...to their own appointed home in one another's arms' (*WK* p.38). This

---

[23] Craik, *The Woman's Kingdom: A Love Story* (1869) (London: Hurst and Blackett, circa 1897). Hereafter WK.

companionate bond provides the only truly moral and reasonable outlet for altruism, the only allowable escape from a solipsistic individualism that is as oppressively lonely for the strong and successful as it is for the weak. Only in marriage does the heroine learn 'the self-control which every human being must learn who has another human being to care for – bound by the only tie which entirely takes away the solitude of individuality' (*WK*, pp.170–1). Marriage alone, unlike any other bond, social or even familial, can justify the 'absorption of self into some other being', that sympathetic absorption, that giving and taking which compromises the integrity of the self, 'which is the foundation of everything divine in human nature'. Marriage finds its essence in its very contrast to all other bonds, in particular the fraternal, which is compared with it to disadvantage time and time again. 'Even if blessed with the closest bonds of fraternity, every soul is more or less alone, or feels so – till the magic other soul appears, which, if fate allows, shall remove solitude forever', 'every one of us is, more or less, intensely alone. Before marriage ...absolutely and inevitably alone' (*WK*, pp.16, 30). The sibling relation lacks the crucial measure of choice that defines marriage: 'there comes a time in a man's life – in all lives – when ties, not only of instinct and duty, but of personal election, are necessary for happiness; when, in short, no tie satisfies, except *the* one which God Himself made to be the root of all' (*WK*, p.118).

This exercise of independent, self-regarding choice is not only desirable, it is also a pre-eminent duty. With characteristic overdetermination, marriage is to be strictly distinguished from all other ties by inclination, the way of the world, *and* by the law of God. Craik polemically insists that family members *ought* to bear in mind that their relations to one another are second-rate:

> each [brother] fortified himself behind his masculine armour of steely reticence, smooth and cold, feeling all the while that within it he was a dull fellow – a solitary fellow – even with his own brother beside him. Such lonely moments come to all people – before marriage ...and it would be well if brothers and sisters, fathers and mothers, recognized this fact – as a law of God and necessity – that all the love of duty never makes up for the love of choice. (*WK*, p.52)

The moralistic stress on the duty of coolness is strange but indicative, and is particularly marked in relation to women. In *A Woman's Thoughts about Women*, Craik remarks that 'For two women ...to be completely absorbed in one another, and make public demonstration of the fact, by caresses or quarrels, is so repugnant to common sense, that when it ceases to be silly it becomes actually wrong'. Sisters above all must keep an eye on their regard for one another. Intimacy between female friends is 'closer' and more allowable than that between sisters, because friendship at least 'has all the novelty of election which belongs to the conjugal tie itself'.[24]

Parents and children also must be careful not to get too close. The mother's tenderness towards her children is confined within definite limits, 'her sons were, after all, less dear to her than was their father'; necessarily, as they are in the end a burden, and must go out into the world as if they had no ties. Edna cheerfully looks forward to her sons leaving home: 'Julius will have one of these days to take his turn in the fever hospital; Will may go in for a Civil Service examination, and be off to India, and Robert turn sheep-farmer. in Australia ... I'll hinder none of you from risking life in doing your duty', or in other words, your job. The practical importance of this highly specific conception of family for a nation whose economic development absolutely demanded the mobility of its middle-class talent could hardly be more explicitly pointed up (*WK*, pp.103, 74, 327, 279, 271).

Craik says that the bond 'closest of all, the love between man and woman' is 'the root of the family life, and the family life is the key to half the mysteries of the universe' (*WK*, p.16). But the 'root' of the family is not really continuous with it any more than it is with the other harsh mysteries of the universe; rather, the opposition between the love match and 'family' in a wider sense is metonymic of its opposition to the rest of the outside world. It excuses or even demands the rupture of all other family ties, as Edna reflects on contemplating an offer of marriage from a man she thinks it possible that her sister also loves:

> A woman who, in such a case, could be influenced by sister or friend – or even parent – who could not ask herself the simple question, 'Do I love him, or do I not love him?' and answer it herself, without referring the decision to any human being – such a woman might be good enough in her way, but she was ...not the woman whom a man like William Stedman would ever care to marry. (*WK*, p.123)

The story in fact contains no authoritarian parents, and no rivalry in love between sisters or brothers, but the possibility of such a rivalry is repeatedly raised, and its implications discussed, through a series of completely implausible and seemingly gratuitous speculations on the siblings' part. The love rivalry in *John Halifax* was seen primarily from the point of view of the

---

[24]   Craik, *A Woman's Thoughts about Women*, p.139

disappointed brother, as a tragedy within the individualistic scheme that the narrative could not but confront. But here the possibility of such a rivalry is almost exalted in, the narrator pre-emptively taking the part of the successful lovers with a jealous rejection of the claims of the rest of the world before they have even been made. Will Steadman is a steady man because he knows his own will in choosing a wife, who similarly knows her Will as a claim to be set above and against all others:

If he does love her and she knows it, she is bound to marry him, though twenty other women loved him, and broke their hearts in losing him. He is not theirs, but hers, and to have her for his wife is his right and her duty. And in this world there are so many contradictory views of duty and exaggerated notions of right, so many false sacrifices and renunciations weak even to wickedness, that it is but fair sometimes to uphold the *right* of love – love sole, absolute, and paramount, firmly holding its own, and submitting to nothing and no one. (*WK*, p.113)

The very devotion and selflessness demanded by the marriage bond, its exorbitant demand of sympathetic relationality, are a defence against all other 'weak' temptations to sympathy, renunciation and self-sacrifice. If the marriage bond is given its due, it will entail a weakening of all other affective and practical relations. It is made clear that, as Ferdinand Mount comments approvingly, 'it is the essence of marriage that it is private and apart from the rest of society. Its "selfishness" or "exclusiveness" is not its undertone but its heart and soul'.[25] 'Those who [marry] have a right to be all in all to each other, to go out cheerfully together in to the wide world, and feel all lesser separations but as a comparatively little thing' (*WK*, p.213).

The continuity between this notion of marriage and a wider classical liberal (or in contemporary terms, libertarian)· ethic of self-assertion and acquisitiveness, of a minimized conception of duties towards others, is at times almost shockingly apparent. As Christopher Cauldwell observes,

'In their early stages bourgeois relations, by intensifying individualism, give a special heightening to sexual love. Before they crystallize out as relations to cash, bourgeois social relations simply seem to express man's demand for freedom from obsolete social bonds ... Sexual love now takes on, as clearly seen in art, a special value as the expression *par excellence* of individuality'.

---

[25]   Ferdinand Mount, *The Subversive Family* (London: Unwin, 1982), p.188.

In marriage, apart from this duteous stepping apart from the world, there is also a miserly joy in having another being all to one's self. With a matter-of-factness which hovers between the questioning and the unquestioning, Craik illustrates Cauldwell's observation that the 'ugly possessive features of bourgeois social relations' give 'bourgeois love a selfish jealous undertone, which the bourgeois ...considers as instinctive and natural'.[26] 'An unaccountable impulse made [Edna] snatch [her lover's letter], and turn away with it; turn away from her sister, – her dear sister, from whom she had not a secret in the world'. '[Julius] betrayed even a wild delight at the idea of having [Letty] all to himself – away from her kith and kin, in the mysterious depths of India' (*WK*, pp.125, 211).

The duty of casting off one's relations, like so many other 'duties' of Craik's world, uncannily falls in with expedient self-interest. The weaker siblings, the convalescent Letty and Julius, without money or means of supporting themselves, are shut out by the marriage of Will and Edna. And it is better for the socially aspiring Will and Edna to be free of them. 'Julius had been ...more anxiety than pleasure', and Will will bear the burden no longer' (*WK*, p.118). Will is grudgingly prepared to give his brother an allowance; one half of a small legacy left to him alone by a relation of whom he was the 'favourite'. But he will not let him live with him:

'No, not with us', was the answer, strong, decisive, almost angry.
'As *she* knows', glancing at Edna, 'there is two hundred a-year, which, if necessary, he can have; part or whole; but I will not have him living with me. Two men in one house would never do'. (*WK*, p.133)

Will's anger is entirely unprovoked. Julius, a brother with whom he gets on very well, has not for a moment suggested living with his married brother. Compelling evidence of the acute ideological tension around these issues is provided by the striking manner in which Craik repeatedly steps outside the probabilities of the situation to make her point. Her most distinctive characteristic as a novelist is her tendency to write like some sort of rhetorical chiropractor, ever ready to crack and bend almost to the point of dislocation the sorest emotional joints.

She shows us Will raging at the very idea, entirely totally unfounded and improbable though it is, that Julius could object to his marriage with Edna:

'I do not contemplate any such impertinent interference on his part.

---

[26] Christopher Cauldwell, *Studies in a Dying Culture* (London, 1938) pp.152–3, 154–5.

But if so, it can make no difference to me. When a man of my age chooses his wife, no other man, not even his own brother, has a right to say a word. Julius had better not; I would not stand it'.

He spoke loudly, like a man not used to talk with or to listen to women; a man who, right or wrong, liked to have his own way. (*WK*, p.134)

The repeated insistence on the right to the independent choice of a partner – with regard to a thoroughly eligible match, to which no one is in the least likely to object – reveals the intimate connection between this kind of marriage and an ideology of self-determination and liberal freedom.

As in *John Halifax*, and many of Craik's other novels (for instance, *A Life for a Life*, in which Dora marries her brother's murderer), the achievement of full self-hood is marked by the linked impulses of choosing a partner and indulging in murderous aggression towards siblings. In an almost absurdly compulsive confrontation with the most disturbing interpretation of her own ideas, Craik, in excuse of Will's almost fatal neglect of his brother, makes yet another of her allusions to the famous biblical fratricide: 'Cain's appeal, "Am I my brother's keeper?" though uttered by a murderer, is not wholly untrue or unjust. Beyond a certain point no human being can help or save another ... In God's hands alone are the spirits of all flesh, their guidance and their destinies' (*WK*, p.281).

In this novel, Craik bites the bullet of this biblical *reductio ad absurdum* of her position. The 'broad, tall and manly', 'strong and resolute' Will at all stages shows a 'masculine' intolerance towards dependence or weakness. 'The dominant hardness which was in his nature, as it is in the nature of every strong man' is part of his perfection, an extension of the manly perception of Justice. After all, Will himself 'had never starved, never been in debt; for neither alternative often happens to an unmarried man who has ordinary health, honesty and brains ...if it does, he has usually only himself to blame' (*WK*, pp.23, 178, 143). As a doctor, he suggests, and his wife agrees, that even ill-health is usually a matter of feeble psychology and moral weakness.

Julius, Will's weaker and more passionate brother is, like Phineas, destined for tragedy, because in his weakness he cannot attract a woman, being himself too much like one; 'As bad as a woman ... Not half a man, and never shall be' (*WK*, p.51). Again, despite her overt rejection of the idea that women are more dependent than men, Craik allows femininity to figure as a reminder of less independent modes of existence: 'that was the key to the whole nature – that sensitive, loving, delicate nature. He could do almost anything, with somebody to help him; without that, nothing'. Will carries Julius around during his illness 'as if he had been a woman or a child' (*WK*, pp.204, 47). Invalids figure repeatedly in Craik's fiction – Julius is aligned not only with the eponymous heroine of *Olive* but also with Phineas and with the Earl in *A Noble Life*. Sickness, womanhood, and childhood all figure, as for Herbert Spencer, as anomalies in the pattern of self-owning individualism.

But Craik gives such anomalies a central place in her fiction, where the feelings of guilt and tenderness that they awaken struggle with the strict individualism of the explicit ideology, to produce a powerful and painful dynamic. *The Woman's Kingdom* starts out as a paradigm escapist romance in which the inequalities and hardships of the world are glossed over in a focus on the perfect love match. But the love-story is wound up early in the novel, on a note of almost absurdly hum-drum modesty – Edna's success in persuading Will not to buy a carriage on credit – that cannot but undermine the heroism of the love match. From this bathetically contracted vision of the woman's kingdom, we move to the world shut firm outside that kingdom, and find a bleak environment of selfish loneliness.

Julius comes to symbolise the suffering of the weak in an individualist society:

> *Lost* – how sad a word it is – how sad and yet how common! And who are the lost? ...the sinners, who have been over-tempted and have fallen – the sinned against, who have been haunted and tortured into crime – the weak ones, half good, half bad, with whom it seems the chance of a straw whether they shall take the right way or the wrong. Who shall find them? (*WK*, p.264)

Not married people, that's for sure. In a society where duty means non-interference, the opium-drugged wretch is 'just allowed to go his own way, – to work or be idle – feed or starve – live or die, as it please himself and Providence' (*WK*, p.264).

Craik suggests that all such misery is the result of the unnatural alienation of real human connections, though she sees such alienation as inevitable. Julius 'haunts' his brother's practice 'as a ghost might haunt its body's grave'. When the brothers confront one another, Will tells his unrecognized brother 'I don't remember your face'. Julius has become a representative of the weak in a winner's world, the needy in a scheme of self-owning individualism: 'Nobody knows me, I may go among them all as harmlessly as a ghost' (*WK*, pp.264, 266).

In this novel, to be a 'burden upon other people' apart from your own spouse, is 'a condition …ten times worse than death'. And so Julius ends his tragic life alone, the subject of a painting that emphasizes the exclusions by which that distinctive compound of peculiar properties, the 'nuclear' family, is brought about:

> It was called 'In another Man's Garden', and was simply a suburban cottage-door, painted with the intense realism then altogether pooh-poohed and despised. Thereat − also modern and real, down to coat, hat and stick − stood a young man, bidding adieu to his wife and child before going to business, − a happy, intensely happy little group, safely shut inside the rose-trellised walls. While outside, leaning against the gate, was a solitary figure − a broken-down, dust-stained, shabby man − gazing with mournful yearning into 'another man's garden'. (*WK*, p.150)

The suburban scene is truly 'modern'. The novel presents with 'unflinching realism' a vision of a society in which the dependent or erring are no more than superfluous onlookers at the success of their stronger brothers. This, comments the narrator, 'is a busy and self-engrossed world: it has quite enough to do with its own affairs, and it likes to get the full value for all it bestows' (*WK*, p.124). The marriage bond, as depicted by Craik, is at the very heart, and is the vivid symbol, of such self-engrossment. Though we have been told that it is weak and wrong to sympathise too much with our weaker brothers, the narrative induces us to do just that, at the expense of our engagement with the married bliss of the hero and heroine.

Craik's fiction constantly surprises with its naïve confrontations of its own most conflicted premises. Her overt, crude and comprehensive partisanship with the dominant social and domestic ideology of her time is accompanied by an emotionally acute, if totally untheorized, probing of that ideology's sorest points. In her fiction, the personal and emotional subject-matter of the domestic genre, resonating as it does with each one of its reader's own experiences of childhood, parenthood, brotherhood and sisterhood, wakes the most basic social instincts but cannot harmonize, contain or put them to rest. This subject-matter brought out in Craik the expression of half-unconscious fears and tendernesses of which we find no trace in her confident and composed prose writings. Poignantly distorted − like the bodies of her suffering invalids − by the lens of her partisan ideology of family and society, we can trace in her fiction the expression and elicitation of the instinct to respect, compassionate, aid and love other persons not as rational self-asserting independent spirits but as needy and embodied social creatures. It is hard to deny Craik reciprocal compassion.

iv. Recognising the family ghosts

The contours of the struggle over the family and the nature of the human subject, so starkly outlined in Craik's novels, are recognizable not only in other fiction, but also in nineteenth-century philosophical and scientific discourses. In this context, for instance, we can see that the competitive and murderous dynamic of Freud's model of family relations is closely related to a particular political ideology. His vision appears in this light not so much a challenge to bourgeois domestic piety as a naturalization and scientific legitimisation of its fantasy of egotistical, self-asserting human nature. His thought offers yet another illustration of the way in which such a conception of man implies the admission of competition into the family, and the prioritization of the impulse for sexual union and possession, closely identified with the definition of the self-owning ego, over all other affective bonds.

In Friedrich Engels's utopian vision of the future of the 'family' also, we find an emphasis on the sexual relation between the sexes, which he conceives as its only valuable and persistent reality. His social utopia, just like Craik's, is characterized by the unfettered expression of 'mutual inclination' in 'sex love', which he proclaims to be 'by its very nature exclusive'. Though in saying this he perhaps refers only to the exclusion of other sexual relations, it is clear that he has a wider exclusivity – an exclusivity as to intimate, personal, 'family' relations – also in mind. For the conditions that allow of 'a girl ...giving herself completely to the man she loves' is the removal of 'all the anxiety about the "consequences"', or in other words, about the children. To accommodate this freedom, 'the care and education of the children becomes a public affair; society looks after all children alike'.[27] Sexual desire is considered a transhistorical fact, copulation an irreducibly private and personal matter, but nurturing maternal love is not. The intimacy and responsibility of parent – child relations gives way to accommodate unbridled sexual inclination. The less easily absorbable 'consequences' of human procreation – the small matter of pregnancy, and of profound emotional bonds between individuals of different generations – are not alluded to. The motivation to bear children at all in this context is not obvious and, on these terms, the advent of effective contraception

---

[27] Engels, *The Origin of the Family, Collected Works* vol. 26, pp.188, 184, 188, 183.

should be a sufficient condition for sexual equality.

We should take Engels's conclusions on this subject not as the logical conclusion of socialist commitment, but as an intervention in a distinctive nineteenth-century debate in which, as Thaden observes, 'the primary conflicts for women ...were generated not, as in our day, by the conflicting demands of career and motherhood but by the conflicts between the role of wife and the role of mother'.[28] Engels goes along with the mainstream of Victorian ideology in imagining the utopian future in terms of a contraction, rather than an expansion of intimate, passionate, family relationships; as a sanctification of the voluntary and equal conjugal relation at the expense of all unequal and involuntary personal ties. The recommendation that reproductive labour become public, rather than that the distinction and the hierarchy between the public and the family be transformed, is simply the logical conclusion of liberalism. Engels is distinctively Victorian in his neglect of the thought that, as Elshtain suggests, 'to require women to surrender an activity that offers them vital human meaning as embodied and sexual beings' is to 'demand an inordinate sacrifice'. Like so many of his contemporaries, he finds it hard to avoid the idea that some kind of self-owning individual 'freedom' comes before embodied biological bonds, and the emotions and subjective attitudes that go with and are cultivated by them.[29]

It is extraordinary how deeply and widely entrenched is what Thaden has shown to be the 'conservative ...typically Victorian view that a wife's [or, for later writers, "a woman's"] primary responsibility was to her husband [or, later, "lover"], not to her child or children', or, indeed, to her parents, brothers or sisters.[30] For the sake of the freedom and self-ownership of husband and sons, Victorian conjugal ideology insisted, mother-love and female nurture must be curtailed. Nietzsche was thoroughly of his time in his assertion that

The free spirit will always breathe a sigh of relief when he has finally resolved to shake off that motherly watching and warding with which women govern him. For what harm is there in the raw air that has so anxiously been kept from him ...compared with the unfreedom of the golden cradle ...*and the oppressive feeling that he must in addition be grateful because he is waited on* and spoiled like an infant? That is why the milk

---

[28]   Thaden, p.109.

[29]   Jean Bethke Elshtain (ed.) *The Family in Political Thought* (Amherst: University of Massachusetts Press, 1982), Introduction, p.11.

[30]   Greer, p.228, Thaden, p.14.

offered him by the women who surround him can so easily turn to gall.[31]

The denial of human interdependence that is at the heart of liberal ideology is closely linked to an inherently misogynistic anxiety about mothering, which has never gone away. Psychoanalysis has founded a 'science' on the extraordinarily Victorian idea that maturing is all a matter of successful separation from the mother (Queen Victoria herself warned her daughter 'not to indulge in "baby worship"'). Juliet Mitchell sums up the psychoanalytic position as implying that 'there can be nothing *human*' until the mother-child bond is broken, following Lacan's post-Freudian assessment of mother-love as a psychotic victimization of the child.[32] Craik's portrayal of family, superficially so 'Victorian', looks forward to our own time's fetishisation of sexual freedom.

Because Craik's view of family has been so influential, we have been liable to be rather hard on its rival – a rival that challenges Craik's contraction and marginalization of family relations, and the picture of the atomic, self-owning human subject that goes with it.

v. Charlotte Yonge's tracts against the nuclear family

Despite (or rather because of) the individualism she espouses, Craik presents us with what *we* recognize as a comparatively 'liberated' vision of the role of women. Most of her heroines are strong and independent, with the mental power to earn a living and choose a husband; they break unwanted ties, and never allow themselves to be constrained by their biology. They literally conquer their bodies, not only dying at will, but, in the case of the eponymous heroine of *Olive*, overcoming a curvature of the spine through sheer force of determination. Only in marriage is selflessness demanded, and that is demanded to an equal extent of men. Sympathy and altruism, for men and women equally, is strictly confined within the marital relationship.

Charlotte Yonge, on the other hand, has a formidable reputation as an anti-feminist novelist because of the altruistic role she sets out for her

---

31   Friedrich Nietzsche, *Human, All Too Human*, trans. RJ Hollingdale (Cambridge: Cambridge University Press, 1986), 7:429, p.158, italics mine.

32   Elizabeth K Helsinger, Robin Lauterbach Sheets and William Veeder (eds.), *The Woman Question: Society and Literature in Britain and America, 1837–83*, 3 vols (Chicago and London: University of Chicago Press, 1983), I:72; Juliet Mitchell, 'Introduction – I' to Jacques Lacan, *Feminine Sexuality*, eds. Juliet Mitchell and Jacqueline Rose (New York: W.W. Norton, 1982), pp.1–26, p.23.

heroines and her championship of what have been considered 'traditional' ideas of family. In her introduction to the *The Heir of Redclyffe*, Catherine Wells-Cole comments that 'Yonge's sympathetic concern for the demands of home and parents …is an indication [that] she is not a feminist'. Shirley Foster, too, in her classic feminist study, alludes to the general impression that Yonge's 'prime interest in family, rather than sexual, relationships – perhaps a result of the apparent lack of romantic experience in her own life …suggests that she has little of relevance to say about issues of particular concern to women'.[33] Both these comments reveal the narrowness of our common-sense contemporary conception of feminism. Given that women are commonly the most committed parents, and occupy a place at the core of the family, why would these concerns be irrelevant to feminism?

Certainly, Yonge's ideas about the family chime far less well with rights-based feminism than do those of Craik. However, I hope I have said enough to make it clear that this assumption that sexual coupling and/or individual autonomy is the beginning and end of biological politics, and the 'natural' focus of feminism (to the extent that any straying from these concerns can only be explained by a freakish 'lack of romantic experience') is too directly descended from Victorian liberal ideology to act as an objective standard by which to judge the 'progressiveness' of Victorian fiction.

Liberal resistance to Yonge's view of family and of the individual runs from Craik and her fictional faction, through QD Leavis, who was horrified by Yonge's 'inhuman theory' and 'moral ethos where everybody's first duty is to give up everything for everybody else', to the critics of our own time who dismiss her out of hand as a conservative anti-feminist. If we mean to understand and master our own Victorian political inheritance, we should also review our placing of Yonge.

'It seems incredible that Charlotte Yonge's novels could be taken seriously as literature … Yonge was a daydreamer with a writing itch that compensated her for a peculiarly starved life', wrote Leavis, disgusted by the 'typical pattern' of Yonge's fiction: 'a permanent invalid who is a hero or heroine …tubercular invalids are peculiarly saintly and frequently an idiot is idealized; the most blessed marriages are those in which one party is diseased or physically incapable'. She abhorred the tendency of Yonge's heroines to 'renounce a possible husband in order to devote herself to her

---

33   Catherine Wells-Cole, Introduction to Charlotte Yonge, *The Heir of Redclyffe* (Herefordshire: Wordsworth Classics, 1998), p.vii; Foster, p.20. Yonge's anti-feminism is an assumption behind most of the critical studies of Yonge, and is the explicit premise of Valerie Sanders in *Eve's Renegades: Victorian Anti-Feminist Women Novelists* (Basingstoke and London: Macmillan, 1996).

relatives, even if they are only imbecile grandparents', and, most of all, what she saw as Yonge's 'refusal to allow anyone ...moral or spiritual privacy or freedom'.[34] Her account of the characteristics of Yonge's fiction cannot be argued with. The only possible defence of Yonge must come from an interrogation of the value-judgements that Leavis simply takes as given.

The normative scheme of familial relations presented in Yonge's fiction is hardly less sexually egalitarian than Craik's. But Yonge demands not that women should become as independent as men in all arenas but the conjugal bond, but rather that men should become as relational and altruistic as women, and that 'Familial' affective, irrational bonds of mutual reliance should spread as widely as possible among human beings who, in the last analysis, want and need each other. Her sentimental novels provide a radically alternative morality to that offered by Craik, embodied in and symbolized by an alternative model of family.

As Barbara Dennis argues, Yonge's 'views on family were so strong as to be almost Roman – one of the standards she applied, in both her life and her fiction, was how an individual related to his family ... Yonge's bond with her family was one of her most notable characteristics'.[35] Her most successful novel, *The Heir of Redclyffe*, is a celebration of Family harmony and interdependence, which the hero dies in protecting.[36]

In Yonge's model of the family, fathers, mothers and children stand in relative symmetry in affective terms. In *The Heir*, indeed, the relationship between Mrs Edmonstone and her husband is much less significant than that between herself and her children. Family bonds are expected to last, siblings cling to each other, children define themselves in relation to their family, and the family circle is potentially ever-expanding, and the very stuff of society. Affective bonds extend both spatially and temporally. The immediate family is not strictly delineated from the extended family – cousins and aunts come and go – and the extended family may absorb other adjacent individuals, not related by blood. Guy, the hero, is brought up with the help of a number of his friends and relations, and is welcomed into the family at Hollywell as an intimate. His own relation to the household and villagers at Redclyffe, 'almost all related to each other', is semi-familial; he feels strong loyalty and affection towards Potts, the schoolmaster who taught

[34] QD Leavis, 'Charlotte Yonge and Christian Discrimination', *Scrutiny* 12 (1944), 152–60, 153, 155, 152–3, 153–4, 155.

[35] Barbara Dennis, *Charlotte Yonge (1823–1901): Novelist of the Oxford Movement* (Lewiston/Queenston/ Lampeter: Edwin Mellen Press, 1992), p.7.

[36] Charlotte Yonge, *The Heir of Redclyffe* (1853) (Herefordshire: Wordsworth Classics, 1998), (hereafter *HR*).

him to read, as well as to the household servants and well-known villagers. He tailors his honeymoon so that his butler may be taken to visit his relations in Switzerland. Deprived of a nuclear family of his own, he does not feel deprived; his grandfather 'never let me miss my parents' (*HR*, pp.253, 23). As the framing narrative of family feud and reconciliation through sacrifice, as well as other plot details such as the founding of the sisterhood and the adoption of neglected children suggest; in this novel the family is not contracting but expanding, through an ethic of expansive sympathy and altruism.

The predominant characteristic of Craik's characters, their proud independence, is cultivated by the fact that they have made their way on their own from youth; John because he is an orphan, and Will because of his parents' wise conduct in sending him to boarding school. In Yonge's novels, on the contrary, boys who triumph at boarding school, like Philip, the villain of *The Heir*, or Norman in *The Daisy Chain*, imbibe a dangerous egoism and even selfishness. In the second, conflicted half of *John Halifax*, Craik seems to enter into this perspective on boarding school; the Halifax boys 'still fondled [their mother] with a child-like simplicity – these her almost grown-up sons; who had never been sent to school for a day, and learned from other sons of far different mothers, that a young man's chief manliness ought to consist in despising the tender charities of home' (*JHG*, p.405). However, Will Steadman, in the more hard-bitten *Woman's Kingdom*, 'had a doctrine – learned at the big public school where he had been educated, fighting his way of necessity from the bottom to the top – that sometimes after a good honest battle ...men, as well as boys, are all the better friends' (*WK*, p.93). His childhood companions are peers with whom he competes, and he wants his own boys to start life with the same character-building struggle for survival.

Yonge's diametrical difference from Craik on the question of boarding school cannot but be read as part of a wider political difference. The upbringing of the hero of *The Heir* is the opposite of that of John Halifax or William Steadman. Guy 'has never been at school; so his thoughts came out in security of sympathy, without fear of being laughed at' (*HR*, pp.93, 37).[37] He has been cherished as the closest companion of his grandfather, to whom 'he told everything freely' and passionately loved; his friends have been

---

[37] 'The dangers of schools and universities as Yonge presents them are partly related to the competitive spirit that is fostered in them as a basic part of their structure. The boys are constantly ranked, and their future depends on their comparative standing.' Jane Sturrock, *"Heaven and Home": Charlotte M Yonge's Domestic Fiction and the Victorian Debate over Women* (Victoria: University of Victoria Press, 1995), p.45.

among the household at Redclyffe and the people of the village. Even undergraduate existence is regarded with extreme suspicion because of its distance from the domestic scene and its regulatory mix of sexes and ages. In Yonge's novels, the home, with its network of mutual obligations and dependencies, is the source and touchstone of a morality that needs no supplementation from schools teaching independence. If Craik preaches the good effects on character of hardship and competition, Yonge insists that it is loving support that breeds kindness and happiness.

Greer points out that 'where Family is strong, individuals take first their friends, and then their lovers from inside its sphere of influence'.[38] This happens time and time again in Yonge's novels; in *The Heir of Redclyffe* alone at least three marriages between cousins are mooted. In sharp contrast, Will and Edna in *The Woman's Kingdom* 'dislike the idea of cousins marrying' (*WK*, p.357). The love of Amy and Guy is built out of, and is continuous with, rather than (as by Craik) explicitly opposed to wider Family affection. 'It was a special delight to Amy that Hollywell and her family were as precious to [Guy] *for their own sake as for hers*' (my itals., *HR*, p.330)

Guy's chosen bride, Amy, is less self-possessed, more lacking in 'firmness and self command' than Craik's heroines, or than her sister Laura on whom Yonge frowns. Amy is said by Philip to have 'no bones' in her character; like Guy she is pliant and adaptable, and relies greatly on others; 'she did not know what she should have done in her own troubles without mamma and Charlie' (*HR*, p.376). She certainly does not feel herself 'absolutely alone' before marriage, as do Craik's heroines. But when Philip and Guy fall ill abroad, she proves herself as good a manager as a nurse, and when Guy dies he makes her his executor, in which capacity she demonstrates strongly the inadequacy of Philip's patronizing assessment of 'poor little Amy'. Amy is strong precisely because she is not egotistically self-reliant, but accepts help. When, as in *The Woman's Kingdom*, the 'self-reliant' and 'independent' pair, Laura and Philip marry one another, we find that they have been made so unhappy, and led so far astray by their 'rectitude' that they are in fact in need of permanent emotional support from Amy and the rest of the cooperative Family.

For Amy and Guy, the marriage bond is no licence to go forth and care no more for other ties, as it is for Craik's heroes. The couple wish to spend their honeymoon with their parents, (a common tendency in Yonge's novels),[39] and on his death-bed Guy foresees a happy future for his wife, 'I

---

[38] Greer, p.223.

[39] Alick and Rachel in *The Clever Woman of the Family* cut short their honeymoon in order to spend time with Alick's uncle. Alick also, like Guy, is a good nurse.

trust you ...to mamma for comfort. And Charlie – I shall not rob him any longer. I only borrowed you' (*HR*, p.412). Amy does not lie down to die with her husband like Mrs Halifax, as Edna Steadman hopes to do, but instead stays alive for the sake of her child, her Family, and the rest of the community; her love for Guy binds her to them all the more, rather than separating her from them.

Contrast the reception of a written marriage proposal by Edna in *The Woman's Kingdom* – 'Edna closed her little hand fiercely over it – her one possession, foretaste of her infinite wealth to come. It was hers – all her own, and the whole world should neither pry into it, nor steal it, nor share it', with Amy's reception of Guy's proposal: 'Amy flew off, like a bird to its nest, and never stopped till, breathless and crimson, she darted into the dressing room, threw herself on her knees, and with her face hidden in her mother's lap, exclaimed ...'Oh. Mamma, mamma, he says – he says he loves me!' The difference in envisioning the secondary emotional consequences of romantic love and sympathy could hardly be more stark (*WK*, p.129, *HR* p.168).

Yonge's account of Amy's reception of Guy is no sexist infantilization of the young woman. Guy also flies to Mrs Edmonstone's room, and 'repeated the same substance as he had said to Amy ...though with far less calmness and coherence, and far more warmth of expression' (*HR*, p.168). It is little wonder that, rather than feeling that she is losing one of her loved ones, as Phineas feels when he suspects the secret of John's love for Ursula, Mrs Edmonstone feels only 'touched and gratified by the free confidence with which both had at once hastened to pour out all to her, not merely as a duty, but in the full ebullition of their warm young love ...she was sympathizing with them as ardently as if she was not older than both of them put together' (*HR*, p.169). The invalid Charles, of whom Amy is the chief friend and nurse, in the warmth of his sympathy with her joy, parodies the selfish emotions he might be expected to feel in losing her. Unlike Phineas, Charles can truly feel that he is not losing a sister but gaining a brother, and so can ridicule the fictional conventions of jealousy and possessiveness between siblings:

> 'Well, Amy', said he, looking full at the carnation cheeks, 'are you prepared to see me turn lead-coloured, and fall into convulsions, like the sister with the spine complaint?'
>
> Amy was helping him to the sofa, laid him down, and sat by him on the old footstool; he put his arm round her neck, and she rested her head on his shoulder.

'Well, Amy, I give you joy, my small woman', said he, talking the more nonsense because of the fullness in his throat; 'and I hope you give me credit for amazing self-denial in so doing'.

'Oh, Charlie – dear Charlie!' and she kissed him …

' …tell me all – all you like, I mean – for you will have lover's secrets now, Amy'. (*HR*, p.172)

Of course Amy will have no such things. However, her elder sister does enter into lovers' secrets, and in doing so, Yonge suggests, brings upon herself her own tragedy. She is influenced by Philip to prize 'self-sufficiency' above all else, and is so persuaded to enter into a secret engagement which shuts her off from sympathy and confidence with her Family. She is decoyed into Craik's nuclear conception of the absolute precedence of the love match above all else; as her mother scolds her, 'you seem to think you owe nothing to anyone but Philip' (*HR*, p.395). On hearing of Amy's open engagement, Laura can respond only with rigidly repressed jealousy. 'All smooth here! Young, not to be trusted … All will be overlooked! And how is it with us? Proved, noble, superior, owned as such by all, as Philip is, yet, for that want of hateful money, he would be spurned'(172). There is, in fact, no possibility of Philip being rejected by the Family as Laura's lover; even after his deceptions have been revealed, he is still accepted. But, being relatively impoverished, he cannot bring himself to make public a proposal to an heiress that would compromise his public character for proud independence and rigid honour, and Laura is deceived by his representation of himself and her as alone and besieged by an unsympathetic world. Laura's lack of openness, and her privileging of the conjugal bond, are presented as extremely serious errors, not least because they make her deeply unhappy, and pervert and narrow her sympathy in a way that hurts no one so much as herself.

In her role as Editor of *The Monthly Packet*, Yonge rejected stories in which 'the whole turns exclusively on love'.[40] Not one of Yonge's own novels takes marriage, sexual choice or love as its primary concern or structuring force. Where the paradigmatic relationship in Craik's model of family is the freely mated couple, that of Yonge's is the relation between mother and child. At the centre of the Family, in *The Heir* as in so many of Yonge's novels, is the figure of the matriarch, for whom 'sympathy was a matter of necessity'. Yonge was used to the presence of such a matriarch in her own home at Otterbourne, which belonged to her maternal grandmother, Fanny Bargus,

---

[40]   Georgiana Battiscombe, *Charlotte Mary Yonge* (London: Constable, 1943), p.113.

who insisted that her married daughter and husband come and live with her, and that her son-in-law renounce his military career in the cause of establishing the family there. 'Mrs Bargus was the authority who ruled the house, with a position in the neighbourhood based on generations of acceptance and respect'.[41] In *The Heir*, Mrs Edmonstone is the hero's mentor, supporting and guiding him even in the choice of his wife. 'It was your likeness to her that first taught me to love you', Guy tells Amy, affirming the value of human affection as a force more basic than individuality (*HR*, pp.395, 413).

As if to prove that this emphasis on interdependence and the Familial virtues goes deeper than a gendered ideology of separate spheres, in novels in which the mother is dead or absent, Yonge introduces a distinctly maternal male figure in her place – a brother or a father who rules entirely through sensitivity, kindness and gentle persuasion, and who identifies his interests entirely with that of his Family. In *The Pillars of the House*, Dr May, one such figure, compares the idyllic results of the 'maternal' governance of another such figure, Felix, with the disaster and suffering caused by the authoritarian guardianship of *The Trial*'s Henry Ward.

In Yonge's fiction, the altruistic love of a mother for her child, and the loving dependence of a child on its mother are the ideal models of human relation not only among women, or between women and men, but also between adult men. She boldly gives her hero the role of caring for children and nursing an old enemy at the cost of his life, linking him with a tradition of heroines such as Gaskell's Ruth, and Anne Brontë's Helen Huntingdon. The sick-bed scenes between Guy and Philip are ennobling to both, as Amy reflects: 'her feelings towards Philip were touched, by seeing one wont to be full of independence and self-assertion, now meek and helpless, requiring to be lifted, and propped up with pillows, and depending entirely and thankfully upon Guy' (*HR*, p.381). Likewise, Charles the invalid, unlike Phineas and Julius, is the very centre of the household at Hollywell, his couch the focus of all merriment and enjoyment, especially after the cheerful influence of Guy has cured him of the notion that his existence is worthless. In the expansive Family, independence is neither demanded nor even considered possible, emotional or physical dependence is no more a humiliation for any Family member than it is for the new-born child, and help is not a matter of mere duty but of affective bonds.

Unlike his cousin Philip, or any of Craik's heroes, Guy is not cut out to fight his way to the top of the school. He is sensitive, and extremely

---

[41]   Dennis, p.9.

uncomfortable with the least sense of competition or animosity. At Oxford he is 'backward and unlikely to distinguish himself'. He is 'not nearly so tall or so handsome' as his soldier cousin Philip, and because of his 'complete absence of self-consciousness' is always liable to make himself ridiculous by exaggerated enthusiasm, or by falling asleep in his chair. Further, he has a fault absolutely inimical to heroism in Craik's narratives: he 'always seem[s] short of money'. He is unable to clear himself of Philip's accusations of gambling by giving evidence of his expenditure, because 'the accounts had not been kept at all. Guy had never been taught to regard exactness as a duty, had no natural taste for precision'. This carelessness about money, and about preserving his own public character, is part of a general openness and lack of focus on his own interest that is his primary and heroic characteristic, for which he suffers throughout the novel, and by which he is eventually killed. Philip regards his whole character as extravagant, and is repelled by its emotional gratuity; 'I don't like such excess of openness about his feelings; it is too like talking for talking's sake' (*HR*, pp.234, 254, 276, 182, 225, 37).

But at Hollywell, that idyllic locus of Family affection, 'anything of extravagance in love met with sympathy'. Guy's openness is of a piece with his need for relation to, and help from others; 'He was quite confidential with Mrs Edmonstone, on whom he used to lavish, with boyish eagerness, all that interested him, carrying her the passages in books that pleased him, telling her about Redclyffe affairs, and giving her letters from Markham, the steward'. He makes her his closest confidante: 'I want to ask something – a great favour ... You see how I am left all alone – you know how little I can trust myself. Will you take me in hand – let me talk to you – and tell me if I am wrong ...?' Guy's willingness to ask for help, his struggle to escape from loneliness, and his diffidence about his own self-control are in sharp contrast with the characteristics of John or Will Steadman, where the only expression of such impulses is secretly contained within the conjugal relation. Guy is always aware that his own virtue is contingent upon the kindness and help of others, that he may be led astray by hardship or bad company, or torn apart by the conflicts within himself. It is precisely this lack of self-sufficiency, this relational subjectivity, that Yonge marks out as the heroic quality, if it can rightly be called such, standing as it does so much in opposition to heroism as popularly conceived. No worldly success rewards such feelings, but Guy is 'supported by the forgetfulness of self' to such an extent that even his death hardly seems a tragedy (*HR*, pp.398, 26, 24. 406).

Guy's claim to heroism is all in the quality of his feeling; his attitude towards the world is one of 'unreasoning adoration'. For him, 'feeling' is the 'great point', and so is extended even to parts of creation towards which he cannot be construed as having any contracted duties. 'Never had man such delight in the "brute creation"' as Guy: '"There was the seagull, and the hedgehog, and the fox, and the badger, and the jay, and the monkey, that he bought because it was dying ...and a toad, and a raven, and a squirrel, and –"' (*HR*, pp.49, 291, 35). He hot-headedly risks his life in trying to save a drowning ram, which kicks him so viciously that they are both saved from the current only by catching on a branch, from which they are both in turn rescued by a St Bernard's dog. As this ridiculous incident suggests, Guy's heroism is the result not of principled or egoistic self-sacrifice but of 'complete absence of self-consciousness', which makes him feel united with the whole world by the warmest sympathy. His goodness is not a matter of calculated principle, 'not merely...duty, but...the full ebullition of [his] warm young love' (*HR*, p.169). Rather than deriving his moral life from his status as rational being, he is strongly bonded with irrational creation, being compared variously to a hawk, a young lion, and a horse 'prancing' in the hall. He 'basks' in human sociability, which he considers a delightful mystery of animal nature such as one see when watching 'what one only half understands – a rook's Parliament, or a gathering of sea-fowl on the Shag Rock' (*HR*, p.25). Guy's moral qualities are continuous with, rather than opposed to, his passionate animal nature.

Guy's rival Philip, on the other hand, despises the sentimentality manifest in novels like *Dombey and Son*, considering such books tolerable only because though their 'principles are negative...[they are] not likely to hurt a person well armed with the truth' (*HR*, p.27). 'True' morality, he considers, is available through exercise of reason and subjugation of emotion. In Philip's view, Guy's goodness hardly ranks as such – he rates partial, emotional and affective motivation as morally neutral; Guy 'has many admirable qualities' but these sentimental virtues are no 'compensations for faults'. Affective tendencies are not to be held to Guy's credit because they may be hereditary, and not the result of individual will or reason. 'I never heard that any in his family...were deficient in frankness and generosity...I wish to be perfectly just; all I say is, that I do not trust him till I have seen him tried'. Philip is resistant to the attraction of Guy's openness and warmth; he aspires to absolute rational impartiality in his judgement, considering that in books and men 'The actual merits are better seen by an unprejudiced stranger than by an old friend who lends them graces of his own devising' (*HR*, pp.31, 133).

Philip's virtue, unlike Guy's, is self-regarding; integrity always comes first: 'It was satisfactory to see his opinion justified, so that he might not feel himself unfair'. Be it in asking for help or in offering it, whenever 'Love [draws] him one way, and consistency the other', it is the latter that triumphs (*HR*, pp.133, 320). Morality is an extension of his sense of himself as an independent individual, and of his sense of other people's sense of him as such. His reputation for goodness is founded partly upon his self-sacrificing act in resigning an academic career in favour of a more immediately lucrative one in the army, which allows him to support his sisters. However, Mrs Edmonstone disapproves this act, committed secretly and without consultation, because it might have been rendered unnecessary by asking Guy's grandfather for help. She judges it 'done in a hasty spirit of independence'. Unlike Craik, she thinks independence may be taken too far, so that it becomes an indication of pride and delusive self-assurance, a symptom of unwillingness to acknowledge human relation. Philip 'was always reserved; open to no one', his self-dependence leading to 'a severity, an unwillingness to trust'. He operates according to a moral scheme aligned with Craik's, but out of harmony with Yonge's (*HR*, pp.20, 50). Yonge presents Philip's aspiration to impartiality as so misguided and unrealistic that it leaves him biased towards no one but himself. 'Cool and prudent', he is too apt to view morality as a game of calculation, in which he can objectively measure and value both himself and others, and feel free to do all he can to apportion the rewards.

The narrative constantly questions the value of this calculated virtue, connecting it with an ethos of self-assertion, self-reliance and, ultimately, a misery-making selfishness. Where Craik's novels make economic success, discretion and probity almost synonymous with virtue, Yonge's explicitly pulls these qualities apart. Guy's bailiff Markham remarks that he wishes his master 'had more such tenants as Todd', ...

'Pays his rent to the day, and improves his land'.
'But what sort of man is he?'
'A capital farmer. A regular screw, I believe; but that is no concern of mine'. (*HR*, p.246)

In Yonge's novels, being a good *man* is more or less directly at odds with being a successful player in the civil arena. Her plots distinguish material reward and moral desert as explicitly as Craik's bind them together. The entail on the estate means that Philip inherits when Guy dies young, while Amy is left to return to her Family to bring up a daughter, and to remain a support to Laura and Philip.[42] Yonge is suspicious of all 'virtue' that

---

[42] Much to the detriment of her reputation as any kind of feminist, see for example Wells-Cole, vii.

forwards individual material interests, or even leaves them untouched. Dr
May, in another of her novels, *The Daisy Chain*, warns his son of the dangers
of becoming 'a mere machine, with a moving spirit of self-interest': 'Take
care the love of rising and pushing never gets hold of you; there's nothing
that faster changes a man from his better self'.[43] Craik's heroines and heroes'
regard for the future is their chief heroism; Edna's womanly sway of virtue is
manifest in her success in persuading Will not to borrow money, and John
Halifax's greatest badge of honour is his survival of the economic crash
through his economic caution. On the contrary, Yonge's model of a virtuous
life is embodied in the action of the impoverished Miss Wellwood, 'not
spending a quiet, easy life making her charities secondary to her comforts,
but devoting herself to them time, strength and goods; not merely giving
away what she could spare, but actually sharing all with the poor, reserving
nothing for the future' (*HR*, p.188). This 'burning and shining light' has
dared to look 'beyond the ordinary range of duties and charities', to teach,
nurse, and comfort the poor; gathering orphans into her house and visiting
at all hours of day and night the most disreputable parts of the town. She
does not win respect for her ministering. The 'tyrannous hate' of the world
views her unconventional behaviour as an aggressive bid to become the
'general subject of animadversion'; Philip's sister Margaret accuses her of
rendering the orphans she adopts unfit for their station, and condemns her
for unwomanly lack of propriety (*HR*, p.177). This is a far cry from Craik's
obsequious submission to the standards of public opinion.

Yonge's narrative is an implicit comment on the fiction that helps to
entrench the equation of worldly success with moral worth. Characters
repeatedly compare the mean Philip with the 'the good boy in a story book'
who always gets rewarded, the 'perfect hero', 'living very happy ever after'
(*HR*, pp.82, 27, 472). *The Heir of Redclyffe* might have been written as a satire
of Craik's novels. Yonge continues the critique of the fictional alignment of
virtue and expediency begun by Fielding in his jibes at Richardson. Guy
derides Sir Charles Grandison (one of John Halifax's literary ancestors) as 'a
piece of self-satisfaction' (*HR*, p.27). Yonge's villain Philip is a more subtly
though hardly less vividly delineated version of Blifil in *Tom Jones*, and, like
many of Fielding's characters, is as much a comment on literary as on real-
life personality. In Yonge's *The Clever Woman of the Family*, the heroine
criticizes the common fictional depiction of heroism: '"No words have been
more basely misused than hero and heroine. The one is the mere fighting
animal whose strength and fortune have borne him through ...the other is

---

43   Charlotte Yonge, *The Daisy Chain* (1856) (London: Macmillan, 1892), p.117.

only the subject of an adventure, perfectly irrespective of her conduct in it.'"
The word, she thinks, should be applied to those '"who in any department
have passed the limits to which the necessity of their position constrained
them, and done acts of self-devotion for the good of others."'[44]

This ideal, one might note, is not gender specific. Here we have evidence
of the implications of Yonge's views on family for the role of women. Yonge
is very happy to see women engaged in roles outside their own immediate
family. But hardly surprisingly, given her critical view of the world of
commerce and public business, her claims for women lie in a radical
extension of Family values. Miss Wellwood's greatest claim to moral respect
is her foundation of a secular sisterhood, a prime example of the
Familiarisation of the public arena. If it is clearly true, as Sturrock points
out, that 'the aims of the sisterhoods ...were a world away from later
[feminist] concepts of the virtues of self-direction and self-fulfilment', that
should tell us something about the partiality of those later concepts.[45]
Yonge's novel might be aligned with Ruskin's 'Of Queens' Gardens' (1865),
which, although it has recently been read 'as a classic statement of the high
Victorian ideal of woman', was, as Helsinger, Sheets and Veeder observe,
'attacked by contemporary critics as violent, "Carlylesque" social criticism'
because of its demonstration that the domestic virtues 'could be invoked to
support a social vision disturbingly different from the Victorian reality'.
Such texts appeal to women to turn the domestic critique of competitive
materialism into reforming action, 'the angel is invoked not as a
conservative force in a changing society, but as a potentially subversive force
in the culture which imagined her'.[46] Yonge's fundamental critique of
individualism leads her to argue for an extension of the Familial world to
include not only men but also public functions, rather than to plead for
women's emancipation from caring roles and freedom to enter the world of
self-assertive competition. Amy, Mrs Edmonstone and the Miss Wellwoods
are powerful and talented women, who stand at the centre of expanded
domestic scenes.

In other novels, Yonge chastises, albeit with sympathetic understanding,
heroines who place their own egotistical desire for importance above the
duties that come in their way. Although she shows sympathy for her
heroines' search for self-fulfilment, however, it is true that ultimately she
seeks to demonstrate that they can do no good for themselves or for anyone

---

[44] Yonge, *The Clever Woman of the Family* (1865) (London: Virago, 1989), p.141.
[45] Sturrock, p.57.
[46] Helsinger, Sheets and Veeder, I:77–78.

else through egoistic independence. Most obviously, Ethel May of *The Daisy Chain* and Rachel Curtis of *The Clever Woman of the Family* find that their ambitious plans of self-improvement clash with their social duties, and that they overestimate their own independent capabilities. Both women, however, find that their domestic responsibilities can be made continuous with a wider round of social work, as long as it is engaged in with a spirit of earnest sympathy rather than self-exultation.[47] We rather beg the question against Yonge if we assume that the fact that she recommends work outside the home as 'devoted service rather than ...a career in its own right' indicates a lack of insight or concern for the lot of women.[48] For she maintains her insistence that egoistic, self-regarding action and ambition can never bring happiness to either women or men, though they may bring a worthless sort of power. She maintains this insistence more strongly in her treatment of Philip than in any of her portrayals of women. Repeatedly, she shows men resigning their own immediate fame and success for their families and communities, particularly for their parents, brothers and sisters, in ways which Craik would have frowned on as an 'unnatural' straining of duty: Norman in *The Daisy Chain*, Tom in *The Trial*, Felix and Lance in *The Pillars of the House* (who makes the ultimate novelistic sacrifice, conventionally associated with women, by resigning an artistic career to look after his Family), are among numerous examples. As Sturrock puts it, 'use and domesticity are finally placed above both prestige and success'.[49] The healthfulness of action is judged according to the impulses that drive it and the worthiness of the cause, not by the success in winning the Hobbesian garland of the foremost.

Yonge is certainly no advocate of the self-owning rights and independence of individual women. But neither is she an advocate of the rights of the individual as an ultimate principle more generally; such priorities would be radically inconsistent with her assessment of what human subjects are like, and how their interaction should thus be viewed and

---

[47] Sturrock comments that Yonge, 'Rather than undercutting domestic ideology ...extends it far beyond its conventional limitations and represents the domestic – and by implication, the feminine – as morally, spiritually, and culturally central for male as well as female. She moralizes and thus universalizes the home.' She shows 'the domestic as the supreme masculine as well as the supreme feminine quality, and portrays those women who are most committed to domesticity as also committed to work', and that in her fiction 'men like women are seen as more properly directing their attention to the private rather than the public sphere,' pp.25, 34.

[48] Foster, pp.22–3.

[49] Sturrock, p.47.

conducted. Her 'good' characters are, definitively, conscious of being emotional creatures who are radically dependent on one another. They know that their wills are weak, and their judgement fallible, being as it is subject to confusion from outside themselves and emotional turmoil within.

If there is no assertion of individual rights in *The Heir*, neither is there expectation that individuals embody perfect virtue. Only persistent delusions of self-sufficiency are beyond comfort and forgiveness. Yonge's heroes, so unlike Craik's, are fallible and faulty creatures, liable to be misled, and exorbitant in their emotional dependence on the love of those around them. There is no question of Guy's holding Philip's ill conduct against him, and his forgiveness is a matter not of principle but of spontaneous generous feeling. Yonge challenges the notion of individual desert as the primary rule of society, and substitutes for it the notion of the Family as the substance of society regarded as a cohesive body, which will support all its members, weak or strong. 'Motherly' love becomes the symbol of a comprehensive ideal of mutuality, interdependence and pleasurable altruism, to which both men and women must aspire.

Of course, Yonge's Tractarianism is highly relevant here. Sturrock comments that while 'Societal expectations commonly associated self-effacement and self-sacrifice with the feminine ...Keble's version of Christianity reinforced but also generalized feminine and domestic virtues. In Keble's Tractarianism ...behaviour associated with the feminine and the domestic became prescribed more generally as Christian behaviour'.[50] The downplaying of Protestant assertions of free-will and rationality is also of a piece with high-church thinking.

However, there was never a picture of Christian virtue of more practical worldly import or warmer human appeal than Yonge's. Her choice of an altruistic heroic trajectory for her heroes and heroines does not come across, like Sewell's, as resignation to earthly misery, or endurance in expectation of the world to come. Yonge's hopes for this world, indeed, seem stronger than Craik's. Whereas the latter's hopes for this world are founded on the idea that God has made the material world to fit us, so that material distribution will come to reflect our deserts and desires, Yonge's hopes for this world are founded on the idea that God has made us to fit each other. There simply should be no tension between making ourselves happy and thinking of and acting for others; in fact, a true view of things will reveal these two things to be two sides of the same coin. Happiness, in Yonge's novels, lies in mutual

---

50   Sturrock, p.23. For further discussion of her relation to the Oxford Movement see
      Dennis.

dependence. Individualism, for Yonge, is not only wrong, it is also uncomfortable. The newly 'self-reliant' Laura cannot find peace: 'though solitude was oppressive, everyone's presence was a burthen'. Amy wonders, on the topic of the secret engagement, '"How could she help telling mamma? ... Not only because it was right, but for the comfort of it"' (*HR*, pp.392, 369). Guy considers his very senses, the most private part of consciousness, as public property. He promises to tell his sofa-bound brother-in-law of all the sights he will see on honeymoon. Charles observes with gratitude '"your sight-seeing is a public benefit. You have seen many a thing for me"' and Guy replies that '"that is the pleasure of seeing and hearing, the part that is not fleeting"' (p.332).

Guy's bouncing enthusiasm throughout the novel, so uncharacteristic of a virtuous hero ('never anyone a greater capacity for happiness than Guy'), in combination with the immediacy of the domestic scene, the appealingly developed characters and conversations, persuade us that entering into the sympathetic, Familial bonds is not an 'unnatural' or weak act of renunciation, as Craik would have it, but the clear path to natural joy. Philip comments that Guy as a child was always 'rushing about, playing antics, provoking the solemn echoes with shouting, whooping, singing, whistling' (*HR*, pp.94, 9). For Yonge, we have sociable joy in our natures. Happiness will come with an open heart and forgetfulness of self, whereas stern morality is the symptom of an inhumanly rigid self-regarding spirit which blights such fragile, transient human delight, as Philip, early in the novel, knocks the single flower from Amy's nurseling camellia.

Yonge's picture of Family life, then, powerfully contests the vision of human personhood upon which liberal public politics and private morality – and the division between the two – are founded. It is clear that there is no principle which contains Yonge's vision of Family feeling within a narrow compass, or which legitimates another sort of standard for the world outside it. Her novels bring to bear on everyday material existence the Tractarian principle of the ethical unity of all areas of life – her Anglo-Catholicism disrupts the Protestant disjuncture of personal morality and economic life.

We should not underestimate the importance of such an ideological challenge. But on behalf of what cause is it made? Does Yonge offer any positive suggestions to advance her negative deconstruction of one conception of social relations? Not many – but this indefiniteness in prescription is hardly a damning failure. It is in fact to the credit of Yonge's fictional vision that it withholds unqualified support from the principal ideological competitor to bourgeois individualism – feudal social paternalism. A zealous attention to the interest of his poorer parishioners is a necessary but distinctly insufficient condition of Guy's heroism. Significantly, Guy always insists that Philip would make a better landlord, and his sanctification seems completed by his resignation of temporal power and authority to Philip. In all Yonge's novels, great wealth, and especially the over-confident exercise of the power it brings, is radically incompatible with goodness. Yonge does use the residual social structures of pre-capitalist society as a setting for her Family ethic that satisfactorily excludes economic competition. But her radically relational conception of human nature leaves no room for the exercise of autocratic judgment. Her fiction does not supply one example of an authoritarian father we are asked to approve. Yonge's powerful fathers are all mothers in disguise, just as Craik's powerless men are women in disguise. Yonge's feminism is deeply concealed, whereas Craik's is consolidated by other concealments.

It is true, however, that Yonge gives us no view of the impersonal structures that govern the social world, but represents only those relations that can be contained within the directly personal paradigm. While we see the good characters earnest in their attempts to meliorate the world they feel their own – and that world is considerably wider than the 'personal' world in Craik's novels – they seem resigned to the evil of the civil arena, and determined to have nothing to do with it. Moreover, Yonge's depiction of the appeal of an interdependent Family, and her foreshadowing of the kind of social relations that might spring from its universalization, is achieved partly through a series of evasions. It is not for nothing that she portrays families of the established gentry. They are part of a society un-ruptured by change and outside influence, not only largely exempt from the more obvious manifestations of capitalist competition, but also sharing common standards of education, conduct and cultural preference. Yonge's charming demonstration of the potential of Familial sympathy and altruism as the basis for a wider social good would have been more rigorous had she conducted it in a different social milieu. If the picture she gives us of family is more attractive, and more coherent, than Craik's, it is also less directly engaged with the dominant economic reality of its time.

vi. Deepest sympathy

I hope I have shown that domestic fiction, and the Victorian attitudes to family that it embodies, are not the settled and serviceable instruments for the displacement of politics that so much recent theory has taken them to be. Despite their diametrically opposed political corollaries, Craik and Yonge's fictional illustrations of the two competing Victorian models of family share a peculiar emotional intensity which bubbles insistently to the surface of the narrative. Family feeling, as manifested here is not merely the displaced discursive product and/or prop of the public political scene. It is, rather, a compelling emanation of a struggle behind that scene over the most basic and persistent, most immanent and gripping practical questions about the nature of the human subject and of social relations. The domestic focus, the details of intimate relationship, and the emotional presentation of these texts allow for a uniquely impassioned exploration of the conditions and passions of everyday life. If we ignore their invocation of an intimate, emotive dimension of experience, insisting that public political discourse comes first, we evade the difficult problem of whether man is first and foremost an abstractly rational and self-assertive, or a sociable, material and feeling, being. Such an evasion is surely unwise, for it is upon our answers to this question that the shape of our political endeavours is most crucially dependent.

CHAPTER 5

The Personal, the Political and the Human, Part III:
'The Torn Nest is Pierced by the Thorns'– Sympathy after the Family

i. 'Daylight on the wreck': The Family in decline

Yonge's investigation of the potential of Familial altruism as the basis for social good is incomplete because of the sheltered social milieu within which it is conducted. In *The Mill on the Floss*, a novel thematically permeated by economic and social friction, George Eliot undertakes a more rigorous exploration of the same theme. She examines the tension between individual will and communal bonds – between the notion of the human subject as rational agent of self-regarding choice on the one hand, and as constituted by given material and emotional relationships on the other – with particular regard to an identifiable debate about what the family really is or should be.

The clannishness of the Dodsons is the besieged and etiolated remnant of the spirit of the traditional Family. Judith Lowder Newton has noted that the 'Dodson creed' 'confers status upon the production and the producers of domestic goods …a vestige from another time, when the comfortable middle-class family was an economic unit and when women of the middle ranks had greater status as persons making visible contributions to the subsistence and income of the family'.[1] The Dodsons put great store by their own 'particular ways of bleaching the linen, of making the cowslip wine, curing the hams and keeping the bottled gooseberries; so that no daughter of that house could be indifferent to the privilege of having been born a Dodson' (*MF*, I:vi:38). Newton shows how the status of each of the Dodson sisters is inversely related to the extent of her husband's engagement with

---

[1] Judith Lowder Newton, *Women, Power and Subversion: Social Strategies in British Fiction 1778–1860*, (New York and London: Methuen, 1985), pp.130–31.

the new spirit of entrepreneurial capitalism.[2] The sisters themselves illustrate a historical process with all its ramifications for female status.

The Dodson creed sets itself against the individualist scheme that allots reward according to merit:

> in the matter of wills, personal qualities were subordinate to the great fundamental fact of blood; and to be determined in the distribution of your property by caprice, and not make your legacies bear a direct ratio to degrees of kinship, was a prospective disgrace ...it was one form of that sense of honour and rectitude which was a proud tradition in such families – a tradition which has been the salt of our provincial society (*MF*, I:xiii:113).[3]

The Dodsons still assume that the business of one is the business of all, and some financial interdependence remains amongst them despite the pressures of an increasingly individualist economy. Mrs Glegg has 'been used to boast that there had never been any of those deadly quarrels among the Dodsons which had disgraced other families; that no Dodson had ever been 'cut off with a shilling', and no cousin of the Dodsons disowned' (*MF*, I:xii:107).

However, the Family instinct, by its economic marginalization, has shrunk down to little more than an instinct to interfere for the sake of it. Tom can only borrow money from the Gleggs on commercial terms, and his uncle Deane thinks nothing of his Family relation to his nephew, refusing to let personal considerations lead him to 'carry out business on sentimental grounds' (*MF*, III:vii:213). Mrs Glegg helplessly looks on as one after another sister drops Family custom after Family custom. With little to do for the communal material wellbeing of the Family, she has no outlet for her importance but troublesome fussiness over the mundane details of the lives of the rest of the family.

The Family under pressure, Eliot suggests, is no idyllic realm of unquestioning affection, but a selfishly exclusive clan, a powerful force which demands absolute conformity of its members: 'There were some Dodsons less like the family than others – that was admitted; but in so far as they were "kin", they were of necessity better than those who were "no kin"' (*MF*, I:vi:38). When the Family offers so little sympathy to its members, it can hardly appear as anything more than an imposition upon their freedom.

---

[2]   Newton, pp.130–5.

[3]   cf. The inheritance that gives Will Steadman the start over his brother Julius in *The Woman's Kingdom*, left to him precisely at the 'fancy' of a relation whose 'favourite' he was.

ii. 'Perplexing freedom'

It is in this context that Mr Tulliver determines to break free of the matriarchal shackles of the Family: 'a male Tulliver was far more than equal to four female Dodsons, even though one of them was Mrs Glegg' (II:ii:138). Tulliver, an old-fashioned man determined to modernize himself, admires his brother-in-law Deane, a true new man, and itches to engage in the struggle for his rights with the help of the rising tribe of lawyers. With newfangled suspicion of traditional Familiar customs, he is unwilling to have his son brought up to take his father's place; like the Steadmans, he foresees the possibility of being 'pushed from his stool' by Tom: 'if I made him a miller an' farmer, he'd be expectin' to take to the mill an' the land ... I've seen enough o' that wi' sons. I'll never pull my coat off before I go to bed ...he may make a nest for himself, an' not want to push me out o' mine' (*MF*, I:iii:15). So, again like the socially aspiring Steadmans, he sends his son off to school to learn independence of the Family: 'the lad must learn not to think too much about home' (*MF*, II:i:127). He makes the choice of Tom's schooling the grounds of an assertion of independence from his wife's Family: '"I shall ask neither aunt nor uncle what I'm to do wi' my own lad," said Mr Tulliver, defiantly' (*MF*, I:ii:9).

However, Mr Tulliver's history illustrates the elusiveness of independence. In the first place, no matter how well he arms himself with the arguments of bourgeois individualism, he cannot throw off the ties of affection that breach its scheme. Riding to Basset to retrieve his debt from his brother-in-law, a necessary corollary of his assertion of independence from his wife's Family, he remarks to himself on the anomaly, given the individualistic scheme, and a (Craikean or Spencerian) equation between wealth and moral desert, of the un-chosen nature of blood relation: 'poor relations are undeniably irritating – their existence is so entirely uncalled for on our part, and they are almost always very faulty people' (*MF*, I:viii:72). He justifies self-assertion in the moralistic terms of beneficial discipline that are also so evident in Craik and Spencer: 'he got up a due amount of irritation against Moss as a man without capital, who, if murrain and blight were abroad, was sure to have his share of them ... It would do him good rather than harm, now, if he were obliged to raise this three hundred pounds: it would make him look about him better' (*MF*, I:viii:68). But although he tells Mr Moss 'I must look to my own business and my own family', and tries to put himself into the frame of mind of a 'man of business', Tulliver cannot help feeling that the very essence of those (nuclear) family relations which he holds so dear, and which provide the justification for his business activities, is threatened by assertion of his rights at the expense of his sister's Family (*MF*, I:viii:72, 68). The thought of Mrs Moss's children provides the conceptual leverage, available even within the nuclear family, for a projection of sympathy that makes clear the difficulties of accepting the individualist scheme. His mind running on the ethic of self-reliance, Tulliver bemoans his sister's superfluity of girl children:

> ' ...they must turn out and fend for themselves', said Mr Tulliver, feeling that his severity was relaxing, and trying to brace it by throwing out a wholesome hint. 'They mustn't look to hanging on their brothers'.
>
> 'No: but I hope their brothers 'ull love the poor things, and remember they came o' one father and mother: the lads 'ull never be the poorer for that', said Mrs Moss, flashing out with hurried timidity, like a half-smothered fire. (*MF*, I:viii:71)

In the end Tulliver does 'not like to give harsh refusals even to a sister, who had ...come into the world in that superfluous way characteristic of sisters, creating a necessity for mortgages'. Although 'conscious of being a little weak', Tulliver is inchoately aware that his own beloved daughter may also come to be 'superfluous' to a scheme of self-assertion and self-advancement, and that only the cultivation of feelings that outrun the strictures of individualism can guarantee that she will find help from her brother once the siblings are separated by the formation of a new generation of nuclear families (*MF*, I:viii:67–8). Once again, Family feeling ruptures individualist ideology.

Another obstacle to Tulliver's independence is the fact that even his desires are determined for him by the forces he struggles to be free from. He is continually in reaction: to popular opinion, to the authority of his wife's sisters – 'it was a guiding principle with Mr Tulliver to let the Dodsons know that they were not to domineer over him' –, or to the infringement on his right by Pivart. Mrs Tulliver, we are told, with mocking reference to the doctrine of female influence that comes with the nuclear family, has considerable influence on her husband; she can be sure of making him do the opposite of what she wants. While a worthless power for her, this 'influence' considerably degrades the value of Tulliver's freedom (*MF*, II:ii:138).

The third, and decisive, obstacle to Tulliver's independence is his human frailty. The picture of the bullish Tulliver reduced to childlike reliance on his family for emotional and economic support is central to the novel. Mr and Mrs Tulliver manifest the vulnerability of human happiness in an unforgiving, individualistic world, bonded together by the only tie in that world that withstands changes of fortune. "'Poor Bessy …you was a pretty lass then – everybody said so – and I used to think you kept your good looks rarely. But you're sorely aged … Don't you bear me ill will … I meant to do well by you … We promised one another for better or for worse'" (*MF*, III:viii:227).

iii. Independence: An expensive commodity

The harshness of civil life and justice is highlighted in the plight of the Tullivers. Mr Tulliver 'fails' largely through bad luck, driven to live and die by a system of arbitrary competition in which even water, the element of life, must be competed for:

> The taxing-masters had done their work like any respectable gunsmith conscientiously preparing the musket, that, duly pointed by a brave arm, will spoil a life or two. Allocaturs, filing of bills in Chancery, decrees of sale, are legal chain-shot or bomb-shells that can never hit a solitary mark, but must fall with widespread shattering …even justice makes its victims, and we can conceive no retribution that does not spread beyond its mark in pulsations of unmerited pain. (*MF*, III:vii:212)

Civil society, Eliot suggests, is a transmuted state of war. Its justice is to be questioned, as Mr Tulliver, in his failure, finds his good deeds of generosity held against him, and as mankind, 'not disposed to look narrowly into the conduct of great victors', visits disproportionate unhappiness on those who go wrong, hurting not only them but those close to them (*MF*, III:vii:219). It seems a medium of awful implacability for the ageing Tullivers. They find themselves neglected by their neighbours, for

> there is a chill air surrounding those who are down in the world, and people are glad to get away from them, as from a cold room: human beings, mere men and women, without furniture, without anything to offer you, who have ceased to count as anybody, present an embarrassing negation of reasons for wishing to see them, or of subjects on which to converse with them …there was a dreary isolation in the civilized Christian society of these realms for families that had dropped below their original level, unless they belonged to a sectarian church, which gets some warmth of brotherhood by walling in the sacred fire. (*MF*, IV:iii:245)

It is *brotherhood* that is lacking in the alienated, 'civilized' community, in which human beings cannot feelingly relate to one another as members of a human family, but only through the mediation of the goods, chattels and social hierarchies of the cash nexus. The inhuman inexorability of the consequences of economic failure, so apparent in the context of the scope of a human life, cannot be completely made up by the limited domestic sphere in which forgiveness and unconditional love still have a hold: "'Oh dear, dear father!' said Maggie ...'bear it well – because we love you – your children will always love you ...'" She felt her father beginning to tremble – his voice trembled too, as he said, after a few moments – "Aye, my little wench, but I shall never live twice o'er"' (*MF*, III:viii:225–6). Tulliver, unfitted by a lifetime of combative self-assertion to set his mind in a different track, can only digest his social failure and cling to his family: "'Give me a kiss, Bessy, and let us bear one another no ill will: we shall never be young again ...This world's been too many for me"' (*MF*, III:viii:228).

The impact of the gendered division of labour on Maggie in this crisis is more indirect, though no less real, than is usually suggested. Her misery is not the result of her exclusion *as a woman* from the world of productive employment; initially she does her paid sewing, and we can hardly imagine that the rebellious girl would enjoy such highly disciplined and competitive work as Tom's were it available to her. As her parents lack the funds to continue her education after thirteen, even had she been a man the only intellectual career open to her would have been teaching, which, when she takes to it, she hates as alienated and badly rewarded. She suffers from the discomfort and cheerlessness of poverty and social exclusion caused by her father's failure in the struggle of the civil arena, and from her thwarted striving after the middle-class world of education and leisure: she is 'as lonely', in her intellectual aspiration 'as if she had been the only girl in the civilized world' (*MF*, IV:iii:252). And as a woman in the home she is faced with a burden of comforting and attempting to cheer her parents; a burden created by their maiming in the economic struggle, shirked as they are by society at large, and even, increasingly, by a Family that is withered to a husk, unsympathetic, and alienated by Tulliver's determination to go it alone. Maggie's suffering as a woman is just one part of the wider suffering of the losers in the individualist struggle.

The history of the Tullivers challenges the bourgeois individualist idea, illustrated by the career of John Halifax, that through rightful exercise of our own powers of self-assertion we will get the place in life we deserve. Moral value is almost inversely related to economic success in this novel; generosity and warmth are not rewarded, and morally neutral characteristics like

Maggie and her father's 'entire want of prudence and self-command' are harshly punished (*MF*, IV:ii:241). As Mrs Moss observes, from her own bitter experience of conscientious but inescapable dependence, "'the right doesn't allays win …[it's] the rich mostly get things their own way'" (*MF*, II:ii:137–8).

Mr Tulliver fails not because his 'will was feeble, but because external fact was stronger … Mr Tulliver had a destiny as well as Oedipus, and in this case he might plead, like Oedipus, that his deed was inflicted on him rather than committed by him' (*MF*, I:xiii:114). The myth of human self-determining within the civil arena is exposed. Mr Moss, a man of no capital, has never even had a throw of the dice; his life is one continual, inevitable bearing of humiliating necessity:

> Basset had a poor soil, poor roads, a poor non-resident land-lord, a poor non-resident vicar, and rather less than half a curate, also poor. If any one strongly impressed with the power of the human mind to triumph over circumstances, will contend that the parishioners of Basset might nevertheless have been a very superior class of people, I have nothing to urge against that abstract proposition: I only know that in point of fact the Basset mind was in strict keeping with its circumstances. (*MF*, I:viii:68)

The abstract plausibility of the bourgeois scheme of equal rights peopled by rational and autonomous agents bears no relation to the material mechanisms of existence. Tulliver asks Mr Moss, who has the 'unexpectant air of a machine horse', why he doesn't make better plans for his land. 'He answered in a patient-grumbling tone, "Why, poor farmers like me must do as they can."' For the poor the chances of self-determination are radically limited. Eliot ridicules the suggestion that such people should 'take responsibility' for themselves and the burden they place on others (*MF*, I:viii: 72).

Physical as well as economic weakness demonstrates the failure of the ideology of rights to bring self-determination in practice. Asked by his son for his blessing for his efforts to win Maggie, Wakem senior angrily tells his son

> ' …you are independent of me: you can marry this girl tomorrow, if you like: you are a man of six-and-twenty – you can go your way, and I can go mine. We need have no more to do with each other'.
> … 'No: I can't marry Miss Tulliver, even if she would have me – if I

have only my own resources to maintain her with … I can't offer her poverty as well as deformity'.

'Ah, there is a reason for your clinging to me, doubtless', said Wakem, still bitterly …

'I expected all this', said Philip. 'I know these scenes are often happening between father and son. If I were like other men of my age, I might answer your angry words by still angrier – we might part …you have an advantage over most fathers: you can completely deprive me of the only thing that would make my life worth having'. (*MF*, VI:viii:373)

Philip cannot validate his self-hood through the proud independence of choosing a partner in the manner of Craik's characters. Like Phineas in *John Halifax* and the various invalids of *The Heir of Redclyffe*, he draws attention to the limits of an ethic of self-reliance. Philip is dependent on those around him.

But the novel also suggests that even those with the power to exercise choice are, however unaware of the fact, radically dependent on their fellow creatures. The observation that Mr Deane 'had been advancing in the world as rapidly as Mr Tulliver had been going down in it', certainly insinuates that there may be some indirect connection between the gains of some and the losses of others (*MF*, III:iii:180). Even for the rich and healthy, self-sufficiency is an absolute illusion. In rejecting Stephen, Maggie simultaneously rejects a place amongst those whose freedom is premised upon the exploitation of those, like Lucy and Philip and the labouring poor, whose lot is determined for them: 'I cannot take a good for myself that has been wrung out of their misery' (*MF*, VI:xiv:419). There is no comfortable freedom from obligation; to act as though one were in fact independent is necessarily to exploit others; to lose sight of one's interrelation is to be alienated from the truth of one's existence. The bourgeois life of unconstrained action and individualist pleasure is a

very expensive production; requiring nothing less than a wide and arduous national life condensed in unfragrant deafening factories, cramping itself in mines, sweating at furnaces, grinding, hammering, weaving under more or less oppression of carbonic acid – or else, spread over sheepwalks, and scattered in lonely houses and huts on the clayey or chalky corn-lands, where the rainy days look dreary. This wide national life is based entirely on …the emphasis of want, which urges it into all the activities necessary for the maintenance of good society and light irony: it spends its heavy years often in a chill, uncarpeted fashion, amidst family discord unsoftened by long corridors.

The experience of this arduous mode of existence, where labour is a necessity and not a mode of self-expression, where personal interrelation is unmediated by civilized distance, and choice is hardly an issue at all, brings into question the naturalness of self-ownership and self-regard as a primary human attitude. Faced with scarcity, and with the unalienated reality of human relationship, Eliot suggests, human societies require 'something …that lies outside personal desires, that includes …active love for what is not ourselves', something like the sympathetic mutuality that characterises Family relationships (*MF*, IV:iii:255).

iv. 'A Duet in Paradise': The critique of the love-plot

Maggie takes after her father in her problematic pursuit of freedom and, in particular, of independence from the Family as it is represented by her aunts. Despite her initial sense that the Family is the place to look for pity and help, when she finds that her aunts will not volunteer any substantial material assistance to stave off the sale of the furniture she determinedly tells them 'we'll do without you' (*MF*, III:iv:189). Like her father, however, she continually finds the form of her rebellion taking a shape determined by others.

The vexing question of Maggie's choice of Stephen becomes newly legible when it is considered in relation to other literary depictions of the love match. Where Craik uses the love match as the embodiment and legitimation of the freedom of the individual, Eliot turns this convention on its head, using it as the prime instance of the individual's inextricable relation to the world around him or her. *The Mill* demonstrates that sexual love is not the refutation but rather the exemplum of the maxim that 'there is no creature whose inward being is so strong that it is not greatly determined by what lies outside it'.[4]

Far from being providentially guided from the start to meet her true partner, it is only too clear how large a share the pressure of 'hard, non-moral circumstance' plays in Maggie's 'choice', which latter, rather than confirming the integrity of her selfhood, sets her past against her present and her egoism against her sympathy for others.

Before he meets Maggie, Stephen is complacent in his contemplation of

---

[4]   Eliot, *Middlemarch*, VII:finale:824–5.

the enjoyment of discrimination in choosing a wife; like Will Steadman and John Halifax, he knows what 'sort of woman' he would have, and perceives his exercise of selection as a validation of his individual status and freedom:

> A man likes his wife to be accomplished, gentle, affectionate, and not stupid; Lucy had all these qualifications. Stephen ...was conscious of excellent judgement in preferring her to Miss Leyburn, the daughter of the county member, although Lucy was only the daughter of his father's subordinate partner; besides, he had had to defy and overcome a slight unwillingness and disappointment in his father and sisters – a circumstance which gives a young man an agreeable consciousness of his own dignity. Stephen was aware that he had sense and independence enough to choose the wife who was likely to make him happy, unbiased by any indirect considerations. (*MF*, VI:i:326)

When Stephen meets Maggie, however, the whole egoistic dynamic of choice takes on an alienated force of its own. The subtle frisson of self-assertive defiance that Stephen feels in his connection with Lucy becomes a very ecstasy in his relation with Maggie; his exercise of will finds a new and compulsive challenge.

The attraction between the two of them is an impersonal result of their relative circumstances, not of their unique individualities. Stephen, who has little to do in life but *autograph* cheques, has been bred up to do little else than assert his superior individuality. He meets in Maggie a 'strange, troublesome' creature, not liable to acknowledge the absolute value of his social status, whom he becomes anxious to 'subdue'. Maggie, on the other hand, has been shut off from any admiration or communion emanating from her intellectual equals, and has gone through a course of social humiliation, in which she has been initially shamed as an accessory to her father's 'failure', and after that forced into unfulfilling work. She meets a representative of the culture and freedom she desires who, despite himself, seems susceptible to her fascination. The 'vanity' his attention stirs in Maggie deserves the name of 'ambition', Eliot tells us. 'I am afraid there would have been a subtle, stealing gratification in her mind if she had known how entirely this saucy, defiant Stephen was occupied with her: how he was passing rapidly from a determination to treat her with ostentatious indifference to an irritating desire for some sign of inclination from her' (*MF*, VI:vii:359, ix:383, vi:352, vii:367).

Their initial meeting is a power struggle in which each seeks to impress the other, the power shifting from Stephen to Maggie, as she feels herself 'for the first time in her life, receiving the tribute of a very deep blush and a very deep bow from a person towards whom she herself was conscious of timidity', back to Stephen, as she realizes there has been a joke against her, and then back again to Maggie, as Stephen has his compliments scornfully rejected and his arguments undermined. Whereas his self-esteem has been only too well nourished, hers has been reduced to a fragile attitude of resistance. The interaction of such differently nurtured egoisms is bound to result in catastrophe.

> [Maggie] had been hearing some fine music sung by a fine bass voice
> ... And she was conscious of having been looked at a great deal ...
> Such things could have had no perceptible effect on a thoroughly well-
> educated young lady, with a perfectly balanced mind, who had had all
> the advantages of fortune, training, and refined society ... In poor
> Maggie's highly-strung, hungry nature – just come away from a third-
> rate schoolroom, with all its jarring sounds and petty round of tasks –
> these apparently trivial causes had the effect of rousing and exalting her
> imagination in a way that was mysterious to herself. It was not that she
> thought distinctly of Mr Stephen Guest, or dwelt on the indications
> that he looked at her with admiration; it was rather that she felt the
> half-remote presence of a world of love and beauty and delight, made
> up of vague, mingled images from all the poetry and romance she had
> ever read. (*MF*, VI:ii:330, iii:337–8)

Maggie is overwhelmed not only by Stephen but by the luxury and freedom of bourgeois life that he personifies. Margaret Homans has noted as much. Staggeringly, though, she claims this awareness that 'gratification of [Maggie's] emotions is economically contingent' as a radical critical insight into the work's political unconscious; Eliot is actually complicit in the widely-diagnosed bourgeois attempt to use the romance plot to disguise the wish for economic and social power as a matter of personal psychology, and to 'glamorize middle-class consumer lust as natural desire'.[5] This view seems positively churlish. Eliot could not be more explicit or consciously revealing in her exposé of the romantic bourgeois fantasy:

> Maggie was introduced for the first time to the young lady's life, and
> knew what it was to get up in the morning without any imperative
> reason for doing one thing more than another. This new sense of

---

5   Margaret Homans, 'Dinah's Blush, Maggie's Arm: Class, Gender and Sexuality in George Eliot's Early Novels', *Victorian Studies* 36 (1993), 155–78, pp.173, 174.

leisure and unchecked enjoyment amidst the soft-breathing airs and garden scents of advancing spring ...could hardly be without some intoxicating effect on her, after her years of privation ... Life was certainly very pleasant just now: it was becoming very pleasant to dress in the evening ...there were admiring eyes always awaiting her now; she was no longer an unheeded person, liable to be chid, from whom attention was continually claimed, and on whom no one felt bound to confer any.

We are repeatedly reminded that Maggie's attraction to Stephen is distinctly impersonal; she loves him as an embodiment of admiration, of her ability to give pleasure and to choose; as a key to the social power she has always felt the lack of, and to freedom from the alienated drudgery that is her customary existence. Her love-story is not, Eliot stresses, an emanation of her natural 'character' but of her 'history' (MF, VI:vi:352).

While Eliot would agree with Homans and Armstrong that the personal and psychological dimensions of romantic love mask impersonal and social desires that are denied recognition or satisfaction as themselves, she sees them also as the ideological regulators of another order of impulse. It is not only the political will to power that is ideologically managed by the narrative of bourgeois love. There is another, diametrically opposed, but equally pervasive, original and fundamental dynamic that is disguised, turned on its head, and made to fit the social order through the ideal of the conjugal bond.

The mixed expression of Maggie's gaze at Stephen, 'defying and deprecating, contradictory and clinging, imperious and beseeching', encapsulates the duality contained within the romance narrative. The duel of self-assertion between Maggie and Stephen has, in each encounter, its reflex in an ostentatious display of loving concern, concession and vulnerability on Stephen's part. His conventional gallantry appears to promise mutual support and reliance in a world of competitive self-assertion. Forced early into lonely independence, with no power of offering or of receiving support from those she loves, Maggie is extremely vulnerable to the language of bourgeois courtship. Eliot has received outraged feminist criticism for her observation that 'there is something strangely winning to most women in that offer of the firm arm: the help is not wanted physically at that moment, but the sense of help – the presence of strength that is outside them and yet theirs, meets a continual want of the imagination'. Yet such outrage misses the subtlety of Eliot's gesture. If Eliot's satire – and satire is unmistakably there – is qualified, it is so by a profound and feeling insight into the cruel penetration of the roots of this shallow bourgeois fantasy, their parasitic sapping of the best potentials of human feeling and self-awareness. She acutely delineates the tragedy of a society in which all impulses of reliance and affection, all concessions to human interdependence, are rigidly contained, by both material and ideological structures, *within the gendered conjugal relationship*. The novel as a whole, as a portrayal of human vulnerability, shows us why 'the presence of strength that is outside them and yet theirs' should indeed constitute a 'continual want' of the human imagination; this perception of human interdependence is an essential part of any criticism of the competitive individualist society that injures women. The tragic irony lies in the fact that the fantasy of bourgeois love contains and betrays such perception (*MF*, VI:vii:359, 358).

Eliot is poignantly satiric on the hollow and trivial conventionalities that exploit and play on women's sense of powerlessness and isolation: their desire to be given and to give support and affection. Bourgeois courtship reduces sympathy, which ought, for Eliot, to be the vital principle of a whole society, to something narrow and trivial indeed:

> Maggie, feeling the need of a footstool, was walking across the room to get one, when Stephen ...guessed her want, and flew to anticipate her, lifting the footstool with an entreating look at her, which made it impossible not to return a glance of gratitude. And then, to have the footstool placed carefully by a too self-confident personage ...who suddenly looks humble and anxious, and lingers, bending still, to ask if there is not some draught in that position between the window and the fireplace, and if he may not be allowed to move the work-table for her – these things will summon a little of the too-ready, traitorous tenderness into a woman's eyes.

While Stephen's gallantries are exposed to a bitter commentary on a treacherously sexist society in which 'women are at once worshipped and looked down upon', Eliot refuses to be hard on Maggie's vulnerability to them. Even if Maggie could understand the strategic deceptions that gallantry represents, the urgency of her 'soul hunger' for a loving and relational existence – with which we feel Eliot strongly identifies – might not, in the face of this beguiling masquerade, be liable to the self-restraint suggested by sceptical reason. The simultaneous authorial distance and involvement that has been regarded as an artistic or ideological flaw in this novel is explained by the fact that Eliot portrays Maggie's adventures in love from the dual, irreconcilable, perspectives set up by liberal ideology.

Narrator and reader on the one hand judge Maggie rationally as a self-assertive reasoner and, on the other, sympathize with her as an emotional, susceptible human being who has limited options and is in desperate need. But here, unlike in Craik's novels, there is no happy marriage in which these opposing perspectives can find comfortable resolution.

Eliot's intimate sympathy for Maggie's impulse is proportional to her fury at its betrayal by shallow and alienated social conventions. The narrative of bourgeois courtship is despicable because it cynically conceals a scornful marginalization of the dependence, neediness, vulnerability and sympathy that are all part of the human condition. For her own lack of such cynicism Maggie is the richer, if also the more vulnerable (*MF*, VI:vii:367–8, 360).

In urging Maggie to marry him, Stephen uses the same arguments as Craik for the absolute primacy of sexual attraction over all other social passions or ties: "'Maggie! Dearest! If you love me, you are mine. Who can have so great a claim on you as I have? My life is bound up in your love. There is nothing in the past that can annul our right to each other.'" The formation of the conjugal bond is framed both as an assertion of individual right and as an act of providence construed as duty. As in Craik, 'nature' is invoked to legitimize the privileging of sexual love, and self-regarding choice, as above all else. "'We have proved that the feeling which draws us towards each other is too strong to be overcome: that natural law surmounts every other; we can't help what it clashes with.'" Stephen speaks for a natural law that, rather like Locke's, is founded on the imperative to look out for Number One no matter what the cost to others. And just as Locke reinforces his rationalist picture of the law of nature with reference to the will of God, Stephen justifies choice by denying that there can be any choice in making it: "'See how the tide is carrying us out – away from all those unnatural bonds that we have been trying to make faster round us – and trying in vain ... Everything has concurred to point it out to us. We have contrived nothing, we have thought of nothing ourselves'" (*MF*, VI:xiv:418, 417, xiii:408). As we have already seen, the notion of material determinism is by no means so in contradiction with individualism, or so naturally aligned with the critique of the capitalist status quo, as anti-humanist critics sometimes seem to think it is. Indeed, quite the contrary. Define the human subject as an atom that, in collision with its environment, unreflectingly moves itself 'forward', and you have reconciled the two schemes. Indeed, the competition and self-assertion upon which capitalist societies are based found early justification in the Calvinistic notion of predestination.

But for Maggie, a clear-eyed acknowledgement of the determinants of her situation leads to quite a different subjective attitude. She sees Stephen's attempt to lead her into unreflecting submission to immediate, egoistic desires as an attempt, precisely, to deprive her of 'choice'. Choice in Stephen's sense appears to Maggie no more than criterionless 'caprice' (a word that recurs in this novel). Choice, for her, involves a wide-ranging consciousness of claims and dependences, and a feeling reflection upon them: a discrimination between the proper result of such feeling reflection, and blind, mechanical reaction to egoism and 'hard, non-moral circumstance'. To give up such discrimination, to behave like a social atom 'with no law but the inclination of the moment', is to let that distinctively human ascendancy over non-moral circumstance, which has its roots in sympathy, sleep. At the heart of Maggie's rejection of Stephen lies a rejection of his conception of what it means to be human: 'Love is natural; but surely pity and faithfulness and memory are natural too'. Maggie's choice is not a matter of subordinating human desire to inhuman duty, but of privileging the 'calmer affections' and social longings which, as the narrative has shown, are, at the very least, as 'authentic' and 'natural' as sexual desire (*MF*, VI:xiii, xiv, xi). Our true self-determination, as a sociable and interdependent species, is realizable through an acknowledgement of our own dependence and our own ties, not through a rejection of all such as unnatural fetters on a natural freedom that is defined by its lack of relation to anything beyond itself, or of any criterion of value other than self-advancement.

The alternative, complex, thick conceptions of the human subject, human desire and self-consciousness, provide a distinctive perspective on the conditions for individual, as well as social well being. Philip knows, as well as the reader, that Stephen is no 'match' for Maggie, and Maggie confirms that she does not love him with her whole self: '"not with my whole heart and soul, Stephen ... I have never consented to it with my whole mind."' Maggie rejects the assumption that the road to happiness is the self-asserting right to follow the self-regarding whim of the moment: '"We can't choose happiness either for ourselves or for another: we can't tell where that will lie. We can only choose whether we will indulge ourselves in the present moment or whether we will renounce that ... for the sake of being true to all the motives that sanctify our lives."' Though Maggie's rejection of Stephen is painful, to go with him would not be to 'choose' authentic personal happiness, 'not a choice of joy, but of conscious cruelty and hardness; for could she ever cease to see before her Lucy and Philip, with their murdered trust and hopes? Her life with Stephen could have no sacredness: she must for ever sink and wander vaguely, driven by uncertain impulse; for she had let go the clue of life – that clue which once in the far off-years her young need had clutched so strongly' (*MF,* VI: xiv:418, xiv:418–9, 413).

This 'clue' is the truth of human interdependence, of the reliance of human happiness upon trust and sympathy. Maggie chooses not helpless suffering, but the 'patient loving strength' of clear-sighted acknowledgment of the limits of independence (*MF,* VI:xiv:413). In rejecting Stephen's Craikian rhetoric of the privileging of conjugal pairing over all other obligations, Maggie rejects the inauthenticity of bourgeois freedom. She clings to a set of values associated with a wider conception of Family, which even in its discords provides a standing ground from which the elusiveness, narrowness and inhumanity of individualist liberty, its limitations as an ultimate ideal of the good, become visible. The family narrative at the centre of *The Mill* illustrates the human *need* for care, pity, loyalty and sympathy; the centrality of values based on motives other than rational, individual self-assertion.

v. Sympathy versus 'justice by a ready made, patent method'

Eliot's relational, interdependent model of human nature also implies, however, that inasmuch as Maggie's humanity is constituted by extensive attachments and responsibilities to her loved ones, they and, if it is to be a truly humane, her society, should feel such attachments and responsibilities towards her. The coherence of the liberal scheme of rights hinges upon the notion that our actions are the very manifestation of our property in ourselves, and that as such we must be brought to account for them. But for Eliot, as for Dickens, along with the qualification of the scope of human independence comes a reassessment of the appropriateness of blame, and of a rigid and mechanical scheme of reward and punishment. There is an ongoing struggle between Maggie and Tom throughout the book over such a scheme, and the family is the microcosm in which it is worked out. This microcosm is, however, profoundly embedded in a wider social arena where the same tensions must also be worked out.

The harshness of the world's punishment of his father perpetuates itself in Tom's disposition. Like John Halifax, 'he shunned comradeship, lest it should lead him into expenses …strode along without swerving, contracted some rather saturnine sternness, as a young man is likely to do who has some premature call upon his self-reliance'. As he moulds himself into the perfect employee, the humanity is drained out of him: his 'young pink-and-white face had its colours very much deadened by the time he took off his hat at home'. His domestic existence shrinks to no more than a condition of his working life: 'no wonder he was a little cross if his mother or Maggie spoke to him' (*MF*, III:vii:214). In stark contrast to Maggie, he has confidence in his self-reliant judgement and conduct, and feels himself to be a person of well-consolidated integrity: '"I'd do just the same again." That was his usual mode of viewing his past actions; whereas Maggie was always wishing she had done something different' (*MF*, I:vi46).

Tom, driven into material and emotional independence, has a rationalistic and abstract sense of 'justice' – 'he would punish everybody who deserved it: why, he wouldn't have minded being punished himself, if he deserved it' – which is sometimes exercised in positive ways, as when he pays the Mosses and Luke after his father's calamity. However, that quality of which Tom has 'more than the usual share', and which is given the 'fine name' of 'boy's justice', is also inextricably wound up with the 'desire to hurt culprits as much as they deserve to be hurt, and is troubled with no doubts concerning the exact amount of their deserts' (*MF*, I:v:33–4, x:88, vi:46). Tom's 'growing experience' of the harsh civil arena leads him to regard himself, and others, as self-owning, simple atoms, with strict contractual duties towards each other. 'A character at unity with itself – that performs what it intends, subdues every counteracting impulse, and has no vision beyond the distinctly possible – is strong by its very negations' (*MF*, V:ii:272–3).

Maggie pits herself radically against the whole notion of calculated justice as a final standard. She seeks a personal, emotional, sympathetic response; she always 'wanted Tom to forgive her because he loved her'. Tom, however, is continually mindful of the limits of what he *owes* his sister, though he sometimes exceeds them: '"Wasn't I a good brother, now, to buy you a line all to yourself? You know, I needn't have bought it, if hadn't liked."' He resolves to exercise the same prerogative to pick and choose his relatives as is adopted by Craik's heroes and heroines. Maggie is haunted by the conditional nature of his affection: '"I won't love you"', he threatens; '"But you oughtn't to hate me, Tom; it'll be very wicked of you, for I shall be your sister." "Yes, but if you're a nasty disagreeable thing, I shall hate you"' (*MF*, I:v:32, 30, II:i:129).

Maggie cannot bear the coldness of a world run only according to justice, 'a world where people behaved the best to those they did not pretend to love and that did not belong to them ...if life had no love in it, what else was there for Maggie?' The familial sympathy for which Maggie yearns is expansive, not exclusive. Her favourite aunt Moss, 'besides being poorly off, and inclined to "hang on" her brother, had the good-natured submissiveness of a large, easy-tempered, untidy, prolific woman with affection enough in her not only for her husband and abundant children, but for any number of collateral relations' (*MF*, III:v:205, II:ii:137).

Maggie and Tom's responses to their father's bankruptcy illustrate two distinct moral schemes, their respective relations to the ethic of individualist self-ownership, and the scope that each accords to family relations. While Maggie feels extra tenderness for her father because of the frailty manifested by his misfortune, Tom infers from that misfortune error on his father's part, and judges him accordingly:

> Tom was very unhappy: he felt the humiliation as well as the prospective hardships of his lot with all the keenness of a proud nature; and with all his resolute dutifulness towards his father there mingled an irrepressible indignation against him … Since these were the consequences of going to law, his father was really blamable …and it was a significant indication of Tom's character, that …he felt nothing like Maggie's violent resentment against [his aunts] for showing no eager tenderness and generosity. There were no impulses in Tom that led him to expect what did not present itself to him as a right to be demanded. Why should people give away their money plentifully to those who had not taken care of their own money? Tom saw some justice in severity; and all the more, because he had confidence in himself that he should never deserve that just severity … He would ask no one to help him, more than to give him work and pay him for it. (*MF*, III:v:196–7)

Here is the proud self-reliance so familiar from Craik's novels. Tom's intolerance, as well as his 'upright' determination and independence, is founded upon confident strength.

The Family regards such independence as arrogance. In response to Bessy's faint echoing of such independent rhetoric, Mrs Glegg snaps, 'it's fine for you to say as you've never asked us to buy anything for you; let me tell you, you *ought* to have asked us. Pray, how are you to be purvided for, if your own family don't help you? You must go to the parish, if they didn't. And you ought to know that, and keep it in mind, and ask us humble to do what we can for you, i'stead o' saying, and making a boast, as you've never asked us for anything" (*MF*, III:iii:184).

Although Maggie baulks at the lack of sympathy with which the Family ethic is pressed, she comes to feel the benefit of unconditional Family support from her Aunt Glegg after her elopement. She is even more grateful for the affectionate way in which her mother offers it, without any claim of merit or questioning of her desert: "'Eh, my dear," said Mrs Tulliver, leaning towards the warm young cheek; "I must put up wi' my children – I shall never have no more; and if they bring me bad luck, I must be fond on it – there's nothing else much to be fond on, for my furnitur' went long ago.'" Misfortune, for Maggie, provides an absolute claim for extra care and love, 'even aunt Glegg would be pitiable when she had been hurt very much'. Her sympathy for misfortune, and even for wrongdoing, springs from a sense of her own frailty and her own need for human support: "'I shouldn't like to punish anyone, even if they'd done me wrong; I've done wrong myself too often.'" 'Maggie hated blame: she had been blamed all her life, and nothing had come of it but evil tempers' (*MF*, VII:iii:441, I:iv:25, VII:i:430, III:ii:180).

The Mill on the Floss is briefly referred to by Carol Gilligan in illustration of her empirical findings in a study of moral reasoning in women.[6] Gilligan observed that women scored consistently worse than men in tests designed to measure moral development. These tests were designed according to the idea, generally accepted in moral psychology, that a moral person is one who can effectively manipulate abstract principles of justice and fairness, construed, after the contract theorists and Kant, as universal rules available to human reason, which mediate between the rival interests of rational independent persons. Gilligan found that women were more inclined than men to construe morality as a response not to rights but to *needs*, manifested not by an abstractly conceived 'generalized other' but rather by particular others, embedded, like the moral agent herself, in a context of particular relationships. Gilligan calls this attitude 'the ethic of care', and she presents it as a challenge to the exhaustiveness of the description of morality in terms of justice.

Gilligan had no space to illustrate how perfectly *The Mill*, and Eliot's oeuvre more generally, illustrates, and indeed imaginatively elaborates and outruns each strand of this theory of female moral reasoning and its opposition to theories of rights. Maggie, in her struggle with Stephen, constantly bears in mind her particular relation to Lucy and Stephen; they trust her, they love her, she has led them to depend on her. As I suggested in Chapter Two, Eliot consistently critiques the reduction of concern for human welfare to what one of Gilligan's male subjects calls 'a math problem but with people'. 'Moral judgements must remain false and hollow, unless they are checked and enlightened by a perpetual reference to the special circumstances that mark the individual lot'.

---

[6] Carol Gilligan, *In a Different Voice* (Cambridge Mass.: Harvard University Press, 1998).

the mysterious complexity of our life is not to be embraced by maxims
...to lace ourselves up in formulas of that sort is to repress all the divine
promptings and inspirations that spring from growing insight and
sympathy. And the man of maxims is the popular representative of the
minds that are guided in their moral judgement solely by general rules,
thinking that these will lead them to justice by a ready-made patent
method ...without any care to assure themselves whether they have the
insight that comes from a hardly-earned estimate of temptation, or
from a life vivid and intense enough to have created a wide fellow
feeling with all that is human. (*MF*, VII:ii:438)

The 'divine promptings' of sympathy once again take centre stage –
sympathy as a distinctively human mode of understanding that dissolves the
boundaries of the self, and unites humanity. Sympathy that shows the way
round the idea that other human beings can be objectively known, or worse
(as this context emphasizes), objectively judged.

Gilligan's opposition between justice and care correlates with the value-
judgements of different modes of family relation in the other novels looked
at earlier. In Yonge's *The Heir of Redclyffe*, Philip Morville's sins spring from
over-confidence in judging where the right lies: he 'had acted, not perhaps
kindly, but as he thought, rightly and judiciously'. In confessing his guilt to
the hero, however, he finds 'neither an accuser nor a judge, not even one
consciously returning good for evil, but a friend with honest, simple,
straightforward kindness, doing the best for him in his power, and dreading
nothing so much as hurting his feelings' (*HR*, p.375). Craik, on the other
hand, reverses the priority of care over justice – in *A Woman's Thoughts*, she
says that although 'kindness, unselfishness, charity, come to [women] by
nature ... I wish I could see more of my sisters learning and practising
...common justice'.[7] There is 'one right alone' that John Halifax holds
'superior to the right of love – duty'; he is 'always tenacious of trenching a
hair's breadth upon any lawful authority' (*JHG*, pp.523, 369). This
conception of rights is self regarding; the right is held up in order that the
individual may seem upstanding and consistent in his own eyes and those of
others. Will Steadman has a 'heart, which yet, under all its tenderness, had a

---

[7] *A Woman's Thoughts about Women*, p.94. Craik expresses this plea for justice with
regard to women's stinginess about paying a fair price for a piece of work. Once
again the real potential for social improvement implicit in the focus on rights is
evident, but so is the implicit narrowness of scope that is assumed to delimit
kindness, unselfishness and charity. There is no reason why an extension of these
principles would not lead women to pay *at the very least* a fair price.

keen sense of right and wrong, honour and dishonour, that no warmth of friendship or nearness of blood could ever set aside' (*WK*, p.279). In the same vein, Tom Tulliver's sense of self, 'in which family feeling had lost the character of clanship in taking on a doubly deep dye of personal pride' finds its legitimation in the exercise of judgement and meting out of punishment; as he tells Maggie, 'I will sanction no such character as yours: *the world shall know* that *I feel the difference* between right and wrong' (*MF*, VII:iii:439–40, i:427 my itals).

The Mill prompts a vivid consciousness of the embeddedness of human reason and human value, and constitutes a powerful critique of the crude objectivist rationalism that would divorce the normative from the particular and the human. Eliot explicitly associates this consciousness of embeddedness with family life; and rationalism and the opposition of self to world, with the imperial expansion of capitalism. Even the independent Tom, on arriving home from school, is open to

the happiness of passing from the cold air to the warmth and the kisses and the smiles of that familiar hearth, where the pattern of the rug and the grate and the fire-irons were 'first ideas' that it was no more possible to criticize than the solidity and extension of matter. There is no sense of ease like the ease we felt in those scenes where we were born, where objects became dear to us before we had known the labour of choice, and where the outer world seemed only an extension of our own personality: we accepted and loved it as we accepted our own sense of existence and our own limbs. Very commonplace, even ugly, that furniture of our early home might look if it were put up to auction ...and is not the striving after something better and better in our surroundings, the grand characteristic that distinguishes man from the brute – or ...that distinguishes the British man from the foreign brute? But heaven knows where that striving might lead us, if our affections had not a trick of twining round those old inferior things – if the loves and sanctities of our life had no deep immovable roots in memory. One's delight in an elderberry bush overhanging the confused leafage of a hedgerow bank, as a more gladdening sight than the finest cistus or fuchsia spreading itself on the softest undulating turf, is an entirely unjustifiable preference to a nursery-gardener, or to any of those severely regulated minds who are free from the weakness of any attachment that does not rest on a demonstrable superiority of qualities. (*MF*, II:i:133–4)

Eliot suggests that value judgements may be as irreducible as sense impressions; not in the sense that Kant described aesthetic knowledge, as disinterested and impersonal, but as profoundly related to human affection and social pleasure. Morality, and the sympathetic projection of feeling beyond ourselves, may be arrived at not via reason and 'the labour of choice', but constructed from the primary instincts of existence within the family. Human comfort, human need, and human love may not be satisfactorily accommodated by a scheme of rational claims, choices and rights. The Holy Virgin rewards Ogg because, as she tells him, "'thou didst not question and wrangle with the heart's need, but wast smitten with pity, and didst straightway relieve the same'" (I:xii:102).

vi. Crux: The containment of sympathy?

Gilligan hypothesises an explanation of the gendered distribution of these separate modes of moral reasoning that is based on Nancy Chodorow's neo-Freudian theory of object relations. She does not make any concerted attempt to rank the two moral schemes, or to provide a functional explanation for their distribution. She suggests that male and female developmental trajectories in moral reasoning, although they take different paths, nevertheless 'progress' towards a shared rapprochement between rights and care, and that moral 'maturity' is attained when the female subject makes 'the discovery that separation can be protective and need not entail isolation', a process observable in Gilligan's empirical studies of contemporary women.[8] This growing individual maturity she sees also, strangely enough, mirrored in the historical progress of liberal feminism. Whereas George Eliot and other women of her time who were sceptical about liberal individualism were, she considers, still guilty of a 'confusion between self-sacrifice and care inherent in the conventions of feminine goodness', since that time women have learned to take on board the message of Elizabeth Cady Stanton, that 'Self Development is a Higher Duty than Self-Sacrifice'. Gilligan sees the opposition between justice and care, individualism and altruism as ahistorical: 'attachment and separation anchor the cycle of human life [and] the psychology of human development …appear in adolescence as identity and intimacy and then in adulthood as love and work'.[9]

In the end, then, Gilligan sees an ethic of care as reconcilable with the

---

[8]   Gilligan, p.39.

[9]   Gilligan, pp.74, 129, 151.

bourgeois conceptual and material scheme that separates identity and intimacy, love and work. However, liberal rights and care are not merely the divergent bi-products of typical human patterns of nurture, but are in fact structurally opposed to one another in constituting the liberal society in which Gilligan's opposition of 'love and work' is institutionalized; in which families, or, at least, sexual partners, provide love and care (at least, ideally), while the world of politics and work is regulated by justice. As such, these values cannot be integrated by the growing 'maturity' of the individual independently of social change.

Joan Tronto has demonstrated that it was the rise of modern capitalist society that led to the marginalization of a sympathetic moral-sentimental ethic of care and its confinement within the domestic arena; the same political setting that led to the establishment of the boundaries between public and private and between the moral and the political.[10] Each one of these divisions is at once a material and a theoretical necessity supporting the structures of our society: they are conditions of our economic system and presuppositions behind moral and political thought. Whether a sympathetic ethic of care is radical or conservative comes down to the effectiveness with which it is contained within a domestic and gendered arena.

To get away from the sex-difference essentialism implicit in Gilligan's perspective, theorists such as Tronto and Annette Baier have looked back to a period prior to the confinement to the home of the sympathetic ethic. Baier's discussion of Hume casts further light on the tension between Family and the liberal individualist scheme, and, through its demonstration that there is a long-established alternative to the ethics and politics of rights, suggests a further historical, as opposed to female-biological, source for the ideas of Eliot and Yonge on this point.[11] Sentiment and sympathy did not

---

[10]   Joan Tronto, *Moral Boundaries* (London: Routledge, 1993).

[11]   According to Haight's *Biography of George Eliot* (Oxford: Oxford University Press, 1968), Eliot read Hume's essays (p.100). She certainly owned a copy of his *Philosophical Works: Including All the Essays* (see William Baker [ed.], *The George Eliot-George Henry Lewes Library: An Annotated Catalogue of their Books at Dr. Williams's Library, London* [New York and London: Garland, 1977], entry 1069 p.100), and Lewes dealt at length with Hume in his *Biographical History of Philosophy* (London: Knight, 1845–6, 4 vols.). WE Henley, towards the end of the century, said that Eliot's novels seemed 'dictated' by 'the ghost of David Hume' (*Views and Reviews: Essays in Appreciation* [London: Macmillan, 1890], p.132). It is possible that Eliot's many reviews of philosophical works published in her own time have given a distorted impression that she was influenced philosophically by her contemporaries alone. But, of course, there was little reason for Eliot to bring Hume to the attention of a public that already regarded him highly. And her lack of reference to him could be explained

die out of the novel tradition at the end of the eighteenth century. On the contrary, in a certain strand of domestic fiction we see those distinctively eighteenth-century conceptions reanimated and brought into fruitful synthesis with the profound social engagement that had grown to characterize fiction in the interval.

As I have suggested already, whether a scheme of morality prioritizes justice over care, or care over justice, depends ultimately upon which of two distinct conceptualizations of man it is founded. The concept of self-owning rights that justifies the capitalist economy posits man as first and foremost a rational being looking after himself. It represses bodily and emotional needs, pleasures, passions and the rest of animal nature, and turns man into an abstract function of economic productivity. Man is functionally conceived, and his function, as in Spencer, is individual survival; he is a 'thin' entity, little more than the locus of reasoned self-assertion. The more moral the man, the more pristine his intellectual freedom from passion, the more complete his regard for his own integrity and independence of others. The concept of care, on the other hand, is foreshadowed in Hume's model of man as an animal whose reason is the invaluable, but utterly secondary, slave to passion. Passions provide the motivating force behind every action, and many if not all of those passions are sympathetic.

Likewise, Eliot's passionate evocation of childhood embodies a vision of the human race as a loving species. In her de-emphasis of man's status as rational and autonomous spirit, Eliot, like Yonge, sees fit to compare her heroes and heroines with animals:

> We learn to restrain ourselves as we get older. We keep apart when we have quarrelled, express ourselves in well-bred phrases, and in this way preserve a dignified alienation, showing much firmness on one side, and swallowing much grief on the other. We no longer approximate in our behaviour to the mere impulsiveness of the lower animals, but conduct ourselves in every respect like members of a highly civilized society. Maggie and Tom were still very much like young animals, and so she could rub her cheek against his, and kiss his

---

by her being so familiar with his ideas that they had just become part of her background of assumptions. Although it is certain that Eliot was familiar with a range of Humean arguments via Comte, who rated Hume very highly, giving him a place in the Positivist Calendar (Wright, *Religion of Humanity*, p.8), any theory of direct and conscious influence must remain, at present, speculative. What cannot be doubted, however, is that Eliot participates in a distinctive approach to morality in which Hume played a formative role.

ear in a random, sobbing way; and there were tender fibres in the lad
that had been used to answer to Maggie's fondling; so that he behaved
with a weakness quite inconsistent with his resolution to punish her as
much as she deserved: he actually began to kiss her in return, and say –
     'Don't cry, then, Magsie – here, eat a bit o' cake'.
     Maggie's sobs began to subside, and she put out her mouth for the
cake and bit a piece: and then Tom bit a piece, just for company, and
they ate together and rubbed each other's cheeks and brows and noses
together, while they ate, with a humiliating resemblance to two friendly
ponies. (*MF*, I:v:34)

Eliot's quiet satire of the 'alienation' (and from the translator of Feuerbach
we should expect this word to carry its full weight of implication)
characteristic of a 'civilized' society, 'humiliated' by the social animal
instincts that ought to provide the grounds for its cohesion, would be biting
if the moving image did not itself carry the day without need for the
negative argument.

With this naturalization of moral sentiment comes a deconstruction of the
opposition between selfishness and self-sacrifice that does not need to route
itself through a recognition of the rights of the self or the notion of a
contract. It allows for a re-integration of morality with notions of the good
life, from which theories of rights and self-ownership seem so radically
estranged, and thus allows for a criticism of social practice that takes as its
positive value the human capacity for unselfish social pleasure, and as its
negative the obstruction of such instincts. As we have seen, Yonge is insistent
in her association of the relational existence with happiness, on the misery of
egoism and self-sufficiency, and on the joy of sharing everything, down to
one's very sense impressions, with loved companions. Her characters are
humanely caring not so much from duty, as for 'the comfort of it'. Eliot also
gives us a central character whose happiness is absolutely reliant on loving
and being loved.

For Hume, neither morality nor a healthy political society is
fundamentally a matter of following rules suggested by reason. Both are the
outcome, rather, of the cultivation of the human capacity for sympathy.
What he counts as the standard for a justifiable rule is not its capacity to
guarantee the autonomy of the self-owning individual, but its potential for
redirecting energy from anti-social self-interest into more mutual impulses.
All rules and rights depend for their very viability upon the pre-existence of
such impulses. Schemes of rights, therefore, are not eternal and absolute, a
matter of natural or transcendental reason, but alterable by human will and

growing human sympathy. In Baier's words, 'the moral and critical stance Hume encourages us to adopt to, say, the property rules of our society …comes not from our ability to test them by higher more general rules, but from our capacity for sympathy, from our capacity to recognize and sympathetically share the reactions of others to that system of rights'. [12] Political relations for Hume, as Baier describes them, are 'possible because the persons involved …have already learned, in the family, the advantages which can come from self-control and from cooperation …were there not minimally sociable human passions such as love between man and woman, love of parents for their children, love of friends, sisters and brothers, the Human artifice of justice would not be constructed …at the very heart of Hume's moral theory lies his celebration of family life and parental love'. [13]

Baier suggests that John Rawls's recent overwhelmingly influential updating of contract theory 'like so many other theories of obligation, in the end must take out a loan not only on the natural duty of parents to care for children …but on the natural *virtue* of parental love (or even a loan on the maternal instinct?) The virtue of being a *loving* parent must supplement the natural duties and the obligations of justice, if the just society is to last beyond the first generation'. [14] She also traces this insight back to Hume, who argued that the self-assertion posited in the state of nature must always be supposed to rely on altruism within the family.

The notion of the family as the foundation of a sympathetic political and social ethic has roots that both reach beyond and undermine the division of spheres. The politico-moral power of *The Mill* is founded upon its development of this awareness. Maggie Tulliver's history graphically illustrates Baier's argument that, in a society that recognized only minimal, self-owning structures of rights as mediating between individuals, 'the long unnoticed moral proletariat were the domestic workers, mostly female'. [15] With the decline of her parents, Maggie is isolated and shut out by a society embarrassed by human need, and is left to bear the whole weight of a burden that has been rendered ignominious. It is in the cause of a critique of the individualistic standards of her society that Eliot resists granting her

---

[12] Annette Baier, 'Hume, the Women's Moral Theorist?' in E Kittay and D Meyers (eds.), *Women and Moral Theory* (Maryland: Rowman and Littlefield, 1987), pp.40, 41.

[13] Baier, 'Hume', p.42.

[14] Annetter Baier, 'What Do Women Want in a Moral Theory', in Roger Crisp and Michael Slote (eds.) *Virtue Ethics* (Oxford: Oxford University Press, 1997), pp.263–77, pp.267–8.

[15] Annette Baier, 'The Need for More than Justice', *Canadian Journal of Philosophy*, Supplementary Volume 13 (1978), 14–56, 49–50.

heroine an escape from all this into a triumphant 'independence' achieved through a successful career or a social-climbing marriage. Eliot's deeply sympathetic rendering of the Tullivers' plight makes it clear that sympathy and altruism cannot be discarded as ideological illusions *tout court*. Rather, civil society should reject defining itself in terms of rights alone, and should accept care as part of its *raison d'être*, so that another Maggie's share in her parents' fate could be part of a more lightly-carried, meaningful and cohesive social experience.

vii. Judging Maggie

The critical response to Maggie's suffering has shown the extent to which the contradictions and inadequacies of liberal individualism, the brunt of which are felt in the domestic sphere, remain unexamined even by writers overtly critical of that stance.

Newton's more or less professedly Marxist feminist study gives clear voice to a number of widely felt critical objections to *The Mill*. She comments, in the first place, on Eliot's unfairness to Maggie: 'even her relation to Stephen is taken to task, both because Stephen deprives her of power and because she fails to sacrifice herself for Lucy and Philip'.[16] Newton sees a contradiction where Eliot sees an extension of a single principle: the need to critique the egotistical power relations that are perpetuated by an inhumanly individualistic society. Though it is the callous containment of sympathy, interdependence and support within the narrow, egotistical range of sexual courtship, along with the unequal distribution of wealth, confidence and freedom of choice that at first draw Maggie to Stephen, it is also her consciousness of having suffered herself under this inhuman dynamic that leads her to reject the possibility of taking advantage of the suffering of others to clamber into the parasitic ease of wealth. It does not follow that because you yourself are victimised, you should assert yourself by victimizing – rather, the reverse is true, and the human capacity for sympathy makes this clear. 'I see – I feel their trouble now: it is as if it were branded on my mind. *I* have suffered, and had no one to pity me; and now I have made others suffer' (*MF*,VI: xiv:419). This dynamic is prefigured at Garum, where Maggie is tempted to re-enact the cruelty of which she has been a victim at Tom's hands. She cannot do so as she would like, that is, by slapping Tom, and so is forced to use Lucy as an instrument of her revenge. Despite the feminist applause that has greeted her violence towards the

---

16   Newton, p.153.

blonde and mouse-like Lucy, the passions that urge her on are real demons for Maggie. She has felt too much of the suffering of the helpless animal herself not to be made miserable by participating in the process of victimization that has proved an 'attribute of so much promise for the fortunes of our race' (*MF*, I:ix:80). The novel is a chronicle of Maggie's search for a more productive transformation of the impetus of her own suffering.

Newton remarks that 'Eliot's adherence to an ideology which valorizes dependent love curtails her criticism of the traditional love plot ...and this must explain in part why Maggie is not allowed to reject Stephen and the love plot of the novel on the grounds that Stephen and the life he offers her are inadequate to her happiness'.[17] Newton accepts precisely the equation of dependent love with the 'traditional love plot' that Eliot is at so much pains to deconstruct. Certainly Eliot does 'valorize dependent love'; her examination of family life shows that humans are inherently dependent and loving beings. It is the comprehensiveness of this valorization – its resistance to the ideological concentration of all such dependence within the conjugal relationship, and to the illusion that the conjugal choice of choices can secure happiness in an inhumane world – that provides the force and depth of her criticism of the love plot, and of the individualist ideology that makes the self-asserting right to seek one's own happiness *as opposed to the interests of others* the primary value of society.

So constrained is Newton by the liberal assumptions that Eliot critiques, that she reads Eliot's simple central arguments – dependent love is too large and too important to be contained within the conjugal relation, happiness is not to be found by asking 'what will make the independent, self-identical and self-seeking individual *"me"* happy' – as contradiction and confusion. Newton follows the contractarians in assuming that the primary goal of any moral or political scheme is to establish the autonomy of individuals, and to weigh their opposing claims. But, as Baier observes of Hume, with equal application to Eliot,

> the problem morality solves is deeper; it is as much intrapersonal as interpersonal. It is the problem of contradiction, conflict, and instability in any one person's desires, over time, as well as conflicts between persons. Morality, in theory, saves us from internally self-defeating drives as well as from self-defeating interpersonal conflict ...the moral point of view overcomes contradictions in our individual sentiments

---

[17]   Newton, p.152.

over time ...[Hume insists, furthermore, that] our sentiments [are] intrinsically reactive to other persons' sentiments. Internal conflict in a sympathetic and reassurance-needing person will not be independent of conflicts between the various persons in his or her emotional world.[18]

Maggie's story is Hume's picture of morality as both inter- and intra-personal conflict agonisingly vivified. Always wishing she had done something different, the 'impulsive' Maggie struggles to bring meaning and coherence to a lonely and fractured existence in the face of the erratic behaviour that that existence elicits from her. Her dilemma about Stephen is thus not about a choice between happiness and self denial, but about how to preserve a background of moral coherence for her actions.

Maggie's self-will is not only fractured internally, it is also radically permeated by, and fused with, the other selves with which it makes contact. As Hume observes, 'We can form no wish, which has not a reference to society. A perfect solitude is, perhaps, the greatest punishment we can suffer. Every pleasure languishes when enjoy'd a-part from company, and every pain becomes more cruel and intolerable. Whatever other passions we may be actuated by; pride, ambition, avarice, curiosity, revenge or lust; the soul or animating principle of them all is sympathy; nor wou'd they have any force, were we to abstract entirely from the thoughts and sentiments of others'.[19] We may also recall the remarks of both Comte and Marx on the radical sociability of man. Eliot goes beyond them in retaining Hume's emphasis on the collectivity and sociability not only of forms of life and of reason, but also, most importantly, of the passions. Baier draws attention to Hume's belief that 'human desire languishes unless it receives sympathetic reverberation from another ...unless someone sympathizes with my "selfish" pleasures they will not persist. But the fact that another does so sympathize makes that pleasure less purely selfish, more "fertile" for others, and also evokes in me a sympathy with the other's sympathy for me – a "double

---

[18]   Baier, 'Hume', p.45. Hume comments, with regard to this problem, 'Our situation, with regard both to persons and things, is in continual fluctuation; and a man, that lies at a distance from us, may, in a little time, become a familiar acquaintance' *Treatise*, III:I, p.581. Again, the analogy with Eliot's ideas is striking: think of *Middlemarch*, 'any one watching keenly the stealthy convergence of human lots, sees a slow preparation of effects from one life on another, which tells like a calculated irony on the indifference or the frozen stare with which we look at our unintroduced neighbour' (I:xi:93). For both Eliot and Hume, clearly, the 'moral' is not the need for deontological impartiality (wholly compatible with the frozen stare) but a wider sympathy.

[19]   Hume, *Treatise*, p.363.

reverberation"'. Eliot's sketch of Maggie's consciousness reveals exactly such a dissolution of the ego boundaries within which pleasure runs. Maggie's special pleasure in petting rye-necked lambs, because she knows that they are particularly pleased to be petted by her, is an instance not, as some have imagined, of patronizing hypocrisy, but of Hume's mutually reinforcing altruistic pleasure principle.[20]

Newton fails to take on board Eliot's radical critique of individualism as 'immoral' precisely in so far as it is inhuman and unfulfilling. Newton remarks that 'charming or not, Tom has what Maggie does not, the power to survive, and that is a form of autonomy [even] more vital than the power of self-definition ... Tom's mobility, his faith in his power to achieve, his ability to define himself and to feel self-worth, his pleasing sense of control all contribute to that confidence and that ability to adapt which make for a steadiness in surviving young adulthood'.[21] Tom says that business is the only thing he cares about, but he is potentially a winner in the social-Darwinian rat-race, where only a rigid sense of individuality and of one's right to self-assertion can give one a chance of coming out on top. Apparently, for Newton, it is better to win at that game, even if it makes you utterly miserable or emotionally and reflectively dead, than to reject it as an alienated imposition on the sociable human subject.

Newton's reference to 'young adulthood' as a period at which self-definition is essential, is characteristic of the liberal individualism which would transform as completely and quickly as possible the deficiently dependent child into the self-sufficient human mushroom. It also recalls the rather condescending value-judgement, conveyed through the liberal trope of progressive development away from nature and interdependence, to which even Gilligan's theory of care ultimately retreats. Newton's remarks

---

[20] Hume is in favour only of the kind of socially-orientated altruism which (by its nature) brings benefits to both parties. He rejects the 'monastic' virtues, celibacy, fasting, penance, mortification, self-denial, humility, silence, solitude, 'because they serve no manner of purpose; neither advance a man's fortune in the world, nor render him a more valuable member of society ...on the contrary ...they cross all these desirable ends; stupify the understanding and harden the heart, obscure the fancy and sour the temper' (*Enquiries*, IX:I:219, p.270). cf. Philip's remarks to Maggie in her 'resigned' religious phase, 'a way of escaping pain by starving into dullness all the highest powers of your nature ... Stupefaction is not resignation: and it is stupefaction to remain in ignorance − to shut up all the avenues by which the life of your fellow-men might become known to you. I am not resigned: I am not sure that life is long enough to learn that lesson. You are not resigned: you are only trying to stupefy yourself.' (*MF* V:iii:288)

[21] Newton, p.142.

on Eliot's own development are similarly patronising:

> Eliot's family life appears to have made her particularly vulnerable to
> this ideology [of love and care for others] ...she was *scarred* in early life
> by maternal rejection [which] produced an insatiable need for love ...
> Writing fiction ...had to be justified by being 'transformed into both a
> religion and a strict duty'. 'Proof that her writing was a positive
> contribution to society had to occur ...' ...It is this tension between the
> desire for self-enhancing power and *the ideologically influenced need for
> sacrifice and love* which informs, on the one hand, Eliot's potentially
> radical analysis of Maggie's oppression by the community and, on the
> other, her attenuation of protest and valorization of corporate loyalty.[22]

Large but familiar questions are begged by this judgement. It assumes a
particular model of human nature, recognizable from Sarah Ellis and
Spencer, according to which the desire for self-enhancing power is natural,
whereas lovingness and the need for love are unnatural, 'ideologically
influenced', or as Ellis, Craik and Nietzsche would say, 'weak' (although, of
course, if mothers *don't* love their children they will 'scar' them). For
Newton, incoherently, these softer sentiments are both individual
psychological pathologies and ideological effects. Newton suggests that the
female author ought really to write *just* to show off or to gain personal
power, as though the creative impulse were polluted by the desire for social
good. She sets up a dichotomy between childish dependence and adult self-
sufficiency and self-regard, between love-acts that benefit or please others
and 'self-enhancing power'. The obvious rejoinder is the observation that
Eliot's work is a striking example of the non-contradiction between seeking
to do good for others and self-enhancement; Marian Evans would not have
become the towering George Eliot were it not for the humanist moral
commitment that is the heart and soul of her fiction.

Newton complains that 'We are invited ...to feel less about Maggie as a
restricted individual and more about the requirements of the community
which has restricted her'. On the other hand, she also remarks critically of
Brontë's *Villette* that 'Ultimately, the fulfilment of Lucy's quest requires no
confrontation with the ideological and material restrictions of a communal

---

22 Newton, pp.138–9, quoting Ruby Redinger, *George Eliot: The Emergent Self*. Sanders
adopts a similarly patronising attitude towards Charlotte Yonge, of whom she claims
that her 'relationship with her parents never really developed from one of childish
dependency' in so much as 'her work seemed meaningless without their approval',
p.36.

order, for ...in the end both are evoked only to be defined and thereby managed as individual'.[23] The female novelist, it seems, is rather like Maggie's witch on the ducking stool, who loses both ways. She is caught by a contradiction between the liberal feminist and the socialist standards of the critic, a double bind created by precisely the isolated and individualist conception of 'self-enhancement' as, in principle, divorced from or opposed to the needs of the community, that *The Mill* seeks to undermine. Failing to penetrate the rich and radical alternative scheme of thought upon which Eliot bases her social critique, Newton is far from alone in dismissing *The Mill* as just another manifestation of 'separate spheres' Victorian ideology.

Eliot's valorization of corporate loyalty *is* a protest against society in its present imperfect state; the Tullivers suffer because there is something wrong with a society that does not recognize its own corporate responsibility. Maggie's life is a reproach on the restriction of affective and altruistic relations to a constricted family circle, which Eliot figures as a nest pierced and torn by the thorns of the unsympathetic world outside. This restriction deprives family relations, and the individuals caught up in them, of their potential for expansion into self-fulfilling social activities and bonds.

Maggie's return to St Ogg's is not a passive renunciation of agency and of judgement, but an assertion of self in relationship, and of her continuing humanity in the face of ostracism. Had she married Stephen she would have been in the iniquitous position of profiting by callousness; society would have approved her and cast shame on her wronged cousin. To have set out on her own would have been to adopt the individualist self-regard that denies connection, and, for Maggie, to withdraw her claim on society and condemn herself to a meaningless, wretchedly selfish existence, would be to feel that "'I should have no stay. I should feel like a lonely wanderer – cut off from the past ... I will not go away because people say false things of me. They shall learn to retract them'". She returns to reassert her connection with the community and so to challenge its values and boundaries (*MF*, VII:ii:436–7).

Tom's reaction to Maggie's return shows how challenging to the individualist conscience is her bold embodiment of interconnection and affective ties. 'There had arisen in Tom a repulsion towards Maggie that derived its very intensity from their early childish love in the time when they had clasped tiny fingers together, and their later sense of nearness in a common duty and a common sorrow: the sight of her, as he had told her, was hateful to him'. Maggie's death, even more than her life, demonstrates

---

[23] Newton, pp.154, 120.

that human beings are not self-sufficient, invincible or divided, and as a public event it suggests to the whole community the truth of Dr Kenn's observations of the inhumanity of a present in which 'everything seems tending towards the relaxation of ties – towards the substitution of wayward choice for the adherence to obligation'. Lucy recognizes the catastrophe as an effect of conditions beyond Maggie herself, part of the common weal of human interrelation, 'a trouble that has come on us all' (*MF*, VII:iii:439, ii:435, v:449).

viii. Radical sympathy: Beyond Family, beyond gender

Family, and maternal affection, are presented in *The Mill* as living proof of the human potential for sympathy and altruistic love, 'The only thing clear to [Mrs Tulliver] was the mother's instinct that she would go with her unhappy child'. We should not read this emphasis as a reproduction of the ideology of separate spheres. The family plays exactly the same role for Hume, who, unlike Craik, argues that the bond between parent and child is 'the strongest and most indissoluble bond in nature', foremost among blood relationships, 'the strongest tie the mind is capable of'.[24] *This* bond, not the equal and chosen conjugal one, is for him the paradigm of all others, and as such its characteristics have a determining effect on the morality constructed around it. As Baier comments, 'this relationship, and the obligations and virtues it involves, lack three central features of relations between moral agents as understood by ...the contractarians – it is intimate, it is unchosen, and is between unequals'.[25] Much of the passion behind *The Mill* flows from an investment in the ideal of such love, and the proof it offers of the human potential to form bonds and duties divorced from the threat of opposing self-assertion.

Such love comforts the giver and the receiver equally. Mrs Tulliver bears her great disappointment better because her 'heart, so bruised in its small personal desires, found a future to rest on in the life of this young thing, and the mother pleased herself with wearing out her own hands to save the hands that had so much more life in them'. Despite the wide space of culture and character between them, Maggie comes to value her mother's unconditional love as her highest comfort. 'O the sweet rest of that embrace to the heart-stricken Maggie! More helpful than all wisdom is one draught of simple human pity that will not forsake us' (*MF*, IV:ii:242, VII:i:427).

Eliot, like the modern proponents of the ethics and politics of care, again

---

[24] Hume, *Enquiries*, VI:I:197, p.240, *Treatise* II:IV, p.352.
[25] Baier, 'Hume', p.44.

and again comes back to this model of natural altruism. In *Adam Bede* she speaks of how 'the mother's yearning, that completest type of the life in another life which is the essence of real human love, feels the presence of the cherished child even in the debased, degraded man'.[26] However, in this instance she is speaking of a *man's* − and a masculine man's at that − love for a *woman*. The double reversal of gender in this particular metaphor pointedly reveals Eliot's insistence that motherly love is a capacity of men and women both, and that both men and women will, in their time, fall greatly in need of it. In *The Mill*, of course, it is *Mr* Tulliver's pride in and tenderness towards his daughter that first claim our attention; Mrs Tulliver's mothering instinct requires the removal of its alienated social surrogates, in the form of her plate and china, before it can find its true outlet. Josephine McDonagh suggests that 'for Eliot the role of the mother is an emotional one and possibly a practical one too, but it is *not* a biological one, for anyone can perform it, even men'.[27] I think it is a biological one − Eliot is as insistent on the innate human aptitude for sympathy as the contractarians are on the naturalness of rationality and self-interest − but it is not differentially distributed according to sex.

Like Yonge, Eliot resists the ideological containment of sympathetic and altruistic bonds within the gendered domestic arena. She shows that such restriction both victimizes women and alienates men from the truth and joy of human connection. *The Mill* counterbalances Maggie's last caring act with Philip's hopes for his future, which also equate care for others with personal power, happiness and meaning:

> I think nothing but such complete and intense love could have initiated me into that enlarged life which grows and grows by appropriating the life of others; for before, I was always dragged back from it by ever-present painful self-consciousness. I even think sometimes that this gift of transferred life which has come to me in loving you, may be a new power to me. (*MF*, VII:iii:443)

Despite the bleak conclusion of the novel, there is something utopian in Philip's words. The human potential to feel with others, to sympathize, allows for the hope of a future in which many tragedies may be avoided. Again Eliot follows Hume, and Marx, in rejecting the contractarian model in which morality is a matter of weighing opposed interests, in favour of a

---

[26] Eliot, *Adam Bede*, ch.43, p.406.

[27] Josephine McDonagh, *George Eliot* (Plymouth: Northcote House, 1997), p.44.

conception of morality as 'the problem of how to *minimize* opposition of interest, how to arrange life so that sympathy, not hostile comparison, will be the principle relating our desire to those of our fellows'.[28] As Baier comments on Hume's sympathetic morality, ethics are thus at once a matter of personal morals and of social organization

> ...of the social 'artifices' which divide work [and] conjoin forces so that not just collective power but each person's power is augmented ...a 'system of actions concurr'd in by the whole society ...infinitely advantageous to the whole and to every part' ...if we remember those endless satisfactions which sympathetic enlargement of self-interest can bring ...a set of institutions that really did prevent oppositions of interest might indeed bring 'infinite' or at least indeterminately great increase of power of enjoyment.[29]

Marx observed that 'industry, in overturning the economical foundation of the old family system, and the family labour corresponding to it, has also dissolved the old family relationships', but that 'however terrible and disgusting the dissolution of the old family ties within capitalism may appear, large-scale industry ...creates a new economic foundation for a higher form of the family'.[30] *The Mill*, more directly than the other novels dealt with here, examines as a historical phenomenon this 'terrible and disgusting' dissolution, and the options it presents. Eliot's vision of the present is bleaker, her image of the traditional Family less idealized than Yonge's. She remains aware that for a politics of care modelled on Familial relationship the difficulty is to ensure, as Tronto puts its, 'that the web of relationship is spun widely enough so that some are not beyond its reach'.[31] From the early chapters of *The Mill*, the problem of the opposition of inside and outside, of the opposition between the warmth of family and the coldness of civil society, is made a central problem:

> Snow lay on the croft and river-bank in undulations softer than the limbs of infancy ...there was no gleam, no shadow, for the heavens, too, were one still, pale cloud – no sound or motion in anything but the dark river, that flowed and moaned like an unresting sorrow. But old

---

28 Baier, 'Hume', p.51.
29 Baier, 'Hume', p.52.
30 Marx, *Capital*, iv:9:620–21.
31 Joan Tronto, 'Beyond Gender Difference to a Theory of Care', *Signs* 12/4 (1987), 644–63, 660.

Christmas smiled as he laid this cruel-seeming spell on the out-door world, for he meant to light up home with new brightness, to deepen all the richness of in-door colour, and give a keener edge of delight to the warm fragrance of food: he meant to prepare a sweet imprisonment that would strengthen the primitive fellowship of kindred, and make the sunshine of familiar human faces as welcome as the hidden day-star. His kindness fell but hardly on the homeless – fell but hardly on the homes where the hearth was not very warm, and where the food had little fragrance; where the human faces had no sunshine in them, but rather the leaden, blank-eyed gaze of unexpectant want. But the fine old season meant well; and if he has not learned the secret how to bless men impartially, it is because his father Time, with ever-unrelenting purpose, still hides that secret in his own mighty, slow-beating heart. (*MF*, II:ii:134)

Eliot refuses to regard the opposition of a warm inside and a cold outside as natural facts of *human* society. Central to human nature is the potential to build a warm shelter from the coldness of 'hard, non-moral' inanimate nature, and in the fully human society no one will be left out in the cold. Nature has provided the raw materials of sympathetic human sociability and enjoyment: it is for historical change, embodied in 'young natures' acting out of feeling reflection on and participation in human nature (as it is still revealed within the tatters of the Family), to bring about the harvest. The pain of change, the 'suffering, whether of martyr or victim, which belongs to every historical advance of mankind …in every town, and by hundreds of obscure hearths' is also potentially a step towards some wider and more adequate institution of a 'brotherhood'; 'that constitution which is alone fitted to human needs' (*MF*, IV:i:238, VII:ii:435). Maggie's history is an engagement with historical circumstance in the struggle for a new kind of relation that can expand the restrictions and exclusions of the Family and operate in and on the modern world. Her rejection of Stephen, and her death in the arms of her brother, symbolize Eliot's rejection of the conventional bourgeois containment and etiolation of the caring family impulse within a love-plot founded upon the liberal individualist values of self-ownership and egotistical whim.

From the feminine perspective of radical exclusion, Eliot bids, finally, not for powerful individual autonomy, but for a society founded upon something other than individual self-assertion. She is not so conventionally Victorian, so ideologically feminine, in her emphasis on altruism and care as she might seem; many contemporary political theorists have found that the question of justice for women leads inexorably towards a subordination of the rights of the individual, male and female both, to sympathetic principles. Eliot foreshadows a sympathetic ethic that leads, through its deconstruction of the public/private divide, to a 'clear perception of the given-ness of interconnection, in the family and beyond', and to an 'emphasis on our capacity to make others' joys and sorrows our own', and on 'the inescapable mutual vulnerability and mutual enrichment that the human psychology and the human condition ...entail'. Eliot realized already what the liberal feminist tradition has been unable to accept; that the deconstruction of separate spheres ultimately renders 'autonomy not even an ideal ... A certain sort of freedom is an ideal, namely freedom of thought and expression, but to "live one's own life in one's own way" is not likely to be among the aims of persons whose every pleasure languishes when not shared and seconded by some other person or persons'.[32] Domestic fiction in general, and Eliot's *Mill on the Floss* above all, lead us with compelling immediacy towards a subversive truth that we are only just now beginning to recall.

Even Craik recognizes the moral and emotional appeal of the possibility of resigning oneself 'totally and contentedly into the hands of another; to have no longer any need of asserting one's rights or one's personality, knowing that both are as precious to that other as they ever were to ourselves; to cease taking thought about one's self at all, and rest safe, at ease, assured that in great things and small we shall be guided and cherished, guarded and helped'.[33] Domestic fiction draws on this 'delicious' appeal, and more or less directly questions its gender-specificity and the contraction of its status and scope within the nuclear family. Only by rejecting this contraction, these novels suggest, can we protect the women who bear the whole weight of sympathy as a lonely burden, and humanise a society alienated from itself.

---

[32] Baier, 'Hume', p.46
[33] Craik, *A Woman's Thoughts about Woman*, p.73

Envoi: Sympathetic Magic

The mid-Victorian realist novel is the medium par excellence for an exposition of a sympathetic politics of care, and an effective vehicle for the perpetuation of the conditions for its realization. Its realism is orientated towards the caring conviction, which Gilligan observed in her female subjects, 'that the solution to the dilemma will follow from its compelling representation'.[1] Its personal focus, its realist enumeration of particularities and its emotional function make it a form that emphasizes connection and that cultivates the virtue of human sympathy, that weighs the subjective and emotional value of quotidian experience in dense and human terms, and that makes visible the delicate, fragile and underground lacework of social mycelia connecting the autonomous man-mushrooms of civil space. Even when its overt 'message' is individualistic it is led, by the very skill with which it mobilizes its fictional conventions, into an emotive revelation of human connection.

This same revelation is embodied, in different ways, in every novel to which I have turned my attention. It bursts the channels cut for it by any rational scheme of rights, and any rationalistic legitimation of or resignation to the status quo, and it bears the reader inexorably on to a hopeful and active desire for the social realization of human sympathy.

It is only at the level of emotion, finally, that the sympathetic argument can be won. These dimensions of Victorian fiction cannot be understood, let alone 'felt', from the anti-humanist, 'distanced' perspective adopted by much recent so-called 'political' literary criticism. I have tried to show that these novels consistently and powerfully contest the notion of man as atomic, rational and self-asserting, conceived as either imperiously in command of material process, or abjectly prostrated before its inhuman force. Instead, what they embody and describe and address, is feeling, suffering, imagining and loving subjectivity. They stand up, passionately, against the brutalities of all discourse without a truly human subject[2], which,

---

[1] Gilligan, p.30.

[2] I allude to Althusser's highly influential conception of theory as a 'discourse without a subject.'

from political economy to unsympathetic theory, has always remained the enemy of imaginative art and sympathetic protest.

Bibliography

ALTHUSSER, LOUIS, 'Ideology and the Ideological State Apparatus', in *Lenin and Philosophy and Other Essays*, trans. Ben Brewster (London: New Left Books, 1971), pp. 121-180.

ARMSTRONG, NANCY, *Desire and Domestic Fiction* (Oxford: Oxford University Press, 1987).

AUSTEN, ZELDA, 'Why Feminist Critics are Angry with George Eliot', *College English* 37 (1976), 549- 61.

AZIM, FIRDOUS, *The Colonial Rise of the Novel* (London and New York: Routledge, 1993).

'B.A. & J.K.', *Wreck of the 'Royal Charter', Steam Clipper, on her Passage from Australia to Liverpool* (Dublin: Glashan and Gill, 1860).

BAIER, ANNETTE, 'The Need for More than Justice', *Canadian Journal of Philosophy*, Supplementary Volume 13 (1978), 14-56.

— 'Hume, the Women's Moral Theorist?' in Eva Feder Kittay and Diana T. Meyers (eds), *Women and Moral Theory* (Totowa, N.J.: Rowman and Littlefield, 1987), pp. 35- 55.

— 'What Do Women Want in a Moral Theory', in Roger Crisp and Michael Slote (eds), *Virtue Ethics* (Oxford: Oxford University Press, 1997), pp.263-277.

BAKER, WILLIAM (ed.), *The George Eliot-George Henry Lewes Library: An Annotated Catalogue of their Books at Dr Williams's Library, London* (New York and London: Garland, 1977).

BARTHES, ROLAND, *S/Z*, trans. Richard Miller (New York: Hill and Wang, 1985).

— *The Rustle of Language*, trans. Richard Howard (Oxford: Blackwell, 1986).

BATTISCOMBE, GEORGIANA, *Charlotte Mary Yonge* (London: Constable, 1943).

BAYLEY, JOHN, 'Eminent Victorian', Review of Kathryn Hughes, *George Eliot: The Last Victorian, New York Review of Books* 49, no. 16, Oct 21 (1999), pp.59-60.

BELSEY, CATHERINE, *Critical Practice* (London: Routledge, 1980).

— 'ReReading the Great Tradition', in Peter Widdowson (ed.), *ReReading English*, (London and New York: Methuen, 1982), pp.121-135.

BLACKMUR, R.P., Introduction to Henry James, *The Art of the Novel* (New York: Scribners, 1934).

BRANTLINGER, PATRICK, *The Spirit of Reform* (Oxford: Oxford University Press, 1978).

— *Rule of Darkness* (Ithaca and London: Cornell University Press, 1988).

CARLYLE, THOMAS, *Sartor Resartus* (London: Chapman and Hall, 1896).

— 'On History', in *Critical and Miscellaneous Essays*, 5 vols (London: Chapman and Hall, 1899), II:83-95.

— 'On History Again', in *Critical and Miscellaneous Essays*, 5 vols (London: Chapman and Hall, 1899), III.

CARROLL, DAVID (ed.), *George Eliot: The Critical Heritage* (London: Routledge and Kegan Paul, 1971).

CARRUTHERS, PETER, and PETER K. SMITH (eds), *Theories of Theories of Mind* (Cambridge: Cambridge University Press, 1996).

CAULDWELL, CHRISTOPHER, *Studies in a Dying Culture* (London, 1938).

CHEADLE, BRIAN, 'Despatched to the Periphery', in Anny Sadrin (ed.), *Dickens, Europe and the New Worlds* (London: Macmillan, 1999).

COHEN, G.A., *Self-Ownership, Freedom and Equality* (Cambridge: Cambridge University Press, 1995).

— *If You're an Egalitarian, How Come You're So Rich?* (London and Cambridge Mass: Harvard University Press, 2001).

COHEN, MONICA F., *Professional Domesticity in the Victorian Novel* (Cambridge: Cambridge University Press, 1998).

COLLIER, ANDREW, 'Truth and Practice', *Radical Philosophy* 5 (Summer 1973).

COLLINS, K.K., 'G.H. Lewes Revised: George Eliot and the Moral Sense', *Victorian Studies* 21 (1978), 463-92.

COMTE, AUGUSTE, *System of Positive Polity*, trans. J.H. Bridges and others, 4 vols (London: 1875-7).

COTTOM, DANIEL, *Social Figures: George Eliot, Social History, and Literary Representation* (Minneapolis: University of Minnesota Press, 1987).

CRAIK, DINAH MULOCK, *The Ogilvies* (1849), (London: Chapman and Hall, c.1860).

— *Olive and the Half-Caste* (1850), ed. Cora Kaplan (Oxford and New York: Oxford University Press, 1996).

— *John Halifax, Gentleman* (1856) (London and Glasgow: Collins, c.1930).

— *A Woman's Thoughts about Women* (1857-58), ed. Elaine Showalter (New York: New York University Press, 1995).

— *A Life for a Life*, 3vols. (London: Hurst and Blackett, 1859).

— Letter to Margaret Oliphant, 27th October 1865, in collection at the National Library of Scotland, Record MS.23210:36-75.

— *A Noble Life* (New York: Harper and Brothers, 1866)

— *The Woman's Kingdom: A Love Story* (1869) (London: Hurst and Blackett, c. 1897).

CREAVEN, SEAN, *Marxism and Realism* (London: Routledge, 2000).

CROSBY, CRISTINA, *The Ends of History: Victorians and 'The Woman Question'* (New York and London: Routledge, 1991).

CULLER, JONATHAN, Introduction to Tzvetan Todorov, *The Poetics of Prose* (Oxford: Blackwell, 1977).

CURRIE, GREGORY, 'The Paradox of Caring: Fiction and the Philosophy of Mind', Mette Hjort and Sue Laver (eds), *Emotion and the Arts* (Oxford: Oxford University Press, 1997), pp.63-77.

DAVID, DEIRDRE, *Rule Britannia* (Ithaca and London: Cornell University Press, 1995).

DAVIES, EMILY, 'The Influence of University Degrees on the Education of Women', *The Victorian Magazine*, June 1863, reprinted in C.A. Lacey (ed.), *Barbara Leigh Smith Bodichon and the Langham Place Group* (London: Routledge, 1987), pp.415-427.

DAVIES, MARTIN, and TONY STONE (eds), *Mental Simulation* (Oxford: Blackwell, 1995).

DAVIS, LENNARD J., *Resisting Novels* (New York and London: Methuen, 1987).

DELEUZE, GILLES, *Logic of Sense*, trans. Mark Lester, ed. Constantin V. Boundas (London and New York: Athlone, 1990).

DENNIS, BARBARA, *Charlotte Yonge (1823-1901):Novelist of the Oxford Movement* (Lewiston/Queenston/ Lampeter: Edwin Mellen Press, 1992).

DICKENS, CHARLES, *Dombey and Son* (1848), ed. Alan Horsman (Oxford: Clarendon Press, 1974).

— *Bleak House* (1852-3) (Oxford: Oxford University Press, 1948).

— 'The Shipwreck' and 'My Line of Business', in *The Uncommercial Traveller and Other Papers, 1859-70*, ed. Michael Slater and John Drew (London: J.M. Dent, 2000).

— *The Letters of Charles Dickens*, ed. Madeline House, Graham Storey, Kathleen Tillotson, et al. (Oxford: Clarendon Press, 1965-2003).

DISTEFANO, CHRISTINE, *Configurations of Masculinity* (Ithaca: Cornell University Press, 1991).

EAGLETON, TERRY, *Myths of Power: A Marxist Study of the Brontës* (London and New York: Macmillan, 1975).

— *Criticism and Ideology* (London: Verso 1978).

— 'Foreword' to Daniel Cottom, *Social Figures: George Eliot, Social History, and Literary Representation* (Minneapolis: University of Minnesota Press, 1987).

ELIOT, GEORGE, *Scenes of Clerical Life* (1857) (London: Penguin, 1998).

— *Adam Bede* (1859) ed. Carol A. Martin (Oxford: Clarendon Press, 2001).

— *The Mill on the Floss* (1860), ed. Gordon S. Haight (Oxford: Clarendon Press, 1980).

— *Middlemarch* (1872), ed. David Carroll (Oxford and New York: Clarendon Press, 1986).

— *Daniel Deronda* (1876), ed. Graham Handley (Oxford: Clarendon Press, 1984).

— *Essays of George Eliot*, ed. Thomas Pinney (London: Routledge and Kegan Paul, 1963).

— *The George Eliot Letters*, ed. Gordon S. Haight, 9 vols. (New Haven: Yale University Press, 1954-1978).

— 'Ruskin's Lectures', in *George Eliot: A Writer's Notebook (1854-1879) and Uncollected Writings*, ed. J. Warren (Charlottesville: Virginia University Press, 1981).

ELLIS, SARAH, *The Women of England* (London: Fisher, Son and Co., 1839).

— *Wives of England* (London: Fisher, Son and Co, 1843).

— *Daughters of England* (London: Fisher, Son and Co, 1845).

— *Education of the Heart* (London: Hodder and Stoughton, 1869).

ELSHTAIN, JEAN BETHKE, Introduction, *The Family in Political Thought* (Amherst: University of Massachusetts Press, 1982).

ELSTER, JOHN, *Making Sense of Marx* (Cambridge: Cambridge University Press, 1985).

ERMARTH, ELIZABETH DEEDS, *The Novel in History* (London and New York: Routledge, 1997).

EVANS, MICHAEL, *Karl Marx* (London 1975).

FIELDING, HENRY, *Tom Jones* (1749), ed. Martin Battestin and Fredson Bowers (Oxford: Clarendon Press, 1974).

FLEISCHER, HELMUT, *Marxism and History* (London: Penguin Press, 1973).

FLINT, KATE, 'George Eliot and Gender,' in *The Cambridge Companion to George Eliot*, ed. George Levine (Cambridge: Cambridge University Press, 2001), pp.159-180.

FORSTER, JOHN, *The Life of Charles Dickens*, 3 vols (London: Chapman and Hall, 1872-4).

FOUCAULT, MICHEL, *Language, Counter-Memory, Practice*, ed. Donald F. Bouchard, trans. Donald F. Bouchard and Sherry Simon (Oxford: Blackwell, 1977).

— 'Politics and the Study of Discourse', *Ideology and Consciousness* 3 (London: Routledge, 1978).

— *Archaeology of Knowledge*, trans. Alan Sheridan (London: Routledge, 1989).

FREGE, GOTTLOB, *On* Sinn *and* Bedeutung (1892), trans. Max Black, in *The Frege Reader*, ed. Michael Beaney (Oxford: Oxford University Press, 1997).

GALLAGHER, CATHERINE,'The Failure of Realism: "Felix Holt"', *Nineteenth-Century Fiction* 35 (1980), 372-384.

— *The Industrial Reformation of English Fiction, 1832-1867* (Chicago and London: University of Chicago Press, 1985).

— AND STEPHEN GREENBLATT, *Practising New Historicism* (Chicago and London: University of Chicago Press, 2001).

GASKELL, ELIZABETH, *Mary Barton* (1848), ed. Macdonald Daly (London and New York: Penguin, 1996).

— 'Half a Lifetime Ago' (first published in *Household Words*, XII, 6-20 October 1855), in *'The Manchester Marriage' and Other Stories* (Stroud, Gloucestershire: Alan Sutton, 1990).

— 'The Well of Pen-Morfa', in *The Works of Mrs Gaskell*, The Knutsford Edition, ed. A.W. Ward, 8 vols (London: Smith, Elder and Co., 1906), Vol. II.

GAUTHIER, DAVID, 'David Hume: Contractarian', *Philosophical Review* 88 (1979), 3-38.

GERAS, N., *Marx and Human Nature* (London: Verso/New Left Books, c1983).

GILLIGAN, CAROL, *In a Different Voice* (Cambridge Mass.: Harvard University Press, 1998).

GOODE, WILLIAM, *World Revolution and Family Patterns* (London: Collier-Macmillan, 1963).

GREER, GERMAINE, *Sex and Destiny* (Reading: Picador, 1985).

GRIBBLE, JENNIFER, Introduction to George Eliot, *Scenes of Clerical Life* (1857) (London: Penguin, 1998).

HABERMAS, JURGEN, 'The Limits of Neo Historicism', in *Autonomy and Solidarity* (London: Verso, 1992).

HAIGHT, GORDON S., *Biography of George Eliot* (Oxford: Oxford University Press, 1968).

HARDY, BARBARA, *The Novels of George Eliot* (London: Athlone Press, 1963).

HARTMAN, GEOFFREY, *The Sympathy Paradox: Poetry, Feeling, and Modern Cultural Morality* (Texas: University of Austin, 1996).

HEATH, STEVEN, 'Narrative Space', *Screen* 17:3 (1976), 68-112.

HELSINGER, ELIZABETH K., ROBIN LAUTERBACH SHEETS, and WILLIAM VEEDER (eds), *The Woman Question: Society and Literature in Britain and America, 1837-1883*, 3 vols (Chicago and London: University of Chicago Press, 1983).

HENLEY, W.E., *Views and Reviews: Essays in Appreciation* (London: Macmillan, 1890).

HJORT, METTE, AND SUE LAVER (eds), *Emotion and the Arts* (Oxford: Oxford University Press, 1997)

HOBBES, THOMAS, *Philosophical Rudiments Concerning Government and Society* (1651), in *The English Works of Thomas Hobbes*, ed. W. Molesworth (1839-45), 11 vols (London: Routledge/Thoemmes Press, 1992), Vol II.

— *The Elements of Law Natural and Politic* (1640), ed. F. Tönnies (Cambridge: Cambridge University Press, 1928).

HOBSBAWM, ERIC, *The Age of Capital* (1975) (reprinted London: Abacus, 2000).

HOMANS, MARGARET, 'Dinah's Blush, Maggie's Arm: Class, Gender and Sexuality in George Eliot's Early Novels', *Victorian Studies* 36 (1993), 155-178.

HOUSE, MADELINE, GRAHAM STOREY, KATHLEEN TILLOTSON, et al. (eds), *The Letters of Charles Dickens*, (Oxford: Clarendon Press, 1965-2002).

HUME, DAVID, *An Enquiry Concerning the Principles of Morals* (1751), in *David Hume: Enquiries Concerning Human Understanding and Concerning the Principles of Morals*, ed. L.A. Selby-Bigge and P.H. Nidditch (Oxford: Clarendon Press, 3rd edition, 1975).

— *A Treatise of Human Nature* (1739-40), ed. L.A. Selby-Bigge and P.H. Nidditch (Oxford: Clarendon Press, 1978).

HUTTON, R.H., 'Novels by the Authoress of "John Halifax"', *North British Review* XXIX (Nov. 1858), 466-481.

— *The Relative Value of Studies and Accomplishments in the Education of Women* (London, 1862).

JAFFE, AUDREY, *Scenes of Sympathy* (Ithaca, NY and London: Cornell University Press, 2000).

JAMES, HENRY, *The Art of the Novel* (New York: Scribners, 1934).

JENKINS, J.L., and ROBERT SHAVER, '"Mr Hobbes Could Have Said No More"', in Anne J. Jacobson (ed.), *Feminist Interpretations of David Hume* (Philadelphia: Pennsylvania State University Press, 2000).

JOLLEY, NICHOLAS, *Locke: His Philosophical Thought* (Oxford: Oxford University Press, 1999).

LASLETT, PETER, *The World We Have Lost* (London: Methuen, 1965).

— (ed.), *Household and Family in Past Time* (Cambridge: Cambridge University Press, 1972).

LEAVIS, Q.D., 'Charlotte Yonge and Christian Discrimination', *Scrutiny* 12 (1944), 152-160.

LEVINSON, MARJORIE, 'The New Historicism: Back to the Future', in Marjorie Levinson et al (eds), *Rethinking Historicism: Critical Readings in Romantic History* (Oxford: Blackwell, 1989), pp. 18-63.

LEWES, G.H., *Biographical History of Philosophy*, 4 vols (London: C. Knight, 1845-46).

— *Problems of Life and Mind* 5 vols (London: Trübner, 1874-79).

LI, HAO, *Memory and History in George Eliot* (London: Macmillan, 2000).

LOCKE, JOHN, *Two Treatises of Government* (1680-90), ed. Peter Laslett (Cambridge: Cambridge University Press, 1960).

MACAULAY, THOMAS BABINGTON, 'Von Ranke' (*Edinburgh Review*, 1840), in *Macaulay's Essays for the Edinburgh Review* (London, Glasgow and New York: Routledge, 1887), pp.571-593.

MARCUS, STEVEN, *Dickens: From Pickwick to Dombey* (London: Chatto and Windus, 1965).

MARX, KARL, *Grundrisse* (1857) (Harmondsworth: Penguin, 1973).

AND FRIEDRICH ENGELS, *Marx and Engels: The Collected Works*, 49 vols (London: Lawrence and Wishart, 1975-6).

MACCABE, COLIN, *James Joyce and the Revolution of the Word* (London: Macmillan, 1979).

MCDONAGH, JOSEPHINE, *George Eliot* (Plymouth: Northcote House, 1997)

MCGOWAN, J.P., 'The Turn of George Eliot's Realism', *Nineteenth-Century Fiction* 35 (1980), 171-192.

MCKEE, A., *The Golden Wreck* (London: Souvenir Press, 1961).

MCMURTY, JOHN, *The Structure of Marx's World View* (Princeton: Princeton University Press, 1978).

MIDGLEY, MARY, 'Creation and Originality', in *Heart and Mind: The Varieties of Moral Experience* (Brighton; New York; London: Harvester Press, 1981).

— 'Duties Concerning Islands', *Encounter* 60/2 (1983) 36-44.

MILL, JOHN STUART, *The Subjection of Women* (1869), in *Collected Works of John Stuart Mill*, ed. John M. Robson, 33 vols (Toronto: University of Toronto Press, 1963-91), Vol.XXI, 261-340.

— *On Liberty* (1859), in *Collected Works* (1963-91), XVIII, 213-310.

— *An Autobiography* (London: 1873).

MILLER, D.A., *The Novel and the Police* (London: University of California Press, 1988).

MITCHELL, JULIET, 'Introduction – I' to Jacques Lacan, *Feminine Sexuality*, eds. Juliet Mitchell and Jacqueline Rose (New York: W.W. Norton, 1982).

MOUNT, FERDINAND, *The Subversive Family* (London: Unwin, 1982).

MULLAN, JOHN, *Sentiment and Sociability* (Oxford: Clarendon Press, 1988).

NEWTON, JUDITH LOWDER, *Women, Power and Subversion: Social Strategies in British Fiction 1778-1860* (New York and London: Methuen, 1985).

NIETZSCHE, FRIEDRICH, *Human, All Too Human* (1878-79), trans. and ed. R.J. Hollingdale (Cambridge: Cambridge University Press, 1986).

O'DAY, ROSEMARY, *Family and Family Relationship 1500-1900* (Basingstoke: Macmillan, 1994).

OKIN, SUSAN MOLLER, 'Gender, the Public, and the Private', in Anne Phillips (ed.) *Feminism and Politics* (Oxford: Oxford University Press, 1998), pp.116-141.

PAXTON, NANCY L., *George Eliot and Herbert Spencer* (Princeton and Oxford: Princeton University Press, 1991).

PEACOCKE, CHRISTOPHER, 'Imagination, Experience and Possibility', in John Foster and Howard Robinson (eds) *Essays on Berkeley*, (Oxford: Oxford University Press, 1985).

— *Sense and Content* (Oxford: Oxford University Press, 1983).

PERERA, SUVENDRINI, 'Empire and the Family Business in *Dombey and Son*', *Victorian Studies* 33:4 (1990), 603-620.

POLANYI, KARL, *The Great Transformation* (Boston: Beacon Press, 1957).

POOVEY, MARY, *Uneven Developments* (London: Virago, 1989).

POULET, GEORGES, *Studies in Human Time* (Baltimore: Johns Hopkins Press, 1956).

ROBBINS, BRUCE, 'Colonial Discourse: A Paradigm and its Discontents', *Victorian Studies* 35 (1992), 209-214.

— 'Telescopic Philanthropy', in Homi Bhabha (ed.), *Nation and Narration* (London and New York: Routledge, 1990).

RUSKIN, JOHN, 'Of Queens' Gardens', in *Sesame and Lilies* (1865) (London: George Allen, 1901) pp. 87-143.

SAID, EDWARD, *Culture and Imperialism* (London: Chatto and Windus, 1993).

SANDERS, VALERIE, *Eve's Renegades: Victorian Anti-Feminist Women Novelists* (Basingstoke and London: Macmillan, 1996).

SCHUMPETER, JOSEPH, *Capitalism, Socialism and Democracy* (London: Allen and Unwin, 1943).

SCOTT, JOAN W., and LOUISE TILLY, 'Women's Work and the Family in Nineteenth-Century Europe', in C.E. Rosenberg (ed.), *The Family in History* (Philadelphia: University of Pennsylvania Press, 1975), pp.145-178.

SEWELL, ELIZABETH, *The Experience of Life* (1853) (London: Longman, Brown, Green, 1859).

SHIRES, LINDA M., 'Afterword', in *Rewriting the Victorians* (New York and London: Routledge, 1992).

— 'Form, Subjectivity, Ideology', in *The Cambridge Companion to the Victorian Novel*, ed. Deirdre David (Cambridge: Cambridge University Press, 2001).

SHKLAR, JUDITH, 'The Liberalism of Fear', in Nancy Rosenblum (ed.), *Liberalism and the Moral Life* (Cambridge, Mass.: Harvard University Press, 1991) pp.21-38.

SHOWALTER, ELAINE, 'The Greening of Sister George,' *Nineteenth-Century Fiction* 35 (1980), 292-311.

SHUTTLEWORTH, SALLY, Critical Commentary, *The Mill on the Floss* (London: Routledge, 1991).

SPENCER, HERBERT, 'The Moral Discipline of Children', *British Quarterly Review* (1858–1859) 364-90.

— 'What Knowledge is of Most Worth?' in *Education, Intellectual, Moral and Physical* (London: G. Mainwaring, 1861), Ch. 1

— *Social Statics* (London, 1868).

— *The Principles of Ethics* (London, 1881).

— 'The Comparative Psychology of Man', in *Essays Scientific, Political and Speculative*, 3 vols (London: Williams and Norgate, 1891), I, 351-370.

— *The Man versus the State* (1884) (London, 1950).

SQUIRES, JUDITH, *Gender in Political Theory* (Cambridge: Polity, 2000).

STIERLE, KARLHEINZ, 'The Reading of Fictional Texts', in Susan R. Suleiman and Inge Crosman (eds.), *The Reader in the Text* (Princeton: Princeton University Press, 1980).

STURROCK, JANE, *'Heaven and Home': Charlotte M. Yonge's Domestic Fiction and the Victorian Debate over Women* (Victoria: University of Victoria Press, 1995).

THADEN, BARBARA Z., *The Maternal Voice in Victorian Fiction* (New York and London: Garland, 1997).

THOMPSON, E. P., 'The Poverty of Theory', in *The Poverty of Theory and Other Essays* (London: Merlin Press, 1978).

TILLOTSON, KATHLEEN, *Novels of the Eighteen Forties* (Oxford: Clarendon Press, 1954).

TOCQUEVILLE, ALEXIS DE, *Democracy in America* (1835), trans. Henry Reeve, ed. Phillip Bradley (New York: Vintage Books, 1945).

TODOROV, TZVETAN, *The Poetics of Prose* (Oxford: Blackwell, 1977).

TRONTO, JOAN, 'Beyond Gender Difference to a Theory of Care', *Signs* 12/4 (1987), 644-663.

— *Moral Boundaries* (London: Routledge, 1993).

TUCHMAN, GAYE, 'When the Prevalent Don't Prevail: Male Hegemony and the Victorian Novel,' in Walter W. Powell and Richard Robbins (eds), *Conflicts and Consensus* (New York: Free Press, 1984), pp.139-58.

WALTON, KENDALL L., *Mimesis as Make-Believe: On the Foundations of the Representational Arts* (Cambridge, Massachusetts and London: Harvard University Press, 1990).

— 'Spelunking, Simulation, and Slime: On Being Moved by Fiction', in Mette Hjort and Sue Laver (eds), *Emotion and the Arts* (Oxford: Oxford University Press, 1997), pp.37-49.

WATT, IAN, *The Rise of the Novel* (London: Penguin, 1979).

WELLS-COLE, CATHERINE, Introduction to Charlotte Yonge, *The Heir of Redclyffe* (Herefordshire: Wordsworth Classics, 1998).

WHITE, HAYDEN, *Metahistory* (Baltimore and London: Johns Hopkins Press, 1973).

WILLIAMS, R., 'Anglesey and the Loss of the "*Royal Charter*"', *Transactions of the Anglesey Antiquarian Society and Field Club* (1959), 21-43.

WILLIAMS, RAYMOND, Introduction to *Dombey and Son* (Harmondsworth: Penguin, 1970).

WILTSHIRE, DAVID, *The Social and Political Thought of Herbert Spencer* (Oxford: Oxford University Press, 1978).

WRIGHT, T.R., *The Religion of Humanity* (Cambridge: Cambridge University Press, 1986).

WRIGHT, TERENCE, *Elizabeth Gaskell. 'We Are Not Angels': Realism, Gender, Value* (Houndsmills, Basingstoke, Hampshire and New York: Macmillan Press, 1995).

YONGE, CHARLOTTE, *The Heir of Redclyffe* (1853) (Herefordshire: Wordsworth Classics, 1998).
— *The Daisy Chain* (1856) (London: Macmillan, 1892).
— *The Trial: More Links of the Daisy Chain* (1864) (London: Macmillan, 1868).
— *The Clever Woman of the Family* (1865) (London: Virago, 1989).
— *The Pillars of the House* (1873), 2 vols. (London: Macmillan, 1907).
YOUNG, ROBERT, *White Mythology* (London: Routledge, 1990).

Index

Adam Bede (Eliot) 109, 113, 155, 235–6

Althusser, Louis 15, 50, 53, 101, 124, 129, 141, 241

altruism 124, 125, 145, 151, 156, 169, 175, 185, 188, 199, 201, 203, 224, 228, 229, 232n., 235, 238

anti-humanism 18, 216, 241

Arbury Hall 90

Armstrong, Nancy 17, 157, 159, 214

Austen, Zelda 156

Autobiography, An (Mill) 152

Azim, Firdous 38

'baggy monsters', novels as 78, 79, 97

Baier, Annette 225, 227–8, 230, 231, 235, 237, 239

Barthes, Roland 18, 19, 75–6, 79, 82, 83–6, 92–3, 99, 120n.

Barton, Amos 71, 103

Battiscombe, Georgiana 191

bedeutung 81, 84–5, 96

bedrooms 72–3, 102

Belsey, Catherine 12–3, 39, 75–6n., 119–20

Bentham, Jeremy 141

Blackmur, R.P. 96

Bleak House (Dickens) 52

bourgeois 1, 133, 134
  hegemony 1, 2, 8, 64, 66, 158
  ideology 3, 15, 67, 124, 126. 143n., 208–10, 218

and mechanistic social determinism 152

anglo- 165

and care 224–5

as 'true man' 140

and family 144–9, 205, 238

and sexual love 178–9, 213–6

Brantlinger, Patrick 38, 115

Brontë, Anne
  The Tenant of Wildfell Hall 192

Brontë, Charlotte 22, 64, 65, 76n., 86, 94, 145
  Jane Eyre 87, 145
  Shirley 66, 86–8, 89–90, 93, 102, 103, 104–5, 114, 120
  Villette 233–4

brothers, see siblings

Cain 170, 180

care 128, 166, 176, 183, 192, 197, 221, 222, 224–9, 232–3, 236–8, 241

Carker, James 54–6

Carlyle, Thomas 29, 41–2, 47, 49, 50, 59

Cauldwell, Christopher 178–9

Cheadle, Brian 52

Cheverel Manor 90

children
  their inability to generalise 63
  socialization and rearing of 128, 134, 135, 137, 138, 144
  instinctual bonds with 150

in nuclear families 159, 160, 166–9, 171–2, 177, 183–5, 206
in the 'Family' 187–94, 208, 219, 221, 228–9, 233
Chodorow, Nancy 224
choice, as expression of self-ownership 129, 130, 147. 161, 203, 223–4
of a sexual partner 135, 163–6, 171, 176–80, 185. 191, 211–9, 229–31, 235
Clever Woman of the Family. The (Yonge) 196–7
Cohen, G.A. 16, 126n., 142
Cohen, Monica F. 159
Collier, Andrew 142
compass 43n.
Comte, Auguste 10, 117n., 151n., 153–4, 226, 231
contract theory 129, 131, 133, 141, 147, 151n, 221, 228, 236

Cottom, Daniel 2–4, 6n.
couple, sexual see love match, love plot
Craik, Dinah Mulock 65, 145, 158–9, 183, 185, 186, 188, 191, 195–6, 200–1, 205, 211, 216, 218, 233, 239
John Halifax, Gentleman 162–174, 175, 177, 180, 188, 196, 208, 210, 222
A Life for a Life 164
A Noble Life 181
The Ogilvies 164
Olive 181, 185
The Woman's Kingdom 164, 174–182, 188, 189–90, 204n., 205, 222–3
A Woman's Thoughts about Women 145, 162, 173–4, 176–7, 222, 239
Creaven, Sean 140

Crosby, Cristina 19, 64–7, 82, 75, 76, 77–8, 79–80, 91
Culler, Jonathan 79–80
Currie, Gregory 112
Cuttle, Captain Edward 43, 45, 56

Daisy Chain. The (Yonge) 188, 195–6, 198
Darwin, 136n. see also evolutionary theory and social Darwinism
David, Deirdre 24, 37–8,
Davies, Emily 62
Davis, Lennard J 1, 19, 61, 66, 75–80, 82, 89, 93–4, 107, 109–11, 116–7, 120
Deane
Mr 204, 205, 210
Lucy 210, 212, 217, 221, 229–30, 235
debt, as a compromise of self-ownership 133, 145, 180, 196, 204–5, 208
Deleuze, Gilles 31
Dennis, Barbara 187, 191–2, 199n.
dependence, physical, of humans on others 143, 144, 172, 192
description, see details, descriptive
details, descriptive 19–20, 25–26, 38, 45, 47, 49, 51, 62–7, 68–121
determinism 43, 115–6, 149, 152, 216
Dickens, Charles 9–10, 64, 65, 218
Bleak House 52
Dombey and Son 19, 23–24, 36–60, 61, 194
Great Expectations 163
The Uncommercial Traveller 25–36
DiStefano, Christine 148
Dodsons 203–6
Dombey

Edith (née Skewton) 48, 50, 53, 54, 59

Florence 37, 44, 51–2, 56, 57, 60

Mr (Paul senior) 48

Paul junior 44, 47, 52, 60

Dombey and Son (Dickens) 19, 23–24, 36–60, 61, 194

domestic economy *see* labour, reproductive

ducks 88, 114

Dworkin, Ronald 126n.

Eagleton, Terry 2–3, 4, 5, 6, 8, 11, 145n.

Edmonstone

Amy 189–91, 192, 195, 197, 199, 200

Charles 190, 192, 200

Mrs 187, 190, 192, 193, 195, 197

Eliot, George

mistreated by critics 3, 6n., 11, 64, 66, 76n., 117

common ground with Marx 10

idea of sympathy 12, 108–9, 112–3, 231–2

affinity with Gaskell 73, 131

not thoroughly 'feminine' in writing style 65

opposition to Social Darwinism 116

on education 117

and the value of art 118

fear of abstract moralising 120–1

and feminism 144–6, 149–51, 214–5, 224, 229–35

evasion of biological determinism 149–52

productive acknowledgement of human nature 149–53, 226–7, 235–6

and Comte 152–3

and the value of reproductive labour 155

and care 221–2, 225–7

family background 232–3

Adam Bede 86, 109, 113, 155, 235–6

Daniel Deronda 112

Felix Holt, The Radical 97–101

Middlemarch 2, 12, 67, 97, 98–9, 121, 123, 211, 231n.

The Mill on the Floss 20, 82, 88–9, 113–4, 143, 203–39

Scenes of Clerical Life 66, 70–73, 90–1, 94, 98, 103–5, 106–7, 109–10, 112, 115, 116, 118, 120, 121

Ellis, Sarah 62, 132–6, 138–9, 153, 233

Elshtain, Jean Bethke 156n., 184

Elster, John 140

empathy, coining of the word 19

Engels, Friedrich 10, 17, 183–4

Ermarth, Elizabeth Deeds 67, 75

essentialism *see* human nature

Evans, Michael 141

Evans, Marian 233, *see also* Eliot, George

evolutionary theory 63, 126, 136, 138, 150

'moral evolution' 150 *see also* Darwin *and* social Darwinism

evolution of society 6, 43, 143

Experience of Life, The (Sewell) 68–71

family 20, 143

domestic fiction's special insight into 21, 158, 206

genesis of modern conception of 125
and contract theory 129–139
as necessary to capitalist society 143–9
Comte and 153
feminist suspicion of 154–5, 157–8, 196
and individualism 155–6
as ethical training ground 153, 224, 228
two types of 158–161. 220, 222,
nuclear 158–9, 161–166–90, 220–1
   couple as core of 159, 164
'Family' 159, 161, 190–206, 218, 220, 225
   under pressure 203–4, 211, 234
   restrictions of 204–206
   dissolution of 237
   Eliot's gestures beyond 237–9
and embeddedness of reason and value 223–4
Hume's conception of 228, 235
Eliot's own 232–3
as proof of human potential for sympathy 235–6
Marx on 237
fathers 37, 60, 134, 160, 169, 176, 177, 187, 192, 201, 205, 206, 208, 210, 212, 220

feminine fiction 19, 62–121
feminism 20, 144–51
   and domesticity 154–6
   and Craik 173–4
   and Charlotte Yonge 185–87, 197–99, 201
   and George Eliot 149–51, 214–5, 229–35
   liberal 224–5

feminist criticism 18, 131n, 144–46, 154–6, 186–7, 195n., 214, 229–35

Feuerbach, Ludwig 10, 11, 227
fictionality 93–5
Fielding, Henry 67, 196
Flaubert, Gustave 83, 86, 98, 99
Fleischer, Helmut 141
Fletcher, Phineas 172–4, 180–1
Flint, Kate 145, 146
Forster, John 39, 48
Foster, Shirley 185–6
Foucault, Michel 30–1, 40, 49, 53, 60
Frege, Gottlob 81, 86, 95, 96, 98n., 102, 113
Freud, Sigmund 6, 150, 183, 185, 224
friendship 11, 165, 176–7, 189, 222–3, 228
frogs 91, 94

Gallagher, Catherine 8, 10, 19, 41, 50, 116, 117–8, 141–2
   on domesticity 15
   on Felix Holt 97–101
games 83, 91, 92, 113
gardens 91, 94, 102, 110, 119, 182, 214
Gaskell, Elizabeth 115, 120
   'Half a Lifetime Ago' 66, 73–4
   Mary Barton 66, 102, 105–6, 107–8, 114–6, 119
   Ruth 192
   'The Well of Pen-Morfa' 36
Gauthier, David 131n.
Gay, Walter 38, 44, 48, 49
Geras, Norman 141–2
Gilfil
   Mr 72, 73
   Mrs (Tina) 71–3, 91, 94, 102, 121

Gilligan, Carol 221–2, 224–5, 232, 241
Gills, Solomon 43–4, 56
Glegg, Mrs 204, 205, 220–1
Goode, William 154–5, 159–60, 164
Grandison, Sir Charles 196
Great Expectations (Dickens) 163
Greenblatt, Stephen 8, 10, 41, 141–3
Greer, Germaine 148, 159, 160–2, 184, 189
Guest, Stephen 210, 211–8, 221, 229–31, 234, 238

Habermas, Jurgen 58
Haight, Gordon S 225n
'Half a Lifetime Ago' (Gaskell) 66, 73–4
Halifax
  Edwin 169–71
  Guy 169–71
  John 162, 163–9, 171–5, 188, 193, 196, 208, 212, 218, 222
  Muriel 167–9
  Ursula 163, 165–7, 172
Hardy, Barbara 76
Hartman, Geoffrey 113
Heath, Steven 120n.
Heir of Redclyffe, The (Yonge) 186, 187, 188–93, 196, 199–200, 222
Helstone, Caroline 87–8, 89, 90, 102, 104, 105, 114
Henley, W.E. 225n
history
  ethics of writing of 1, 19, 23–4, 27, 28–9, 30–1, 36, 39–40, 57–60, 66
  determinism and human agency 15, 17, 41, 49–50, 52–7, 123
  Dickens's conception of 23–60

with a capital H 23–4, 20, 38, 42, 46–7, 61–2, 64–6, 75–8, 115–6 118
  as brute fact 27, 29, 31, 36, 42, 43–50, 68
  of the novel 38
  women's 65–74, 104–5
  as lived experience 120–1
Hobbes, Thomas 129, 141, 165n, 198
Hobsbawm, Eric 144
Hollywell 187, 189, 192, 193
Homans, Margaret 155, 213
Hughes, Stephen Roose 29–30, 32
human nature 6n., 16, 20, 123–32, 134–44, 150–8, 163, 183, 201, 218, 233, 237–8 *see also* evolutionary theory
Hume, David 9–12, 113, 131, 148, 225–232, 235–7
Huntingdon, Helen 192
hurricane 27
Hutton, R.H 63–5, 97, 117, 174
humanism 4, 11, 18, 20, 53, 66, 141

illness, *see* invalids
imagination
  sympathetic 10–12, 32, 108–121
  sensuous 10, 28, 87, 87, 90, 91, 93, 95, 103, 108, 116
individualism 14, 124–8, 134–185, 197–238, 241
invalids 136, 180–1, 182, 186, 190, 192, 210

Jaffe, Audrey 9–10
James, Henry 74, 95–8, 119
Jane Eyre (Brontë) 87, 145
Jellyby, Mrs 10
Jenkins, J.L 131n

John Halifax, Gentleman (Craik) 162–
    174, 175, 177, 180, 188, 196, 208,
    210, 222
Jolley, Nicholas 165
justice, as a realisation of rights 20,
    130–2, 137–141, 144–151, 154–6,
    161–7, 170–181, 198–200, 207–9,
    218–30, 238–9

Kant, Emmanuel 120. 221, 224
Keeldar, Shirley 86–7, 89, 90, 93,
    103

labour, reproductive 126, 127, 143–6,
    149, 154–5, 166, 173, 183–4, 203–
    4, 208–9, 228–9, 237
Lacan, Jacques 185
Laslett, Peter 160–1
Leavis, Q.D. 186–7
Levinson, Marjorie 41, 54
Lewes, G.H. 112, 150, 156, 225n.
Li, Hao .112n.
liberalism 126n., 129–32, 139–43,
    146–9, 158–9, 172, 184
liberal ideology *see* liberalism
liberal humanism 4
libertarianism 126 *see also* liberalism
Life for a Life, A (Craik) 164
Locke, John 129–32, 134, 161n, 165,
    172, 216
love match 175, 177, 211
love plot 163–6, 211–8, 229, 238–9

Macaulay, Thomas Babington 31–2
MacCabe, Colin 75n.
make believe 83
Marcus, Steven 43n.
marriage 69, 71, 132, 135, 163, 166,
    171–3, 175–82, 185–6, 189–91,
    216, 228, 234

Mary Barton (Gaskell) 66, 102, 105–6,
    107–8, 114–6, 119
Marwood, Alice 48, 50, 51, 53
Marx, Karl epigraph, 20, 10, 15–8,
    109, 136n, 139–43, 146–7, 149–53,
    231, 236–7
Marxism 15–7, 18, 142, 144–5, 229

McDonagh, Josephine 236
McGowan, J.P. 98n
McKee, A. 29n
McMurty, John
memory 23, 27, 28–31, 54, 57, 60,
    112n., 168, 217, 223
Middlemarch (Eliot) 2, 12, 67, 97, 98–
    9, 121, 123, 211, 231n
Midgley, Mary 129, 162–3
Mill, John Stuart 146–50, 152
    The Subjection of Women 146–7
    On Liberty 147
    An Autobiography 152
Miller, D.A. 1, 5, 19, 71, 75n.
Mill on the Floss, The (Eliot) 20, 82, 88–
    9, 113–4, 143, 203–39
Mitchell, Juliet 185
Moilfre 34n., 36,
Morfin, Mr 48, 50–1
Morville, Guy 187–96, 199–200
Moss
    Mr 205, 209, 219
    Mrs 206, 209, 219
mothers 29, 50, 53, 135, 148, 156,
    160–1, 167–9, 174, 176–7, 184–5,
    187–8, 190–2, 199–201, 206, 218–
    21, 233, 235–6
mother-child relationship 148–9, 185
Mount, Ferdinand 160, 178
Mullan, John 9n.

Native, the 37–8, 51–2, 54

needs, human 17, 53, 60, 126, 128, 141–2, 156, 161, 181–2, 187, 189, 216, 218, 221, 224–9, 233, 236, 238
new historicism 19, 40–1, 142
Newton, Judith Lowder 203–4, 229–30, 232–4
Nietzsche, Friedrich 50, 138, 150n., 163, 184, 233
Noble Life, A (Craik) 181

O'Day, Rosemary 160
Ogilvies, The (Craik) 164
On Liberty (Mill) 147
Okin, Susan Moller 144, 157
Olive (Craik) 181, 185

Paxton, Nancy L. 137
Peacocke, Christopher 113
Perera, Suvendrini 24, 37, 39
Pillars of the House, The (Yonge) 198
play, see games
plot 37–8, 45, 48–9, 61–2, 66–9, 71, 73, 76, 112, 165, 188, 195, 211, 213, 230, 238
Polanyi, Karl 127n
political economy 15, 115, 118, 140, 142, 143, 242
Poovey, Mary 125–7, 129, 156, 157, 159
post-colonial criticism 18, 38
post-structuralism 80, 99
Poulet, Georges 57n.
poverty 36, 44, 50, 51, 106, 107, 171, 208, 210
proletariat 8, 16
  moral 228
Pryor, Mrs 104
Punch 31–2

railways 27, 42–3

Rawls, John 126n., 228
Rayburn, Eugene 10
rights, see justice
realism, fictional 13–14, 17–19, 37–8, 45, 48–9, 51–2, 57, 61–3, 65–6, 75, 83, 86, 91–101, 113, 116–121 *see also* reality effect
reality effect 76–7, 82, 83–4, 91
relativism 32, 40, 52–3, 58
Religion of Humanity 117n., 151n., 153, 156, 225–6n.
Richardson, Samuel 196
Robbins, Bruce 40, 52–3
Royal Charter 26–36, 40n., 43n., 44
Ruskin, John 197
Ruth (Gaskell) 192

Said, Edward 24, 38–9, 46
Sanders, Valerie 186n., 233n.
Scenes of Clerical Life (Eliot) 66, 70–73, 90–1, 94, 98, 103–5, 106–7, 109–10, 112, 115, 116, 118, 120, 121
Schumpeter, Joseph 56–7
school 188–9, 192, 205, 213, 223
self-help 162–3, 164–5, 168, 205, 208
self-ownership 20, 126n.. 127, 130, 136, 139, 142–6, 148, 161, 165, 171–2, 181, 183–5, 211, 219–20, 226–8, 238
sensations 62, 110–1
Sewell, Elizabeth 65–6, 68n, 69–70, 199
  The Experience of Life 68–71
Shaver, Robert 131n.
shipwreck 19, 25–36, 40n., 43n, 44–5, 48, 60
Shires, Linda M. 13, 50
Shirley (Brontë) 66, 86–8, 89–90, 93, 102, 103, 104–5, 114, 120
Shklar, Judith 130

Showalter, Elaine 140, 145
Shuttleworth, Sally 146
siblings
    bonds 135, 166, 169, 172, 175,
        176,180, 186–7, 190–1, 205–6,
        226–7, 238, 176–7, 179–80, 184,
        189, 190, 192, 195, 198, 204,
        205–6, 219, 228, 238
    rivalry 166, 169–71, 175, 177–8,
        179–82, 190–1, 204n.
significance
    'world of' 19, 56
    and Foucault's 'genealogical
        method' 30
    of events in *Dombey and Son* 45–6,
        48–9
'Significance' and inSignificance 61–
    2, 64, 66–82, 86, 88, 92–112, 117,
    121
simulation 111–3, 117–8
sinn 81–2, 84–5
sisters, *see* siblings
Skewton, Mrs 10, 58
Skimpole, Harold 10
Smith, Adam 9–10
social climbing, *see* self-help
social contract 129–32
Social Darwinism 136, 143
socialism 15–6
    French 10, 152
    utopian 15–16, 17
    as humanism and naturalism 141
    and New Labour 160n
    and the family 160n., 183
Spencer, Herbert 63, 136–9, 142,
    152–3, 168, 181, 205, 226, 233
Squires, Judith 155–6
Steadman
    Will 175, 178, 193, 204n., 212,
        222–3

Julius 179–82, 192
    Edna 177, 179, 181, 189, 190, 196
Stierle, Karlheinz 76n.
structuralism 6, 11, 15, 18, 79–81,
    83, 84–5
Sturrock, Jane 188n., 197–9
Subjection of Women, The (Mill) 146–7
sympathy
    changing sense of the word 9–10,
        225
    false 10
    'vertical' 10
    Hume's definition of 10–11, 113.
        225, 227–8, 231–2, 235–6, 236–7
    as a critical and political virtue 10–
        14, 20. 116–8, 241–2
    between past and present 10–14,
        59–61, 241–2
    as a displacement of political
        engagement 15–7, 20, 201
    necessary for social change 16–17,
        116–8, 125
    and domestic fiction 20–1, 241–2,
        156–85, 188, 190–201, 204, 206
    and the limits of knowledge 51–3,
        56
    and the realism of things 108–14,
        118, 119–21
    Eliot's sense of 108–9, 112–3, 231–
        2
    and simulation 111–2
    and perspective 113–4
    and utopia 121
    debates over status and scope of
        125, 146, 225
    containment within feminine arena
        125, 145, 146, 149–51, 224, 236–
        7, 239
    as a biologically given virtue 150–1,
        218, 226–7, 236

containment within the nuclear
family 156–85, 211–8, 237–9
and the love plot 163–6, 211–8,
229, 238–9
and Family 188, 190–201, 204,
206, 237–9
as opposed to a mechanical
weighing of rights 218–224

tattoo 30–1
Tattoo, Sir Cannibal 31–2, 43
tea 105–8
Tenant of Wildfell Hall, The (Anne
Brontë) 192
Thackeray, W.M 66, 78
Thaden, Barbara Z. 166–7, 183–4
Thompson, E. P. 1, 7–8, 15, 18
Tillotson, Kathleen 39–40
Tocqueville, Alexis de 31
Todorov, Tzvetan 79–81
Tractarianism 199, 200
träger 15, 253–4
Trial, The (Yonge) 192, 198
Tronto, Joan 9n., 225–6, 237
Tryan, Mr 109–10
Tuchman, Gaye 63
Tulliver
Maggie 20, 82, 155, 208–21, 223,
226–38
Tom 204, 205, 208, 218–20, 223
Mr 205–210, 236
Mrs 206, 220–1, 235–36

Ulysses (Joyce) 95
Uncommercial Traveller, The
(Dickens) 25–36
utilitarianism 141

Villette (Brontë) 233–4

vorstellung 81, 84–5, 87, 92, 96, 101,
114

Wakem, Philip 209–10, 232n., 236
Walton, Kendall L. 83, 89, 95, 112
Watt, Ian 67
'Well of Pen-Morfa, The' (Gaskell) 36
Wells-Cole, Catherine 185–6, 195n.
White, Hayden 44
Williams, R. 29n., 33, 40n., 43n.
Williams, Raymond 50
Wiltshire, David 138n., 152
Woman's Kingdom, The (Craik) 164,
174–182, 188, 189–90, 204n., 205,
222–3
Woman's Thoughts about Women, A
(Craik) 145, 162, 173–4, 176–7,
222, 239
women, modesty of 33
their lot determined by material
circumstances 50–1, 53
as recorders of experiential
realities 62–74, 86–121
as excluded from History 64–6, 71–4
and female historiography 104–7
and 'separate spheres' 26–128, 132–
9, 154–6, 192, 197, 208, 225, 228,
234, 236
and individualistic/altruistic double
bind 143–9, 170–1, 173–4, 233
biology of 149–51
Comte's view of 153
and domesticity 154–6, 198–9
and the nuclear family 159, 163–72,
175–85, 188, 191
and the extended 'Family' 185–201,
203–8, 211, 219–21, 239
and romantic love plot 211–8
and moral reasoning, 221–2, 224–5,
229, 241

see also feminine fiction,
inSignificance, mother
Wright, T.R. 117n., 151n., 153, 156,
   226n.
Wright, Terence 74, 114, 120

Yonge, Charlotte 65, 155, 158–9,
   185–202, 203, 222, 225–7, 233n,
   236–7
   Clever Woman of the Family, The 196–
      7
   Daisy Chain, The 188, 195–6, 198
   Heir of Redclyffe, The 186, 187, 188–
      93, 196, 199–200, 222
   Pillars of the House, The 198
   Trial, The 192, 198
Young, Robert 23–4, 31

Lightning Source UK Ltd.
Milton Keynes UK
UKHW050153030323
417923UK00008BA/124